Yet Another Costume Party Debacle

Yet Another Costume Party Debacle

Why Racial Ignorance Persists on Elite College Campuses

INGRID A. NELSON

The University of Chicago Press
Chicago and London

The University of Chicago Press, Chicago 60637
The University of Chicago Press, Ltd., London
© 2024 by The University of Chicago
All rights reserved. No part of this book may be used or reproduced in any manner
whatsoever without written permission, except in the case of brief quotations in
critical articles and reviews. For more information, contact the University of Chicago
Press, 1427 E. 60th St., Chicago, IL 60637.
Published 2024
Printed in the United States of America

33 32 31 30 29 28 27 26 25 24   1 2 3 4 5

ISBN-13: 978-0-226-83683-6 (cloth)
ISBN-13: 978-0-226-83685-0 (paper)
ISBN-13: 978-0-226-83684-3 (e-book)
DOI: https://doi.org/10.7208/chicago/9780226836843.001.0001

Library of Congress Cataloging-in-Publication Data

Names: Nelson, Ingrid A., author.
Title: Yet another costume party debacle : why racial ignorance persists on elite
    college campuses / Ingrid A. Nelson.
Description: Chicago : The University of Chicago Press, 2024. |
    Includes bibliographical references and index.
Identifiers: LCCN 2024021596 | ISBN 9780226836836 (cloth) |
    ISBN 9780226836850 (paperback) | ISBN 9780226836843 (ebook)
Subjects: LCSH: Bowdoin College. | Racism in higher education. |
    College students—Social life and customs. | Stereotypes (Social psychology)
Classification: LCC LB3608 .N45 2024 | DDC 378.1/9829—dc23/eng/20240521
LC record available at https://lccn.loc.gov/2024021596

♾ This paper meets the requirements of ANSI/NISO Z39.48-1992 (Permanence of Paper).

Contents

1 Celebrating Cultural Appropriation at an Elite College 1

2 Multiculturalism or Monoculturalism?
Producing Unmarked Whiteness 28

3 Racism as a Personal Problem 56

4 The Pros and Cons of Civilized Diversity Discourse 75

5 Campus Is Not a Bubble 99

6 Money Talks 126

7 The Aftermath 149

8 Conclusion 168

Acknowledgments 187
Appendix A: Respondents' Gender, Race, and Ethnic Identities 191
Appendix B: Interview Protocol 195
Notes 199
Index 225

1

Celebrating Cultural Appropriation at an Elite College

On a cold February evening, a crowd of undergraduates gathered in a dorm room on a small college campus to drink tequila at a party that, according to the invitation, was "not *not* a fiesta." As with parties held every night at every college, memories may have faded like the resulting hangovers—if not for some little sombreros, a cellphone camera, and Instagram. By brunch the next day, snapshots of white (or white-presenting) students sporting miniature sombreros had circulated campus. Over the next few weeks, national media outlets would broadcast the fallout. To some, this marked another example of white students downplaying racist acts. To others, it represented overly sensitive "PC rats" spoiling good fun. Either way, the controversy hit a nerve, becoming what *The Independent* referred to as "the latest instance of a new mood of censorious political correctness sweeping university campuses."[1] Indeed, twice in the prior two years the same thing had happened on this same campus: Students hosted a racially themed party, inflamed campus dialogue, and endured the widely publicized fallout. The frequency with which similar acts continue to repeat on campuses across the US raises the question: Why do these parties persist, and what, if anything, do undergraduates learn about race and racism from these encounters?

A quick Google search of "racially charged college party" reveals the latest of the ever-expanding list of campuses exposed to firestorms of media attention because images of predominantly white students dressed in racially themed costumes went viral.[2] Although "Gangster," "Mexican," and other themed revelries have gone without garnering media attention for generations, the shifting political and social landscape during the early 2010s brought more public scrutiny.[3] Such parties occurred on campuses of all kinds—public and private, elite and open access, large and small—parading and reinforcing derogatory stereotypes under the masthead of "having a good time." In 2010, fraternity members at University of California San Diego held a "Compton Cookout," mocking Black History Month by dressing up as ghetto stereotypes.[4] In 2013, pictures posted to social media captured sorority members at California State San Marcos dressed as stereotypical "cholas"—wearing bandannas and flannel shirts—and making "gang-like gestures with their hands."[5] In 2013, a Dartmouth fraternity and sorority cohosted a "Crips and Bloods" party where students pretended they were members of the notorious gangs.[6] In 2014, members of an Arizona State fraternity celebrated Dr. Martin Luther King Jr.'s birthday with a party where students promoted stereotypes by wearing basketball jerseys, flashing gang signs, and drinking from hollowed-out watermelons.[7] In 2014, racial tensions at University of Michigan were brought to the fore by a fraternity party inviting "rappers, twerkers, gangsters," and others "back to da hood again."[8] In 2015, a "Kanye Western" event held by a University of California Los Angeles fraternity featured students dressed either as "Kanye West, in baggy clothes, or as Kardashians, in form-fitting outfits and padded behinds."[9] That same month, the University of Louisville president apologized after he and his friends were pictured "wearing ponchos, sombreros, and bushy mustaches" as part of their Mexican-themed Halloween costumes.[10] At Claremont McKenna College, the junior class president resigned under similar circumstances, except that she was merely posing with students wearing sombreros, ponchos, and fake mustaches, and not wearing the costume herself.[11] Each event drew national media attention and sparked campus protests, yet these represent only a fraction of the offending parties. Despite public condemnation by students, administrators, and community leaders, however, the parties kept happening for years.

In a well-publicized incident at Yale, administrators tried to avoid a similar fate. In October 2015, the intercultural affairs committee sent an email asking students to avoid wearing "culturally unaware and insensitive" Halloween costumes, such as feathered headdresses, turbans, and blackface. When an administrator at a student residence—who was also a faculty member—sent a response to her residents arguing that students should wear whatever they wanted even if they offended people, sparks flew. "Is there no room anymore for a child or young person to be a little bit obnoxious . . . a little bit inappropriate or provocative or, yes, offensive?" she wrote in her email. "American universities were once a safe space not only for maturation but also for a certain regressive, or even transgressive, experience; increasingly, it seems, they have become places of censure and prohibition,"[12] she continued. Students protested her email and videos of the protests went viral. Administrators stood by their initial statement. By the end of spring semester, the residential administrator resigned.[13]

In the years following, the controversies lived on[14] and the parties continued. The list of colleges thrust into headlines because their students or administrators turned a culture or stereotype into a party theme or costume continued to grow. But why? Each time, the media replayed now-familiar debates about cultural appropriation, political correctness, freedom of speech, and racism. Administrators issued statements condemning inappropriate behavior and encouraging constituents to rally around idyllic visions of a diverse campus. In many cases, when confronted after the fact, students who hosted the parties claimed they meant no harm. Too often, organizers said they did not know relevant social history as to why their costumes were offensive.[15] Yet little changed.

In this book, I explore why, even after a campus has been called out in the national media for a costume party that perpetuated and celebrated racial stereotypes, similar parties recur. Specifically, this book spotlights a cohort of students on a small, elite, predominantly white campus who, during their first two years, experienced three racially themed parties that garnered media attention.

Some have argued that the massive protests that took place during the summer of 2020 in response to racism and police violence in the US[16] have altered conversations about race such that my questions are no longer relevant. More Americans are now familiar with concepts such as microaggressions and structural racism. And social media has created powerful modes of calling out and amplifying critiques of racists acts and systems.[17] On the other side, white supremacist speech has also intensified as "white America uses race as a public weapon to address its grievance as a targeted group."[18] In this charged and changing context, why should we care about who wore what to an unremarkable college party? The answer lies in what the parties—and the college's reaction—reveal about "the enormity of whiteness"[19] in higher education. Contrary to popular characterizations of elite colleges as liberal bastions of "wokeness," this study illustrates the necessarily conservative nature of such institutions. The reasons for studying racially themed costume parties are therefore less about who gets to wear a mini sombrero, and more about the organizational structures that make these parties possible.

My findings reveal that racialized costume parties are a symptom of deep institutional investments in whiteness, and they keep happening because strategies for addressing racist acts on campus were never intended to address the roots of the problem. In fact, just the opposite. Upending racism at historically white colleges threatens the very fabric of their solvency. To gain legitimacy in an increasingly heterogeneous society that still buys into myths of meritocracy, elite colleges invest in elaborate charades that paint diversity as a core value.[20] All the while, these institutions rely—largely un-critically—on structures and practices that reproduce existing racial and socioeconomic hierarchies. In other words, the parties recur because nothing changes, and nothing changes because those in power benefit from existing arrangements.

The next sections build the groundwork for this argument. First, I review how whiteness has been invented and sustained in the US and, more specifi-cally, in higher education. Second, I show how waves of cultural appropria-tion and anti-PC backlash have bolstered white dominance. Then I introduce the theoretical framework for this study, bringing together inhabited institu-tionalism[21] and racialized organizations[22] theories to highlight the interplay of structures and agency. Finally, I describe my research site and methods, and close by outlining how findings from this study explain not only why racialized costume parties recur and what students learn from them, but also complicate our understandings of equity and justice on elite campuses.

Although the landscape of higher education is vast and varied,[23] elite col-leges graduate a disproportionate percentage of future leaders across a vari-ety of cultural and economic domains.[24] In fact, many elite American firms, including those in law, finance, and consulting, recruit new hires only from the most prestigious colleges and universities.[25] In light of these facts, this book offers an important window into what and how our next generation of cultural and economic leaders are learning about race and racism as under-graduates and, more importantly, why.

How White Ignorance Sustains White Dominance

Because race is a social construct, rather than a fixed biological trait, defini-tions of racial categories and their meanings change over time and across geographies.[26] Race as Americans know it today—specifically, the idea of Pan-European racial superiority—emerged together with capitalism. Al-though Black Africans were first associated with slavery in the early sixteenth century, racial categories were not first legislated in the American colonies until the early eighteenth century.[27] From the advent of the American colo-nies, the ruling class had treated enslaved Africans differently from inden-tured Europeans, even though their conditions were similar. Yet where white and Black people—enslaved and indentured—found themselves with com-mon interests, they behaved toward one another as equals.[28] The only thing more threatening to landowners than "slave rebellions" was the possibility

CELEBRATING CULTURAL APPROPRIATION   5

that indentured servants would join forces with enslaved Africans. To prevent the kind of cooperation between enslaved Black people and indentured white laborers that could facilitate an overthrow, landowning Virginians worked to pit those groups against each other, redirecting the vitriol away from themselves. The plan—known as a "racial bribe"—involved giving white indentured servants marginally more status over enslaved Black people, essentially incentivizing their participation in a racialized hierarchy and enshrining the racial superiority of white people into law.

Thus, whiteness has never been just an individual identity. Whiteness was created as a system of domination and exclusion and circumscribed into law. Focusing only on how individuals conceive of their personal racial identities ignores the ways white supremacy[29] has been written into our bedrock social institutions, even as these systems have changed over time.[30] For example, when enslaved people were emancipated, racial subjugation lived on first through black codes and convict laws enacted by southern states, then (after the brief period of progress brought by Reconstruction) in Jim Crow laws.[31] When massive waves of Irish and then Italian immigrants arrived in the US in the mid to late 1800s, they had to fight for many years to be seen as white.[32] For decades, people from China, Japan, and the Philippines were brought as low-wage laborers, but denied the right to become citizens.[33] Ongoing colonial regimes triggered new currents of voluntary and forced international migration, and definitions of whiteness were repeatedly rewritten by the courts to include or exclude particular ethnic groups until race was finally removed as a criterion for citizenship in 1952.[34] Since then, according to legal scholar Michelle Alexander, the US has been governed by a different kind of racialized system of social control characterized by the mass incarceration of people of color, particularly Black men.[35] Extensive research documents the myriad ways racialized social systems[36] have produced striking inequalities over time, in wealth, income, housing, education, employment, health, justice, and nearly every other social indicator imaginable.[37] Through all these reinventions, whiteness has continued to function as system of domination,[38] an asset akin to a form of property,[39] and an ideology rooted in antiblackness, anti-Indigeneity, and settler colonialism.[40]

As people of color have continued to resist and systems sustaining whiteness have evolved, so have narratives for talking about race. Whereas Jim Crow era segregation was justified through outright claims of white racial superiority, civil rights victories of the 1950s and 1960s pushed such portrayals of whiteness underground, replacing them with framings of whiteness as "normal"[41]—newly invisible, yet still dominant.[42] To bolster racial whiteness in this new political landscape, white Americans began to distance themselves from the kinds of whiteness associated with Plymouth Rock and the founding of the US (e.g., colonization, slavery, and genocide) and more closely identify with the kinds of whiteness represented by Ellis Island (e.g., pulling oneself up by one's bootstraps). Ellis Island remembrance recast the US as a nation of immigrants who survived harrowing personal epics, deserved this nation's greatness, and offered proof of the upward mobility promised by the American dream.[43] It also obscured the truth of this nation's violent founding, shaping a "blameless white identity," such that white people who claimed an immigrant lineage were therefore not accountable for the sins of slavery and genocide.[44] This articulation of whiteness gave rise to the politics of white grievance that have flourished in recent decades—faced with demographic, social, and political advances by people of color, white Americans now seek to be regarded as an oppressed group.

At present, white people have vested political and economic interests both in maintaining the existing racial hierarchy and in obscuring its existence. Philosopher Charles Mills called this the "racial contract,"[45] drawing on the ways white men established global social and economic systems of white supremacy, through both explicit and tacit agreements, marked by the subordination and exploitation of people of color and their lands. Mills argued that *"white misunderstanding, misrepresentation, evasion, and self-deception on matters related to race . . . are in no way accidental, but prescribed by the* terms of the racial contract . . . in order to establish and maintain the white polity,"[46] dubbing this phenomenon "white ignorance." Elsewhere Mills continued, "white normativity manifests itself in a white refusal to recognize the long history of structural discrimination that has left white people with the differential resources they have today."[47] By collectively avoiding and distorting reality, producing and enabling vast racial ignorance, white people evade the moral and practical implications of critical racial consciousness.

Because it is deliberate, structural, and powerful, "white ignorance" is not the same as general ignorance or lack of understanding.[48] White ignorance is the product of both group-based identities and myriad social systems—drawing on the collective power of elite and ordinary white people, individually, organizationally, and institutionally—colluding to produce and defend racial ignorance.[49] In this way, Mills explains, "all whites are beneficiaries of the contract, though some whites are not signatories to it."[50] As sociologist Jennifer Mueller argued, "white ignorance requires real effort and dedication in a world saturated with evidence of racism and the suffering, counter discourse, and resistance of people of color."[51] Thus, the remedy for white ignorance is the same as the remedy for white supremacy—not education, but political struggle.[52]

CELEBRATING CULTURAL APPROPRIATION

Take the example of blackface—a slice of popular culture that has always been harmful but only recently frowned upon by polite (white) society. Blackface and minstrel shows have been part of American popular culture since popular culture emerged in the early nineteenth century. Blackface started with stage performers—first white men, then Black performers—and spread to radio, film, and television, reaching the height of its popularity in the early twentieth century.[53] The first minstrel shows were performed in New York in the 1830s by white performers with blackened faces (using burnt cork or shoe polish) who impersonated enslaved Africans in ways that characterized Black people as, "lazy, ignorant, superstitious, hypersexual, and prone to thievery and cowardice."[54] Minstrel entertainers spawned caricatures that endure to this day, introducing audiences—many of whom never encounter Black people in real life—to stereotypes portraying grinning, dancing, simpletons.[55] Many colleges had student minstrel clubs, even into the 1950s, and throngs of white film and television stars were featured in blackface, including Judy Garland, Mickey Rooney, and Shirley Temple. Although the use of blackface has waned, it has not disappeared.[56]

As part of a pervasive and continuing tradition of what sociologist Raul Perez has dubbed "amused racial contempt,"[57] blackface uses humor to normalize ideologies of white supremacy and antiblackness. Due to the epistemology of white ignorance, many Americans claim not to know the history of blackface and how it has been used to spread derogatory stereotypes for nearly two centuries. "Not knowing" thus allows harmful practices to continue reinforcing, yet minimizing, long-standing racialized oppression.

For example, in October 2018 in a segment about Halloween costumes, Megyn Kelly—a popular television morning show host and former news anchor—lamented on air that the "costume police" were ruining good fun by discouraging people from dressing up as cowboys and Native Americans, among other tropes. She went on to wonder aloud on air why it was inappropriate for white people to dress in blackface, which she claimed was okay when she was young, "as long as you were dressing up as a character." Thanks in part to social media, the backlash was swift. Kelly apologized both in a written statement and on air at the beginning of her next show, but public sentiment viewed the remarks as too callous and NBC canceled her show by week's end.[58] After lengthy negotiations, however, NBC paid Kelly the remaining $30 million in her multiyear contract.[59]

In 2019, Virginia politicians were thrust into the spotlight when photos from their college yearbooks surfaced, picturing them in blackface. The revelation prompted *USA Today* to undertake a massive study of college yearbooks, revealing more than two hundred examples of racist material from yearbooks throughout the 1970s and 1980s, including students dressed in blackface or KKK robes.[60] Later that year, photos emerged of Canada's prime minister, Justin Trudeau, dressed in brownface, turban, and robes at an Arabian Nights party in the 2001 yearbook from the private school where he was then teaching.[61] Although some called for these politicians to resign, all kept their positions. The contrast between what happened to Megyn Kelly for her remarks about blackface and what happened to those male politicians who sported black- or brownface decades earlier, not only shows how epistemologies of racial ignorance have evolved, but also how they continue to function to protect whiteness.

To understand how white ignorance has been produced and sustained, many studies have examined macro-level factors, such as laws and institutions. Yet much of the time those macro-level policies and ideologies are interpreted through meso-level organizations, such as corporations or schools. Conflating the macro- and meso-levels of analysis runs the risk of underestimating the ways that mainstream organizations contribute to the reproduction or disruption of white supremacy. Indeed, organizations—including colleges—are one of the primary battlegrounds for racial contestation in the US.[62]

Racialized organizations theory, developed by sociologist Victor Ray, posits that recognizing organizations as fundamentally racialized "can help better explain the centrality of organizations in accumulating, managing, monopolizing, and apportioning the resources that make up racial structures."[63] Racialized organizations theory thus acknowledges the central role that organizations play in connecting racial ideologies, cultural schemas, and resource distribution, where cultural schemas are defined as a "template for social action," or an "unwritten rulebook explaining how to write rules."[64] Through this lens, white ignorance is not a static social fact, but something that becomes enacted and adapted within different organizational contexts by different social actors, changing as it spreads within and across fields, yet constantly and intimately connected with how people access resources.[65]

Specifically, Ray's theory highlights the ways that racialized organizations constrain or enhance personal agency—and by extension collective efficacy—for different racial groups. The courses of action available to any individual at any given moment are often dictated by organizational policies and norms. For example, employers and schools may formally determine what employees and students wear, how they spend their time, and how workspace is allocated, while also enforcing norms about speech and emotionality. By limiting the agency of subordinate racial groups while magnifying the agency of dominant racial groups, organizations play a critical role in legitimating the unequal distribution of resources—such as time, money, labor, and power. In this way, whiteness acts as a credential within organizations, proffering increased agency and resources for those in the dominant racial group. Although strong affirmative action policies have sought to diminish this link in selective college admissions and hiring, whiteness still acts as a credential in other ways. Namely, Ray's theory calls attention to the ways that formal rules are often "decoupled" from organizational practices in a racialized manner.[66] The disconnect between most colleges' proclaimed commitments to diversity and inclusion and the parties described at the beginning of this chapter are one cogent example of racialized decoupling of formal rules from actual practices.

How Higher Education Sustains White Dominance

Since their advent, American colleges have fit Ray's definition of racialized organizations. As historian Craig Wilder argued, "The founding, financing, and development of higher education in the colonies were thoroughly intertwined with the economic and social forces that transformed western and central Africa through the slave trade and devastated Indigenous nations in the Americas. The academy was a beneficiary and defender of these processes."[67] Not only were many colleges and universities built by enslaved people and using profits from the exploitation of enslaved Africans and lands violently stolen from Native Americans, for centuries most colleges explicitly excluded students of color from matriculating. For these historically and predominantly white institutions (PWIs),[68] legacies of exclusion were crucial to securing public support and financial solvency.

Unlike elsewhere in the world, the US never established a national university—in part because, in the newly formed nation, such an undertaking was perceived as too much big government, and in part because existing colleges resisted mightily. Although some funding for higher education has always flowed from state and federal governments, an 1819 Supreme Court ruling gave colleges broad independence. Without state intervention to limit the establishment and expansion of new colleges, institutions were left to fend for themselves in a consumer-driven marketplace. In his book detailing the rise of American higher education globally, historian David Labaree credits the growing economic, military, and cultural dominance of the US throughout the twentieth century, upsurge of English as the leading international language, and influx of capital to American universities during the two world wars (while European universities were being devastated) and the Cold War. He notes, however, that American colleges and universities were only able to capitalize on these forces because they were structured in ways that allowed them to adapt to the changing marketplace.[69]

Rather than dedicating themselves wholly to educating students (as they could with secure federal funding), American colleges must make survival their first order of business. College governance models have been built to allow institutional leaders to quickly pursue potential sources of funding. Money comes primarily from tuition payments and alumni donations (often feeding generous endowments), which means colleges have a financial imperative to attract and enroll students and, once students have matriculated, keep them happy enough to earn their continued allegiance and generous gifts. Key to this model is the independent board of trustees—made up of alumni and donors (rather than, for example, faculty or government officials).[70]

In short, elite American colleges have never been altruistic havens for higher learning. Rather, they are market-driven organizations, subject to the whims of consumers. During the early years of the American republic, the supply of colleges far exceeded demand. To stay competitive in this crowded landscape, colleges needed to walk the fine line of differentiating themselves from peer institutions without sacrificing legitimacy. This process of imitation and differentiation produced a highly stratified system. Older schools—with established patterns of training leaders, access to and loyalty from wealthy families, and robust endowments—tended to rise to the top. These schools had no incentives to expand access in ways that might risk their reputations; when demand for higher education has surged, the system has expanded by creating new colleges in lower tiers, not by increasing access to elite institutions.[71]

Going to college became the norm for children of upper-middle-class families during the latter half of the nineteenth century. During the post–Civil War era the economy shifted away from small businesses and toward larger bureaucracies.[72] Employers suddenly needed to hire large numbers of managers—people with general verbal and cognitive capabilities, equipped to function in complex bureaucracies. In small firms, newcomers could start on the factory floor and work their way up, but big corporations required more efficient ways of building a managerial class. The college experience provided both elements required of a good manager: the verbal and cognitive skills to function within complex organizations and the interpersonal skills to succeed in leadership roles.[73] With high school enrollments rising, families that had previously relied on secondary education to distinguish their children now required additional credentials. Competing to attract this wave of consumers, colleges modernized curricula and began offering a more gratifying social experience. Myriad extracurricular activities emerged during this era, including fraternities and intercollegiate athletics.

As research universities took shape in the early 1900s (drawing on the German model but adapted for American consumers), the imperative to attract a broad base of tuition-paying undergraduates remained fundamental for survival. Labaree explained: "The key is to provide a campus experience that leads students to identify closely with the university, which becomes for them a status marker, a club membership, a web of social connections, and a badge of learning. They wear its colors with pride, promote its interests in the community, and donate generously to it as their careers advance."[74] Because undergraduates were essential for fiscal solvency, colleges worked hard to make them happy. Labaree continued, "workout facilities, food courts, rock climbing walls, and inflated grades" were not too high a price to pay for the support undergraduates provided the larger institutional enterprise.[75] To remain competitive, elite liberal arts colleges boasted many of the same features as larger universities. Regarding status, however, elite liberal arts colleges came to occupy a distinct market niche, with a hierarchy all their own.

When undergraduates envision their alma maters, they typically think of the grassy quad, a favorite class, or that notorious party. But behind the scenes, American colleges are structured like other large organizations, with mandates to anticipate market changes and, above all, find enough money to keep their lights on year after year. Because elite colleges must cater to tuition payers and donors to remain solvent, racialized exploitation and exclusion have been integral to their founding and evolution.[76] As a result, despite the ways higher education has changed, its central and enduring structures still incentivize and normalize white dominance.

How Cultural Appropriation Sustains White Dominance

One look at the Halloween costumes available from popular retailers confirms that impersonating ethnic traditions and depicting stereotypes are still big business. Perhaps because, for many white people, their ethnic identity exists as just that—something that makes them special or interesting, like a unique article of clothing, recipe passed through generations, or holiday tradition. But for those whose racial or ethnic identity subjects them to discrimination and oppression, dressing up is not just fun and games, it comes at a steep cost. Despite public outcry in response to party themes that riff on racialized typecasting, anyone can still purchase a ready-made "Native American Headdress" or "Mexican Sombrero" for less than $20 at a party supply store.[77] Dressing up in costumes from other cultures may seem frivolous to some, but the act of turning meaningful cultural objects and traditions into party fun reifies white superiority by trivializing their cultural significance.[78]

Cultural appropriation, in its simplest form, is the adoption of elements of one culture by members of another culture. At this basic level, cultural appropriation has been happening throughout human history. But when members of a dominant culture take elements from a culture of people who have been systematically oppressed by that dominant group, benign-sounding metaphors like "cross pollination" obscure the power dynamics undergirding these encounters. Cultural appropriation is not the same as cultural exchange—in cultural exchange, people share mutually with one another. Cultural appropriation is not the same as assimilation either—marginalized people assimilate by adopting elements of dominant culture but do so to survive and make everyday life less of a struggle. In other words, determining whether the act of borrowing from cultures that are not your own is cultural appropriation depends on historical and contemporary power structures. Those power structures, however, are often not known or visible due to systems that promote white ignorance.

Consider the case of cornrows—a style where hair is braided close to the scalp in raised rows. Without knowing history, cornrows may seem to be a hairstyle anyone can try. In 2015, Valentino's show at Paris Fashion Week featured scores of white models sporting cornrows. Countless nonblack celebrities have been photographed wearing cornrows and braids, including Bo Derek in her infamous role in the 1979 movie *10* and Kim Kardashian in 2018. But cornrows are not devoid of history; cornrows date back to ancient African civilizations and have been closely linked with Black culture over the ages.[79]

For African Americans, hair has been not only a venue for self-expression, but also a mechanism for oppression and discrimination. Employers have deemed cornrows unprofessional so many times that the Hotel and Restaurant Union declared cornrows on the job a "workers' rights issue."[80] In 2016, a federal court ruled that employers can legally fire employees or deny job applicants for wearing dreadlocks and other hairstyles commonly associated with African Americans.[81] By 2023, however, twenty-three states had passed the CROWN (Create a Respectful and Open World for Natural Hair) Act prohibiting discrimination based on hair style and texture.[82] When white people wear cornrows, they are rarely subjected to consequences negatively impacting their livelihood. Understanding historical context and continuing discrimination against African American hair texture and styling sheds light on why debates about whether white people can wear cornrows have become so heated.

CELEBRATING CULTURAL APPROPRIATION   13

In the US, cultural appropriation tends to abet white supremacy while causing harm to people of color by trivializing violent oppression, spreading lies about marginalized cultures, and perpetuating stereotypes. As Parul Sehgal wrote in *The New York Times*, "In a country whose beginnings are so bound up in theft, conversations about appropriation are like a ceremonial staging of the nation's original sins."[83] A clear-eyed understanding of US history is critical to deciphering why some acts of cultural borrowing seem amicable and others draw outrage, yet white ignorance often stands in the way.

How Anti-PC Culture Sustains White Dominance

Some people, however, argue that critiques of cultural appropriation are "political correctness" taken to extremes. To them, everyone has become too sensitive, and we should all be entitled to wear whatever costumes or hairdos we please as a matter of free speech. Google's online dictionary defines politically correct as "the avoidance, often considered as taken to extremes, of forms of expression or action that are perceived to exclude, marginalize, or insult groups of people who are socially disadvantaged or discriminated against." The term "politically correct" goes back nearly as far as the founding of the republic, but its meaning has shifted over time.[84] By the mid-1980s, conservatives began adopting the phrase to insult liberal values.[85] Funded by networks of conservative donors,[86] the movement to weaponize "political correctness" entered the mainstream by way of a series of bestselling books taking aim at higher education, and particularly the kinds of changes accelerating in the wake of affirmative action.[87]

In 1991, President George H. W. Bush pushed this narrative when he proclaimed in his commencement address at the University of Michigan: "The notion of political correctness has ignited controversy across the land. And although the movement arises from the laudable desire to sweep away the debris of racism, sexism, and hatred, it replaces old prejudices with new ones. It declares certain topics off-limits, certain expressions off-limits, even certain gestures off-limits. What began as a cause for civility has soured into a cause of conflict and even censorship."[88] In a front-page story, *The New York Times* summarized: "In a speech devoted to three freedoms—enterprise, speech and spirit—the president joined a growing political backlash against the idea that free speech should be subordinated to the civil rights of women and minority members."[89] Critics voiced their opposition, hoping to draw attention to how the president and others were using freedom of speech to problematize the increasing presence of women and people of color at universities. Yet, for the next twenty-five years, conservatives would continue to weaponize anti-PC rhetoric.[90]

Although the attacks of September 11, 2001, turned attention away from debates about political correctness and toward debates about terrorism, political correctness reemerged in the final years of Barack Obama's presidency. As the Black Lives Matter (BLM) movement grew, articles in popular publications began criticizing activists. Critics relied on the same strategies as in the 1990s—complaining other people were creating and enforcing speech codes, while simultaneously attempting to enforce their own speech codes; designating themselves arbiters of which political demands deserved to be taken seriously; continually complaining, in highly visible publications, that they were being silenced. The conversation initially called out universities, as in the 1990s, but the language had changed. Conversations about "difference" and "multiculturalism," were now about "trigger warnings," "safe spaces," "microaggressions," "privilege," and "cultural appropriation." This time, drawing on tropes portraying millennials as spoiled narcissists, students received more contempt than faculty. Elite students were portrayed as sensitive "snowflakes" unable to handle the heat of the real world.[91]

For example, national newspapers picked up a story of undergraduates at Oberlin College, a liberal arts college in Ohio, accusing campus dining services of cultural appropriation when the cafeteria called chicken on a slab of rice "chicken sushi" and pulled pork on ciabatta bread "banh-mi" (a traditional Vietnamese sandwich). The story was initially written by a student for a class assignment and published in the campus newspaper. The dispute was settled calmly via conversations between international students and dining staff members wherein, according to a follow-up story from the campus newspaper, staff agreed to "improve the naming process of meals by not associating excessively modified dishes with specific cultures."[92] The problem seemed to stem from dining services relying on online recipes. Yet conservative critics inflated the story into another example of overly sensitive "snowflakes."[93]

During the 2016 election cycle Republican candidates used political correctness as a "catchall synonym for liberal cowardice or caution."[94] Presidential candidate Donald Trump denounced political correctness so frequently, many argued this alone was his secret to victory.[95] In contrast to when, in 1991, President Bush warned political correctness threatened free speech, Trump not only criticized the idea of political correctness, he said and did the kinds of things PC culture prohibited—such as publicly mocking a man with a disability.[96] Trump's election suggested that many voters opposed political correctness, and a 2016 survey by Pew Research Center confirmed that 59% of Americans agreed: "Too many people are easily offended these days over the language that others use."[97] Two years later, a survey confirmed that

80% of Americans still agreed that "political correctness is a problem in our country." By this time, however, 82% of Americans had come to believe that hate speech was also a problem.[98] These data reveal that, for most Americans, neither extreme feels desirable. But these data also show how effective the discursive machine of the conservative right has been in weaponizing anti-PC sentiments to sustain and promote white dominance.

How Laws Sustain White Dominance on Campus

Conservative organizations have defended the right to be racist on campus through concerted efforts to dismantle racial harassment laws and bias incident response teams. Although hate crimes are clearly defined, any act falling short of those legal criteria forces a college to come up with its own response. Hate crimes are defined as "a criminal offense that is motivated, in whole or in part, by the perpetrator's bias against the victim(s) based on their race, ethnicity, religion, sexual orientation, gender, gender identity, or disability."[99] Under the Clery Act, colleges must report data for eleven types of crimes: murder, sex offenses, robbery, aggravated assault, burglary, motor vehicle theft, arson, simple assault, larceny, intimidation, and vandalism. Yet many acts of racism do not meet the threshold of being considered "hate crimes."

In some cases, institutions have used anti-harassment policies to address racism on campus. Racial harassment policies were built alongside similar policies that prohibit sexual harassment. Unlike sexual harassment policies, however, racial harassment policies have been the target of widespread and coordinated legal challenges from critics arguing that such policies infringe on their rights to freedom of speech. Because of these challenges, the legality of racial harassment policies has been questioned in court to an extent that sexual harassment policies have not. According to sociologists Wendy Leo Moore and Joyce Bell, "this has created contradictions in harassment law and has led to confusion and contradiction in the legal and policy-making environment at colleges." As a result, 71% of US colleges and universities have sexual harassment policies, while only 14% have racial harassment policies.[100] In the absence of such policies, students retain the right to commit racist acts—so long as those acts are not crimes or violations of college policies. For example, at the college depicted in this study, students can be disciplined for, "conduct that threatens, instills fear, or infringes upon the rights, dignity, and integrity of any person," but how those broad terms are defined is left to the discretion of administrators.[101]

What then? Hundreds of colleges, including the one in this study, have voluntarily established bias incident response teams. Bias incidents are acts of conduct, speech, or expression that target individuals and groups based on their actual or perceived race/color, religion, ethnicity, national origin, gender, gender identity/expression, age, disability, or sexual orientation, but are not crimes or even necessarily violations of college policies.[102] While their missions differ, bias incident response teams tend to gather and report data, identify campus resources and coordinate response to each incident, and monitor campus climate regarding inclusivity and safety. Of course, bias incident response teams have also generated pushback from critics arguing that such reporting threatens their rights to freedom of speech.[103]

While many schools have pledged to take bias incidents seriously, deciding which acts to censure and which to allow can be fraught. What words and actions are offensive and hurtful, but allowable under the guise of free speech? When is it okay to dress up in an ethnic- or race-inspired costume and when is it not? And what should the consequences be for crossing the line? As societal norms continue to change and vary by political leanings,[104] college administrators will continue to wrestle with these difficult questions. In this book, rather than prescribing answers to those questions, I widen the lens, seeking to better understand how the organizational context of a college impacts the ways administrators navigate their responses to racially charged controversies.

Framing White Dominance through an Organizational Lens

Until recently, sociologists who study organizations—such as colleges—predominantly subscribed to neo-institutional theory, a macro-level view examining how organizations are influenced by competition and cooperation within broader societal contexts.[105] Elite colleges, for example, stay ever mindful of keeping pace with peer institutions—erecting new admissions' buildings or rock climbing walls—to maintain their status among a certain ilk of schools, but simultaneously work to strategically distinguish themselves in ways that do not threaten their legitimacy.

Inhabited institutional theory continues to recognize these macro-level factors but shifts the spotlight to how social actors bridge local meanings and institutional structures, underlining the meso-level role that organizations play in shaping social policies.[106] In higher education, administrators, faculty, and students must interpret—and perhaps adapt or resist—what we are expected to say and do each day. Because each of us possesses agency, organizational structures are not simply created through top-down edicts or external pressures, but also by our choices. When broad level cultural ideals

CELEBRATING CULTURAL APPROPRIATION   17

have meaning at the ground level and are being practiced, the institution is said to be "inhabited."[107]

Racialized organizations theory reminds us that the ways institutions become inhabited are never race neutral. Throughout this book, I will return to the four tenets of racialized organizations theory. Racialized organizations: limit agency of subordinate racial groups and magnify agency among dominant racial groups, legitimate unequal distribution of resources, treat whiteness as a credential, and decouple formal rules from organizational practices in a racialized manner.[108] The degree to which organizational dynamics rely on racial criteria varies within and across organizations, such that colleges can sustain structures of oppression without appearing explicitly racist.[109] While prior studies have shown how the culture of a campus is shaped by structural factors like student body size, geographic location, and athletic league, as well as by micro-level factors like how students navigate physical spaces, this book will argue that racialization also matters.

Recent studies applying inhabited institutional theory within higher education show how school size impacts students' interactions. In ethnographic studies of how colleges shape undergraduates' political behaviors, sociologists Amy Binder, Kate Wood,[110] and Daisy Reyes[111] compare multiple institutions and find that because small, residential colleges engender strong sense of community and lack of anonymity, activism tends to take the form of deliberation and dialogue—which Binder and Wood dub "civilized discourse."[112] Students identify with the college as a whole so much that campus feels like a bubble, "enclosed and isolated from other communities."[113] Because students are known campus wide by faculty and peers, they worry any misstep might damage their reputation. In contrast, undergraduates at large universities were not tethered to a collective campus community, identifying instead with smaller social pockets; feelings of anonymity freed students to engage in provocative activism, like protests. The relationship between institution size and political behaviors is one example of how structural characteristics become "inhabited."

A college's status also shapes students' interactions. Elite status is not merely granted by institutional ranking systems, like that of *U.S. News & World Report*, it must also be inhabited. Sociologist Shamus Khan's ethnography of a prestigious boarding school argued that contemporary elites prize the ability to be "at ease" in any social setting and highly selective schools socialize students into this practice.[114] To occupy positions of power, students must be comfortable at country clubs and tailgate parties, know opera and Jay-Z, and interact easily with affluent white families as well as everyone else.

Despite access to elite schools opening over recent decades, elite cultural practices still elucidate symbolic boundaries based on social class.[115] Yet because contemporary eliteness emerged as a product of colonial regimes reliant on racialized exploitation, this embodiment of social class is deeply intertwined with productions of whiteness. Becoming elite thus requires not only material resources, but also whiteness or, what scholars Ruben Gaztambide-Fernandez and Leila Angod have a dubbed a "precarious approximation of whiteness."[116] One does not have to possess physical markers of whiteness to become elite, rather a particular performance of whiteness—including gestures and behaviors as well as kinds of knowledge and ways of knowing.

By socializing students to believe that admissions processes reward intellect and hard work, elite schools promote meritocratic beliefs that obscure systematic inequities.[117] Just as scholar Cheryl Harris argued the US legal system endows whiteness as a form of property, scholars Zeus Leonardo and Alicia Broderick have argued that the notion of "smartness," as co-constituted with whiteness, acts as an intersecting ideology of oppression.[118] A study of Harvard Law argued that, based on this meritocratic myth, students were socialized to value collective identity over individual gains, which produced "collective eminence." In other words, students built social networks and strived to maintain their membership within the collective, with long-term hopes of profiting from those connections.[119] As sociologist Lauren Rivera found in her study of elite professional service firms' hiring practices, although employers strived to increase diversity among applicants, hiring processes still prioritized similarity to existing employees regarding background, self-presentation, and extracurricular pursuits.[120] While considerable evidence supports the "strength of weak ties" in social networks generally,[121] elites tend to cultivate dense, robust networks,[122] in part due to these racialized processes of social reproduction.

Although not explicitly situated in organizational theory, critical whiteness scholars have called out the myriad ways the institution of higher education perpetuates white supremacy. In addition to whiteness acting as a racial contract and as property, whiteness has been theorized as structure, ideology, discourse, feeling, and affect.[123] Scholars have shown how "white normativity" operates in higher education, with PWIs acting as gatekeepers of mainstream knowledge, perpetuating monoculturalism, antiblackness and settler colonialism, while protecting and obfuscating the power of whiteness.[124] Similarly, the discourse of whiteness denies the realities of people of color by not naming systemic racism and minimizing experiences of racism, both historically and in the present day.[125] Emotionality permeates these structures and processes; as white feelings—guilt, defensiveness, denial, discomfort, to name

CELEBRATING CULTURAL APPROPRIATION

a few—drive decision-making.[126] Reflecting on the totality of ways white supremacy impacts people of color, scholars Bianca Williams, Dian Squire, and Frank Tuitt call out the parallels between contemporary PWIs and slave plantations, arguing that campuses engage in "plantation politics" by continuing to exploit people of color for economic gain.[127]

This book seeks to bring together insights from critical whiteness studies in higher education with organizational theories, to draw linkages between the ways whiteness manifests in organizations and the associated material effects.[128] While my data do not speak to all aspects of racialized organizations theory, one purpose of this book is to investigate how—in addition to the ways size and status impact students' attitudes and behaviors—racialization matters at elite colleges. I take up Ray's call to investigate whether the "naturalized and unmarked whiteness of mainstream organizations assist[s] in the production of racial ignorance," in the context of higher education;[129] where racial ignorance refers to the ways that "not knowing" buttresses structural white supremacy.[130] To study how the unmarked whiteness of a college incentivizes white ignorance, and in turn racialized costume parties, this book examines the ways organizational structures and scripts work in tandem. Yet even in the context of these coercive structures and scripts, my findings highlight how individual agency matters and, in doing, show how a racialized organization becomes inhabited. The four tenets of racialized organizations theory provide an analytical framework, highlighting the ways colleges: constrain or enhance personal agency for different racial groups, legitimate the unequal distribution of resources, allow whiteness to act as a credential, and decouple formal rules from organizational practices in a racialized manner.

Studying the Experiential Core of the Undergraduate Experience

Intimate connections with empirical reality facilitate the development of relevant and valid theory. Since graduates of highly selective colleges wield disproportionate economic and cultural influence,[131] understanding how these institutions shape students' conceptions of racial inequities on campus and in society may provide critical insight into pathways for social change. Sociologist Randall Collins argued that the struggle between groups within a society is fought both *over* organizations and *through* organizations.[132] Such is the case in the battle for racial justice, being fought over and through many types of organizations, but particularly colleges and universities.

Spurred by Stevens, Armstrong, and Arum's landmark review of the field, sociologists of higher education have refocused on understanding the "experiential core" of college life, uncovering the structures and processes that contribute to the hidden curriculum—the unofficial and often unintended lessons each institution imparts—via book-length case studies.[133] Through nuanced understandings of students' experiences on one or two campuses, this body of qualitative research has inductively revealed contrasts and commonalities within the vast landscape of American colleges. Recent case studies have shown how the history, culture, and structures of individual institutions shape students' political attitudes and strategies,[134] perceptions of social class,[135] friendship networks,[136] ways of talking about race,[137] and career pathways.[138] The nuance revealed by each case study has chipped away at the black box previously obscuring the "experiential core" of the undergraduate experience. My book follows this tradition, presenting an in-depth case study[139] of an elite campus to investigate why racially charged costume parties persist. Even though this book delves into the experiences of students at a single institution, the data reveal both macro- and micro-level structures and processes that shape what and how students learn about race, diversity, and inequality—insights that are beyond the scope of even the highest quality multi-campus survey projects.

Building on sociologists Wendy Leo Moore and Joyce Bell's[140] assertion that racist acts offer windows into institutional processes, Bowdoin College, an elite liberal arts college, offers a theoretically relevant case study. The graduating class of 2018 is the focal point, given the three highly publicized racially themed parties that occurred during their first two years on campus: a pilgrims and Indians–themed Thanksgiving party known as "Cracksgiving," a "Gangster party" (street gang, not Mafia), and the "Tequila party" described earlier. Given the intensity of media attention surrounding these parties, masking the institution's identity was not possible. However, every effort has been made to protect the confidentiality of respondents, including altering or omitting demographic details that were not relevant to the analysis and changing names to pseudonyms. A diverse team of trained Bowdoin undergraduates were involved in study design, data collection, processing, and analysis to ground the findings in the student experience and engage in "respondent validation," a practice shown to increase validity in qualitative research.

Bowdoin's Early History: "Harvard of the North"?

The history of Bowdoin follows the same storyline as other colleges of its era. When it was founded in what is now rural Maine in 1794,[141] its constitution and criteria for admission mimicked Harvard's—Harvard being older (founded in 1636) and wealthier. Enrollments were small and, while the ages

CELEBRATING CULTURAL APPROPRIATION

of applicants varied because high schools were not yet the norm, the student body was otherwise quite homogeneous, made up primarily of the sons of wealthy white merchants.[142] Although the size of the institution would grow over time, the demographic makeup remained similar until the late 1960s. John Brown Russwurm was the first Black graduate in 1826, but Samuel Herman Dreer, the next Black student, did not graduate until 1910—eighty-four years later. The college did not admit women until 1971.

Although Bowdoin was founded with religious ties, it no longer adheres to a specific moral doctrine. As its allegiances were contested by members of various Protestant denominations each time a new president was chosen, all religious ties were severed by the early twentieth century. Since then, the college has had the vague imprint of a Protestant institution but has not been wed to any specific doctrine. For example, the college still refers to the words President McKeen spoke at its opening: "Literary institutions are founded and endowed for the common good, and not for the private advantage of those who resort to them for education."[143] While historian Louis Hatch reminds us there would have been nothing extraordinary about these words when they were spoken, they have been employed on ceremonial occasions as a placeholder for a broadly defined mission, and perpetually adapted to changing times.

How the college portrays its history has also evolved. For example, Joshua Chamberlain (renowned Union General and former president of the college) and Harriet Beecher Stowe (who wrote *Uncle Tom's Cabin* while her husband was on the faculty) are both memorialized on campus, but it is often overlooked that in 1858 the college awarded an honorary degree to Jefferson Davis, US senator who would later serve as the first and only president of the Confederate States of America. Lest that be dismissed as a historical footnote, starting in the 1970s and continuing for nearly forty-five years, the college also awarded a student prize in his name.[144] Many other examples of Bowdoin's diffuse moral compass litter its history, its ever-evolving norms and policies striving to match the standards of its peer institutions and the monied elite that fill its coffers.

Student Body

Today, Bowdoin is a top-ranking liberal arts college, matriculating approximately 1,800 undergraduates. Of those, nearly all are full-time, residential, traditionally aged students. At the time this study was conducted, the six-year graduation rate was 95%. Sixty-two percent of students identified as white (non-Hispanic); 51% were women and 49% men.[145] About 36% of students were varsity athletes.[146] In 2017–18, annual tuition (including room and board) was about $66,000. The college maintained a need-blind admissions policy, meaning that all admitted students' financial needs were met, and need was not a factor in admissions decisions. About 46% of students received need-based financial aid. In addition, the college has maintained a test-optional policy since the 1970s, meaning that applicants were not required to submit SAT or ACT scores. The college's admissions process has become more selective over time (partially due to changes in the Common App and online technologies), with the 24% admit rate in 2001–2 dropping to 15% in 2017–18 and 10% by 2018–19. With its brick buildings, idyllic quad, and robust endowment, Bowdoin presents itself as a quintessential elite New England college.

Like many of its peer institutions, Bowdoin's student body has undergone significant demographic changes over the last twenty years. Fraternities and sororities were phased out in the late 1990s. According to the Common Data Set, during 2001–2, 79% of students identified as white and 14% as students of color. Only two years later (2003–4), 20% identified as students of color, and only two years after that (2005–6), 25%. By 2010–11, 31% of the student body identified as students of color and that number remained about constant for the next decade.

Research Design

To capture the dynamic interplay between organizational structures and individual agency, this case study draws on multiple sources of data, including interviews, surveys, and document analysis.

INTERVIEWS

Interviews were conducted with two samples of students from the class of 2018: a random sample, and a targeted sample. For both samples, the interview protocol (detailed in appendix B) inquired about precollege experiences, social, academic, and extracurricular activities each year on campus, racial, social class, and gender identities, sexual orientation, and experiences on campus linked with these identities. The protocol also inquired about attitudes and experiences related to diversity, discrimination, and segregation on campus; degree of involvement in and reactions to the controversial parties; and impressions of success and belonging at college.[147] Superfluous words such as "like," "um," and other repeating phrases (e.g., "you know") have been removed from respondents' quotes to improve readability, only when removal does not alter the speaker's meaning. Ellipses are used to indicate omissions for the sake of brevity.

Random Sample. First, to capture a range of perspectives on the parties and reduce selection bias, in-depth one-to-three-hour interviews were conducted with a stratified random sample of students from the class of 2018 (n = 57, roughly 12% of the 480-student cohort, response rate = 51%). The roster of matriculated students was stratified by the Office of Institutional Research by gender, such that half of the selected students would be women and half men. The roster was also stratified by race, such that half of the selected students would have identified themselves on their college application as Black/African American, Asian/Asian American, American Indian/Alaskan Native, Native Hawaiian/Pacific Islander, Hispanic/Latino (and any race), or any combination of categories. Although students of color represented less than 35% of the student body, they were intentionally overrepresented in the random sample to better account for the enormous diversity masked by this pan-racial category. Students of color were homogenized into a single group—an act of whiteness in itself—because Bowdoin (and other elite PWIs) presented student demographics this way at the time (e.g., admissions' web page), and students (including the research team) tended to talk about racial/ethnic relations on campus this way. The remaining half of respondents identified as white or from another country, or opted not to indicate their race. Selected students were first contacted via email by me (a white, cis, woman faculty member), with two to four follow-up email solicitations from a student interviewer. Interviews were conducted by trained undergraduates during fall 2017. As much as possible, students of color were interviewed by students of color (though not necessarily matched by race) and white students were interviewed by white students. At the close of each interview, the respondent completed a brief demographic survey.

For some respondents, the information listed in the institutional database did not match their lived identity. During data analysis, I identified respondents according to the race, class, and gender identity self-described during the interview and brief demographic survey, and not as listed in the institutional database. By this measure, of the respondents in the random sample, 47% identified as women, 51% as men, and 2% as another gender. About 9% identified as first-generation students and 37% reported receiving financial aid. In terms of race, 47% identified as students of color, while 53% identified as white. During the interviews however, in response to the question, "How would you describe your racial and ethnic identities?," several students classified as students of color by institutional databases stated that they considered themselves racially white and ethnically Latinx. For example, one respondent described: "You probably can't see it, but my mother is from Argentina, so technically speaking I say I'm from Argentina. But if I ever [said I was Latino] people would be extremely upset, because I would be assigning myself to a different racial identity I never had to deal with." Similarly, another respondent reported: "I'm half-Hispanic, but I identify as white." By this measure, 33% of the random sample self-identified as students of color, 14% were classified as students of color by institutional measures but considered themselves white presenting, and 53% identified as white.

The first time I include a quote from an interviewee in each chapter, I include the race and/or ethnicity and gender they marked on the demographic survey that followed their interview. This is done throughout the book to better capture the complexity of students' racial and ethnic identities. In appendix A, I have also included a brief quote capturing how they described their race and/or ethnicity during the interview. When reporting the student's response would compromise confidentiality, I have noted that. In this way, race as an individual identity is distinguished from race as a credential or as a systemic factor.

Targeted Sample. In addition to the random sample, in May 2018, I interviewed students who were involved in or outspoken regarding one or more of the parties ($n = 11$, response rate = 75%), including many of the party hosts, students who wore controversial costumes, and students who pushed back against the parties. I began by interviewing students who had written publicly about their involvement in the parties in the student newspaper, then built a snowball sample from these contacts. Of the targeted sample, three had been interviewed (in the fall) in the random sample. For these students, I probed more deeply regarding events related to the parties during the spring interview. Of the targeted sample, 46% identified as students of color, 18% were classified as students of color by institutional measures but considered themselves racially white, and 36% identified as white. About 9% identified as first-generation college students and 37% reported receiving financial aid; 73% identified as women and 27% as men. These students are also included in appendix A.

SURVEYS

In addition, in April 2018, a fifty-question survey was distributed using Qualtrics online platform to all Bowdoin students ($n = 973$, response rate = 54%). This anonymous survey included closed-ended questions about friend groups, extracurricular activities, academics, sense of belonging, attitudes about race, social class, affirmative action, affinity groups, diversity, and demographic variables. This survey data helped situate the experiences of interviewees in the context of the general student population and allowed for comparison between the perspectives of the class of 2018 and the three other classes on campus at that time (Classes of 2019, 2020, and 2021). Survey respondents were largely representative of the student body, with 64% identifying as white and 36% identifying as students of color, 54% receiving need-based financial aid, 15% first-generation college students, and roughly 25% from each class year cohort. Regarding gender however, women were overrepresented, representing 60% of respondents; men made up 37%, and less than 4% identified as another gender identity.

DOCUMENT ANALYSIS

My research team compiled and coded documents relevant to understanding structures and policies that shaped the student experience for the four years the target cohort resided on campus (2014–18). These documents included but were not limited to the Bowdoin College web page (spring 2018, all primary pages plus secondary pages within Admissions and Student Life), publicly available speeches and documents (available on the president's web page or linked from articles in *The Bowdoin Orient*), admissions brochures, minutes of Bowdoin Student Government (BSG) meetings, five decennial re-accreditation reviews, other archival documents, media accounts of the controversies, and nearly one hundred issues of the *Orient* (every weekly issue spanning fall 2013 to spring 2018).

THE *ORIENT*

The Bowdoin Orient prides itself on being "the nation's oldest continuously published college weekly," with a new issue released every Friday, totaling twenty-four issues per academic year. The publication is entirely student-run and "editorially independent of the college and its administrators," reporting "news and information relevant to the college community" and "committed to serving as an open forum for thoughtful and diverse discussion and debate on issues of interest to the college community." To this point, the college has no journalism major, no journalism professors, and the *Orient* does not have a faculty or staff advisor. Weekly issues are distributed free of charge on campus, and the website boasts "several hundred" off-campus print subscribers.[148] In 2018, the *Orient* was named College Newspaper of the Year by the New England Society of News Editors and the New England Newspaper and

Press Association. In 2017, the *Orient* had been awarded first runner-up, and in 2016, it received an honorable mention.

While, as evidenced in this study, many students viewed the *Orient* as an important platform for campus-wide communication, others rarely picked up a copy. During the years the class of 2018 was on campus, the *Orient* struggled to remain relevant and undertook internal work to diversify its staff. The *Orient* staff was known as its own social group, associated with specific residential spaces, and comprised mainly of students who had participated in their high school newspapers. Realizing their staff was overwhelmingly white, the editors worked to provide more training for new writers, open their social circle to new members, and encourage opinion pieces and repeating columns from a more diverse cast of students.

BOWDOIN STUDENT GOVERNMENT

BSG was elected annually by popular vote, with turnout rates of 60–70%. Meetings were held once every two weeks and were open to all students, with minutes posted publicly online.[149] Students of color were frequently elected to BSG; in 2017–18, more than half the executive committee identified as students of color. My data suggest that the overrepresentation of students of color in these highly visible, yet largely symbolic roles was likely symptomatic of voters' abstract commitment to performative diversity.[150] Few respondents mentioned BSG in their discussions of campus life, as it was not seen as a powerful unifying or divisive force until it responded to the controversial parties.

The Case of the Missing Structural Response

Drawing from this in-depth case study, this book will show why racialized costume parties persist at PWIs. First, the tenets of racialized organizations theory illuminate how an elite liberal arts college's history and structures inform its present-day culture and practices. Germinating from the civil rights movement and continuing today, elite and historically white colleges have invested in cultivating "diverse" student bodies as a marker of status.[151] In his 1978 "diversity rationale," Supreme Court Justice Powell argued that the educational benefits of learning alongside people different from oneself justify using race as one factor in selective college admissions. Scholars, however, contend that expecting students to benefit simply from proximity constitutes "magical thinking."[152] Even as selective colleges have matriculated more students of color and educators unpack the latent potential of intentionally diverse residential communities, elite campuses remain white spaces—where white norms, values, and cultural representations shape the student experience,[153] enhancing the agency of white students while constraining the individual and collective efficacy of students of color.

Yet my data also show how elite colleges tend to treat racism as an individual problem, concealing the unmarked whiteness of those structures and legitimating the unequal distribution of resources. Administrators rely on discourse that erases institutionalized racism and centuries of exclusion and oppression, by benignly encouraging students to communicate across differences. Administrators further racialized inequities by leaning on the labor of students of color to educate their white peers. When racist acts occur, administrators intervened only with the perpetrators (and occasionally the victims) to avoid disrupting the structures that reproduce white dominance and white ignorance.

In addition, this case study shows that parties recur because even the most idyllic residential campus is not really the "bubble" students believe it to be. Students bring with them preconceived notions of race, status, and merit.[154] They also maintain access to whatever resources and liabilities might be embedded in their existing social networks. When the going gets tough on campus, privileged students draw economic, social, and cultural capital from their networks.[155] Because the American system of higher education is largely privately funded—through donations that serve as tax write-offs for the wealthy[156]—and the broader political and economic machine feeds on racialized exploitation, a college's legitimacy and survival depends chiefly on the largess of donors who have benefited from racialized capitalism. Thus, small colleges have powerful disincentives to engage in anti-racist interventions if they have the potential to alienate major donors.

So, what do undergraduates on a small, white, elite campus learn from racially charged costume parties? As you will see in the chapters ahead, they learn what they are taught. A small number of perpetrators and motivated bystanders soak up educational interventions and begin to acknowledge the sheer enormity of whiteness. Students of color coerced into educating their peers learn that the college will protect its own interests over theirs, regardless of how selflessly they give their time, labor, and intellect. Meanwhile, campus structures and practices encourage most other students to maintain the status quo—the structures, ideologies, discourses, and feelings of whiteness.

2

Multiculturalism or Monoculturalism?
Producing Unmarked Whiteness

While other studies have focused on diversity-related programming on college campuses, this book—by necessity—broadens the scope. Diversity work was still in its early stages at Bowdoin in the fall of 2014, when the class of 2018 arrived on campus. The college had run a Bias Incident Group since 1988, and a committee aimed at increasing diversity in faculty hiring since 2009, but otherwise most of the efforts were concentrated in Student Affairs. In 2014, the Associate Dean for Multicultural Student Programs oversaw nearly all diversity-adjacent work: serving as advisor to all "historically underrepresented student groups," collaborating with faculty and staff to "coordinate resources to support students of color," serving "as a liaison between the college and families of students of color," and overseeing two of three affinity houses. The three other paid staff explicitly supporting minoritized students and/or faculty were part time. During the next four years, diversity-related infrastructure would expand, but clearly a study of only those fledgling diversity-related efforts could not answer the question of why racially themed parties persisted.

Instead, in the next sections, I examine how core organizational structures and prescribed ways of talking about race produced and legitimated white supremacy and white ignorance on campus. First, in line with racialized organizations theory, I delve into the ways core policies and practices legitimate white dominance by limiting agency of subordinate racial groups and magnifying agency among the dominant racial group, legitimating unequal distribution of resources, treating whiteness as a credential, and decoupling formal rules from organizational practices in a racialized manner. Specifically, my data point to selective admissions, National Collegiate Athletics Association (NCAA) Division III (DIII) athletics and other extracurricular activities, and campus housing as core organizational structures colluding to produce and defend normative whiteness on campus.

Second, I document how two scripts for talking about race obscured these structures and sustained white ignorance: the diversity and naturalization scripts. By simultaneously commodifying diversity and explaining social segregation as "natural," organizationally produced scripts erased all mention of the structures producing unequal access, agency, and resources. In sum, this chapter shows how students inhabit a racialized organization, as core structures and policies work in tandem with scripts to dictate and disguise the unequal distribution of power.

Why do racialized costume parties recur on elite campuses? The detailed answer has to do with the interplay between structures and agency. In the latter chapters of this book, you will gain insights into individual's perceptions and behaviors. In those narratives, as in our daily lives, organizational structures are often obscured. This chapter sets the stage, describing the contexts that shape students' interactions on campus, and highlighting the unmarked whiteness of those core structures.

Producing White Monoculture:
Elite College Admissions

Prior research has shown that while elite schools socialize students to believe that their admissions processes reward intellect and hard work,[1] notions of "smartness," have been co-constituted with whiteness.[2] Because elite admissions processes not only dictate who is invited to campus, but also how students think about themselves and their peers, the work of admissions has wide-reaching implications for campus life.

The selective admissions process we know today took shape in the early decades of the twentieth century. Visits by admissions officers to prep schools began during the Great Depression, when colleges were desperate to attract paying customers. During this time, elite universities admitted all students who passed their entrance exams, which effectively limited the field of applicants to sons of wealthy white Anglo-Saxon Protestant (WASP) families.[3] By the 1920s, the most prestigious universities grew wary that too many Jewish students were being admitted and abandoned purely academic criteria in favor of more subjective criteria—such as "character"—that allowed them to regulate the religious composition of entering classes. According to historian Jerome Karabel, Jews were seen as undesirable to many of the WASP patrons top colleges depended upon financially.[4]

Building on this system, elite colleges have tinkered with entrance criteria for the last century—responding to status group struggles in society, but also external stakeholders and organizational interests. According to what Karabel dubbed the "iron law" of admissions, "an institution will retain a particular process of selection only so long as it produces outcomes that correspond to perceived organizational interests."[5] Following World War II, the GI Bill (1944) made financial aid available to throngs of middle- and working-class white men for the first time. This federal investment in higher education attracted students who were more diverse with regard to socioeconomic status, geography, and religion. Not until the monumental civil rights victories of the 1950s and 1960s—when the challenges to "separate but equal" grew louder and more forceful—did historically and predominantly white institutions (PWIs) began to admit previously barred or underrepresented groups in earnest, including Jews, women, and students of color.[6]

The earliest race-conscious admissions policies emerged in the early 1960s—Harvard started in 1961—with more colleges following suit as civil rights movements gathered momentum. Affirmative action policies emerged in response to societal pressures, but variation as to when individual institutions adopted race-conscious admissions policies was filtered through organizational stakeholders. Campuses led by administrators who "were inspired by the civil rights movement and who were unconstrained in their ability to establish programmatic initiatives" became early adopters. Leaders who felt resistance from organizational stakeholders (e.g., donors, trustees) adopted later, with some establishing race-conscious admissions following the Watts riots of 1965, and others not until after the assassination of Dr. Martin Luther King Jr. in 1968.[7] As public sentiment shifted, the number of racially minoritized students on campus soon emerged as a status symbol among elite institutions. Shifts both in rhetoric and student demographics brought a cascade of changes to campus life.

Bowdoin, by my archival research, was a late adopter, not instituting institutionally sponsored recruiting and race-conscious admissions until 1969. That fall, the language in the college handbook shifted accordingly: "Proud of its tradition in educating Maine and New England boys, Bowdoin wants to balance their representation with students from across the nation and the world. Those from the suburbs remain most welcome, but Bowdoin is actively seeking to make their college experience more vital by introducing more students from the inner city and the ghetto."[8] This statement worked to reassure white suburban families that their sons (and their tuition payments) were still welcome, while relying on euphemism to market the notion that students of color from the "inner city and the ghetto" would "introduce" a desirable vitality to the campus experience. In other words, students of color were admitted expressly for the benefit of their white peers.

Progress toward greater racial equity never proceeds without backlash and, by the 1970s, challenges to affirmative action policies had made their way to the Supreme Court. In the 1978 *Regents of the University of California v. Bakke* case, involving admissions procedures at the UC Davis medical school, the Supreme Court agreed that quota-based practices were unlawful but upheld the use of race-conscious practices as a "plus" factor. In Justice Powell's opinion, largely considered the swing vote in favor of race-conscious policies, he rejected three of the four arguments defending the school's practice—reducing the historical deficit of minorities in medical professions, countering the effects of societal discrimination, and increasing the number of doctors practicing in underserved communities—and only agreed with the claim that race could be used in admissions to achieve educational benefits flowing from a diverse student cohort.[9] Even as affirmative action policies began diversifying elite campuses, commitments to whiteness remained prominent.

Powell's "diversity rationale" was endorsed in subsequent cases. In 2003, two related cases came out of the University of Michigan: *Grutter v. Bollinger* and *Gratz v. Bollinger* and together these cases allowed for race-conscious admissions policies to continue, so long as race was part of what the court called "individualized, holistic review."[10] Affirmative action was revisited by the Supreme Court in 2016; in *Fisher v. University of Texas*, the court again ruled in favor of the use of race as one of many factors in holistic admissions decisions to ensure a diverse student body.[11] But challenges to affirmative action continued. In *Students for Fair Admissions v. Harvard*, plaintiffs argued that Harvard effectively set a restrictive quota on the number of Asian American students admitted, and, in 2023, the Supreme Court responded by ruling race-conscious admissions programs unlawful.[12]

Sustaining White Monoculture: Elite Admissions Today

While important, controversies surrounding affirmative action have provided an elaborate distraction; keeping public attention on how race might be used in admissions obscures systems that have explicitly and implicitly advantaged white students. Sociologist Mitchell Stevens's ethnography of the selective admissions process argued that, for students from privileged families, the transition from high school to college has become "a seamless web of interdependencies: between guidance counselors and admissions officers; between youthful athletic talent and athletic league standings; between high property taxes, large tuition checks, and excellent academics."[13] As elite admissions have become more competitive, the hoops wealthy white parents jump through to pass their privilege onto their children—and make it look like their kids earned it in a class-neutral system—are becoming more elaborate and expensive. They start early, intervening on behalf of their children to ensure the best possible outcomes.[14] Indeed, the admissions criteria enforced by elite colleges act as blueprints for childrearing in middle- and upper-class America.[15]

Elite colleges claim to run a meritocratic contest—where the best and brightest earn admission based on objective criteria—but every stage of the process is rigged in favor of white and wealthy families. Admissions decisions are not made about applicants, but about applications—admissions officers can only evaluate the information presented to them. Not only can students with more resources craft more compelling files, but ratings are based on many criteria impacted by systemic racism, and over which privileged parents exert some control: high school quality, curriculum difficulty, grades, class ranking, letters of recommendation, and extracurricular activities.[16]

Although many elite colleges now advertise generous commitments to need-blind admissions and racial diversity, at Bowdoin these priorities were somehow balanced such that white and upper-class students remained the majority. As evidence, 68% of students identified as white, compared to 54% of college-aged Americans.[17] Sixty-nine percent of students came from the top fifth of the income distribution, while only 3.8% came from the bottom fifth.[18] In addition, students from private schools comprised 42% of the student body, compared to only 10% of high school students nationally.[19]

Why focus on admissions in a book about costume parties? Through the lens of racialized organizations theory, selective admissions are one example of how colleges play a critical role in legitimating the unequal distribution of resources—in this case, slots in the entering class at one of the highest-ranking liberal arts colleges in the nation. But admissions decisions also directly impact campus life, as the networks and norms carried over from the disproportionate number of students who attended prestigious New England feeder high schools formed a model for social interactions and played a key role in calibrating students' feelings of belonging. Because belonging and agency were intertwined,[20] admissions priorities were one way the college, as a racialized organization, bolstered the agency of white students and reinforced the ways whiteness acted as a credential on campus.

My interview data show how students' shared perception of the typical Bowdoin student as a wealthy, white, New Englander created a template for social belonging and exclusion. For example, Paige (white woman) noted,

MULTICULTURALISM OR MONOCULTURALISM? 33

"Campus—as a whole—feels pretty white, pretty privileged socioeconomically, and pretty northeastern. . . . If you're outside those categories I think it could be hard [here]." Those who fit the template felt more comfortable on campus than those who did not, but students who lacked physical markers of whiteness could utilize their class status to craft an approximation.[21] Mark (Asian American man) described how his boarding school experience impacted his sense of belonging: "I felt very comfortable here just because it's so similar to a New England boarding school." Jasmine (Black woman) agreed, "I'm not the quintessential Bowdoin student. I mean, I guess I'm what they want. I guess that's why they keep asking for my photo, because I'm what they would like the Bowdoin student to represent. . . . Like, 'Oh she's a Black woman who came here and thrived!' But that's because of my [socioeconomic] privilege." Whiteness acted as credential that led students to experience feelings of comfort and belonging, especially during their first years on campus.

Yet on a campus overpopulated with affluent and white students, "approximations of whiteness" also felt precarious.[22] Even when they were academically successful, students of color often felt less comfortable on campus. Mark described, "It's definitely weird to walk into a party and be the only non-white person there, which is something that happens to me pretty often. I think that might be because I don't have too many Asian friends here." Even compared to his private New England boarding school, Bowdoin stood out: "I was the only Asian student [in a class] for the first time in my life." Elijah (Asian and Hispanic woman), who attended a private high school outside of New England, described her initial transition to campus as "big culture shock," explaining that at home, "everyone speaks Spanish all the time and everyone's brown like me." Whereas on campus, "There's white people everywhere! I look drastically different, and it was just a really hard adjustment." Over time, however, many students of color found or created counter-spaces that engendered a more authentic sense of belonging. Elijah recounted, "The other night I felt super included because there wasn't a single white person around. . . . One of the guys said, 'I really fell for this girl because she smelled like coconut oil and shea butter, and I only smell that at home.' And I'm like, 'Yeah, I feel that.' Maybe not with the coconut oil and shea butter, but my equivalents." Because whiteness pervaded the dominant culture on campus, belonging felt more contingent among students of color.

Prep school culture not only created a template for social belonging, but also gifted some students with preexisting peer networks. When holistic consideration was introduced into elite admissions in the 1920s, one purpose was to preserve the networking opportunities available to the children of WASP elites;[23] contemporary admissions practices continue to serve a similar purpose. For example, Isabella (white woman), who attended a prep school, explained that although her friend group became more diverse during her time on campus, she was "initially friends with all people from New York or Boston suburbs—all affluent [and] predominantly white," who she found through a "these are people who all kind of know each other, they went to camp together, they went to boarding school together," mentality. Because they were already embedded in rich social networks, prep school graduates had more social opportunities from their first days on campus. Through the lens of racialized organizational theory, admissions policies served to magnify those students' sense of agency on campus by reproducing their social networks within the admitted cohort. Meanwhile, students from outside prep school circles were often the only applicant admitted from their high school class; because they arrived knowing no one, their agency was constrained.

The college's admissions priorities also imprinted meritocratic rhetoric on campus. As in prior studies of elite institutions, students echoed the myth of meritocracy when describing the student body.[24] Cody (white man) explained: "You have to be smart because people here are smart and if you're having a conversation and . . . if you sound stupid or you're not engaging then people won't want to hang out with you." The notion that, by virtue of admission, every student must have demonstrated intelligence, hard work, and talent, was agreed upon by most respondents. In this way, meritocratic rhetoric set the standard for how students perceived and judged one another on campus.

But while white students talked about success on campus as being "smart," many students of color also talked about meeting the right people. Erika (Black woman) described with frustration how, "Whenever someone introduces me to someone new [they say], 'Oh yeah, they're really smart!' Like being smart is important." Victor (Latino man) described how success on campus was determined by, "talking to the right people, not necessarily your merits. More so who you talk to and how they're able to help you in the future." Students who were not already embedded in highly resourced social circles hoped that gaining admission to an elite college and meeting the right people on campus would grant them access to elite networks postgraduation.

In sum, prior studies have shown that although elite admissions are marketed as meritocratic contests, highly selective colleges grant considerable advantages to white and wealthy students. My data additionally show that when students arrived on campus, admissions priorities imprinted social dynamics. The system pairing biased admissions criteria with meritocratic rhetoric allowed wealthy, white students the privilege of an easy transition to campus life, while creating challenges for students of color, particularly those from middle and lower-class families. This sense of ease and entitlement among white and wealthy students carried over and, as I will show in subsequent chapters, impacted how students navigated the controversies surrounding the series of racially themed parties that took place on campus. Yet inequities sown by admissions were only the beginning. Social divisions were further exacerbated by structures undergirding campus life—namely extracurricular activities and housing policies. The next sections take up the unmarked whiteness of these structures in more detail.

Sustaining White Monoculture: DIII Athletics and Other Extracurriculars

Once on campus, nearly all students participated in one or more structured extracurricular activities and these activities provided the basis for most students' friend groups. Numerous students made friends through a single, time-intensive activity—such as an athletic team—while others collected friends from many activities. Notably, Bowdoin had no Greek life, as all fraternities and sororities were phased out in the late 1990s. Because extracurricular activities were the most common foundation for students' closest friendships, structures governing extracurricular participation played a central role in social networking. But, like admissions, they too were rigged to disproportionately advantage white and wealthy students.

Peter (white man) succinctly captured the social scene, naming "athletes, nonathletes, [and] kids in the Outing Club" as the three notable factions. With more than one-third of students participating in varsity athletics and about one-quarter participating in the Outing Club,[25] students not on teams referred themselves to as "nonathletic regular people," abbreviated NARP. The next sections describe how, due to historical and contemporary practices, varsity athletics and the Outing Club were overwhelmingly populated by white and wealthy students. And, unlike other extracurricular activities, the college supported them with large budgets, dedicated facilities, massive collections of gear, and professional staff members. While NARPs found friendship through other activities, including racial and ethnic affinity groups, their relative lack of facilities, staff, and funding spotlights how the college, as a racialized organization, legitimated the unequal distribution of resources and magnified agency among dominant racial groups.[26]

DIII ATHLETICS

The NCAA hosts three divisions that "align like-minded campuses in the areas of philosophy, competition and opportunity."[27] At institutions that participate in NCAA Division I play—like Michigan, Ohio State, and Stanford—athletics budgets are huge, many athletes are given multiyear cost-of-attendance scholarships, and only about 4% of students participate in varsity athletics. Televised games, however, give a false impression of player demographics more generally. Even though 60% of athletes in revenue generating sports—namely Power Five conference men's football and basketball—are Black, Black men make up only 14% of NCAA athletes overall. Even among Division I athletes, more than 60% of athletic scholarship recipients are white.[28]

Since the expansion of intercollegiate sporting competitions in the late 1800s, student athletes have occupied a special place in elite admissions because athletic leagues confer status to participating colleges.[29] For example, the Ivy League started as a football league, but the phrase "Ivy League" now conveys a portrait of institutional prestige extending beyond athletics. Bowdoin is one of eleven members of the New England Small College Athletic Conference (NESCAC). The NESCAC was founded in 1971 as a group of "highly selective liberal arts colleges and universities that share a similar philosophy for intercollegiate athletics." Other members include Amherst, Bates, Colby, Connecticut College, Hamilton, Middlebury, Trinity, Tufts, Wesleyan, and Williams. According the NESCAC web page, "The conference is committed to establishing common boundaries to keep athletics strong but in proportion to the overall academic mission of the member institutions."[30] NESCAC tenets are more restrictive than NCAA rules regarding season length, contests per season, and postseason competition. NESCAC colleges are considered prestigious and further evidencing how sports leagues confer status, often referred to as "little Ivies."

Bowdoin has long been known as an athletically minded college but has, over time, adjusted its balance of athletics and academics to remain in step with peer schools. At colleges like Bowdoin where undergraduates take part in DIII play, athletics scholarships are prohibited, and budgets are moderate,[31] but athletes still often get a fast track in admissions. In 2002, NESCAC colleges agreed to reduce the number of recruited athletes given preference in admissions. In a 2005 interview with *The New York Times*, a former dean of admissions explained that NESCAC schools settled on a "slots" system which designates the number of "athletic factor" admits each year. To find a college's allowed "slots," multiply the number of varsity teams by two, then add fourteen if there is a football team. A typical total is in the seventies.[32] When it was instituted, this policy caused the number of "recruited, rated athletes" at Bowdoin to drop by nearly 50%.[33]

The slots for supported athletes are subdivided into "bands" which separate recruits academically. Students whose achievements are on par with other top applicants fall into the "A" band and are not counted in athletic support numbers. For A-band students, coaches can still offer support but, in the revealing words of a former admissions dean, their support "would be no more helpful than the symphony director or the head of the studio art department."[34] Students in the "B" band have slightly lower academic scores, and "C" band recruits are lower still. B- and C-band students count toward each school's athletic cap. Based on this formula, about 15% of students in the class of 2018 were likely admitted based on a coach's support and would not have been admitted on academic qualifications alone.[35] In this way, NESCAC recruiting acts as affirmative action for athletes.

Just as elite colleges have long histories of racialized exclusion, so do elite college athletics. Scholar Kirsten Hextrum's book details the myriad ways athletic recruitment favors white suburban athletes, starting with the role of state-sanctioned residential and school segregation by race.[36] Owing to intergenerational patterns of resource hoarding, white middle- and upper-class communities are more likely to have infrastructure that produces recruitable athletes—such as private clubs, coaching, camps, and selective youth leagues. While sports like rowing, sailing, or hockey have an obvious class bias due to the need for costly equipment and facilities, public narratives often overlook the ways that athletes in sports perceived as more accessible—such as track or soccer—still require costly specialized training and facilities to excel. As Hextrum points out, the common narrative that runners need "only a pair of shoes" obscures the role that private coaching, camps, and competitions play in athletic recruitment at the college level.[37]

Stevens's research further elucidates why athletic recruits come disproportionately from white and wealthy families: Building athletic dominance takes persistent practice over long periods of time. For young people to commit to a sport—including extensive regional and national travel—their parents must have time and resources to support sustained development.[38] As sociologist Annette Lareau argued in her ethnographic study of class-based parenting differences, many contemporary middle- and upper-class families have adapted their lifestyles and budgets to enable exactly these kinds of resource-intensive extracurricular pursuits.[39]

While federal policies were largely responsible for creating segregated and resource-rich suburbs, college policies have incentivized coaches to take advantage of these concentrations of recruitable athletes. Coaches, and DIII coaches in particular, have limited budgets and thus concentrate their recruiting efforts on visits that may yield multiple recruits. Because elite colleges do not admit many students from any single high school (another measure of "diversity"), sports camps have become an efficient way of identifying recruits from across a region. One consequence of recruiting from regional camps, however, is that camps are populated with students whose families can afford the costs of travel, equipment, and registration. Even after NESCAC recruitment budget caps were lifted in 2015 and the scope of recruitment markedly increased,[40] the recruitment process still heavily favors athletes from white suburban communities.

Data from my campus-wide survey support this assertion. Overall, 36% of students are varsity athletes. Recruited athletes were more likely to identify as white,[41] have attended a private high school,[42] have parents who were college graduates (or higher),[43] and come from predominantly white neighborhoods[44] and from homes where English was the only language spoken.[45] They were less likely to be immigrants or children of immigrants,[46] receive need-based financial aid,[47] or have accommodations for disabilities,[48] and all by significant margins. Clearly, there is much diversity among student athletes, yet the generalization painting DIII athletes as privileged white kids holds truth—the symbiosis between affluent families and athletic recruiting practices has created a corps of student athletes that sharply diverge from their NARP peers.

In my interviews, recruited athletes described the college admissions process as relatively straightforward. Athletes figured out which coaches were interested in them, the team hosted a campus visit, and if both parties were interested, they committed. A key component of this process was the "early read"—a preliminary assessment from admissions of whether an applicant qualified as A, B, or C band.[49] Courtney (white woman) gave a behind-the-scenes peek: "My coach now, he reached out to me while I was in high school and requested all of my unofficial transcript and stuff like that, and my resume, extracurriculars or whatever, and then whatever test scores that I might have had. . . . It was very informal, just sent stuff in an email as an attachment. And my understanding of it now is that he then passed it over to admissions . . . then admissions gave a response to him saying what level of support he would need to give me for me to be able get into the school, and then he communicated that to me. And then I technically applied [early decision] but at that point . . . I knew that I was going to get in, so it wasn't stress." NESCAC rules state that no coach can "offer, promise, or otherwise guarantee" admission, but many recruited athletes applied early decision, and, with their coach's support, acceptance came as a matter of course.

This matters for understanding racially themed parties because the ways that athletes, in aggregate, differed from NARPs exacerbated the social rifts on campus that were initially sewn by admissions. Athletic teams—due to their intensive practice and competition schedules—tended to not only work out together, but eat together, live together, and party together. Because of how much structured time athletes spent together, teams ended up feeling like impenetrable cliques, both for those on teams and those who were not. Erika relayed: "People push the idea that if you have a sport, that it will make your life easier. You just follow what the team's going to do." In interviews, student athletes described how they became folded into the team's circuit early, without necessarily realizing the all-consuming nature of "the athlete experience." Rachel (Asian American woman) described how being an athlete facilitated social integration, "I was on the [varsity] team, so I had some automatic friends which was really nice. We started captain's practice the first day of school, so [I] jump[ed] into that. I think my experience would have been different if I had to completely make friends [without the help of the team]." After her first season ended, however, Rachel was "feeling pretty alone." Rachel continued, "After the [team's] season ended, I just didn't stay as close with [my teammates] that year, and I was like, 'Oh wow! I don't have that many other friends!'" When the team's season started up the following fall, Rachel relished having her crew back. Although she was friends with her first-year roommates, Rachel became closer with her teammates, and by senior year the team lived together and comprised her entire social life.

While the team offered Rachel a fulfilling social experience, its members were not diverse. When asked whether she was close friends with anyone of a different social class, she responded: "I think that [my sport] disproportionately has people from decent backgrounds, just because sports in general are like privileges." Rachel's use of the euphemism "decent" suggests not only that her teammates were from upper-class backgrounds, but also that the families of less wealthy students were somehow indecent. When asked about racial diversity, Rachel replied: "Pretty much all my friends are white and everyone in [my sport's] world is white. We have the most diverse team in the NESCAC and it's me and just one other person [of color]." Because teams were predominantly comprised of upper-class white students and presented an all-consuming social experience, athletes tended to have homogeneous friend groups. And when their teams or friend groups threw parties, they tended to draw a homogeneous crowd.

Tyler (white man), a two-sport athlete, emphasized how much participating in sports limited his social circle: "I feel like I know nobody in my grade. People do the 'name game' or people are spewing hot gossip and it's like, 'Who are you talking about? I've never heard of that person before.' . . . And I know for a fact it's because I was on the two teams and have always had these preordained social groups." Tyler explained the homogeneity of his friend circle similarly to Rachel, but without euphemism, "On my team there's a strong preponderance of people who are in the middle- or upper-middle class, with definitely a few soundly upper-class people stuck in there as well. But I think that the [sports] team is very far from representative of Bowdoin." My campus-wide survey data support Tyler and Rachel's observations about the racial and socioeconomic homogeneity of athletic teams. Among varsity athletes, 76% claimed that zero or one of their four closest friends were students of color (80% of white athletes and 65% of athletes of color), compared to nonathletes, where 53% claimed zero or one of their four closest friends were students of color (65% of white nonathletes and 33% of nonathletes of color).

What does this mean for athletes of color? Athletes of color tended to find themselves split between two worlds, feeling like they did not wholly belong within their team, yet knowing their campus identity was inextricably tied to their sport. Erika explained, "I was an athlete, but . . . my best friends were never athletes. I always felt like I was able to navigate both. But that means I was never just from one . . . [*hesitates, searching for the right word*] . . . side?" She ended up leaving her team after a couple seasons, however, because of the pressure. When asked how she thought diversity impacted life on campus, she implicated admissions: "If we had more of it, we wouldn't have the problem of so many students who feel like they didn't fit in or can't find their place on campus or [are] hesitant of joining groups that aren't diverse. Or joining them and not feeling comfortable and dropping out, which is obviously why I dropped out of [my team]." Erika continued, "I did not feel comfortable anymore going to athletic parties, or parties that I knew was just going to be a majority of, white, cis-gendered people." Leaving her team changed her social network, and relieved Erika of the pressure of having to straddle divergent worlds.

In contrast, Lily (Asian American woman) described her journey to acceptance among athletes. "I was constantly uncomfortable and unhappy, and I wasn't able to be comfortable because I felt like I didn't really belong. And maybe the lack of belonging came from not being the right race." Like Rachel, Lily stayed with her team, growing more comfortable each year. When asked if students of different races mix, she pondered, "I only have white friends pretty much. And I know that's also not diverse, but because I'm not white it feels like that's kind of a mixture in itself, right?" While some athletes of color managed to find their footing within athletic circles over time, they uniformly acknowledged how, due to the lack of diversity, belonging came at a steep cost.

THE OUTING CLUB

The whiteness of varsity athletics was closely rivaled by the whiteness of the Outing Club, a long-standing outdoor excursion group. The Outing Club had a dedicated facility on campus, two paid staff members (who trained student leaders and oversaw facilities, gear, and operations), and huge collection of outdoor gear (e.g., kayaks, lifejackets, and skis) for members to borrow. While membership was open to all students and not formally determined prior to matriculation, the precollege investments in training, camps, travel, and gear required to have the skills and comfort necessary to join a club featuring white-water kayaking, cross-country skiing, and other intensive outdoor pursuits, meant that, like varsity athletics, membership was dominated by white and upper-class students. This divide was especially apparent in outings that required more gear, time, or training. While the Outing Club recognized its exclusivity—even designing leadership training programs specifically for students of color and others who lacked experience[50] and eventually getting rid of the nominal annual membership fee—such programs had not significantly diversified its membership or disrupted its status as a white space.

Many participating students formed close bonds within the Outing Club, particularly those who were selected for the semester-long program that certified excursion leaders. Jeff (white man) boasted, "We had such a great [leadership training] group. We all got very, very close—actually to the point that the rest of the Outing Club thought that we were really exclusive. But that's fine! [*laughs*] . . . Doing [leadership training], I was forced to be away—backpacking, or canoeing or whatever—every weekend for two and a half months. And it was so good for my mental state!" Caleb (white and Asian American man) considered transferring colleges his first year but decided not to, "because I did [leadership training] through the Outing Club, and I had a really supportive group of friends there." Both men conceded that being involved with the Outing Club meant their friend group was not diverse. When asked, Caleb said campus did not feel diverse because, "in the Outing Club, they do try to be diverse, but I don't think it's successful. . . . In terms of class, I felt like everybody else was wealthy. And then skin color, I think I was the only person of color." Jeff agreed, "There are a lot of environments that I feel comfortable in or that I haven't had to think about existing in that students of color are not comfortable in or have to think a lot about." When asked for examples he said, "The Outing Club—that's a big one . . . [it's] pretty white." Because the Outing Club's activities predominantly drew students with preexisting comfort and experience with gear-intensive outdoor pursuits, leadership training required first responder certification that cost hundreds of dollars, and time-intensive excursions acted to incubate peer groups, students who were heavily involved in the Outing Club tended to have homogeneous friend groups regarding race and socioeconomic status. The resources the college dedicated to the Outing Club mark another example of racialized organizational structures allocating resources to a program that disproportionately benefited white students.

In sum, racial and socioeconomic divisions seeded by admissions practices and supported by the college's investments in facilities, gear, and professional staff were reinforced by the large number of racially and socioeconomically homogeneous students participating in either varsity athletics or the Outing Club—more than half the student body in total—creating a de facto segregated campus, dominated by white, upper-class norms. Jacob (white and Latino man) summarized, "A big divide on campus is athletics and athletics is pretty white, so then automatically that creates a pretty big [racial] divide. . . . Athletics provides this structure at Bowdoin in the same way that the Outing Club does—people create that structure through racial identity. A lot of that structure is formed through the groups on campus." In this way, the college's extracurricular investments supported its racialized social hierarchy. When each of the racialized costume parties shook campus, these homogeneous and well-resourced networks played an instrumental role in organizing how students responded.

OTHER EXTRACURRICULAR ACTIVITIES

In contrast, most other activities were student-led, funded by a mandatory student activities fee (which was apportioned by an elected student committee), regulated by the Office of Student Activities, and not necessarily directly supported by or affiliated with faculty or staff in their formal capacities. While the Office of Student Activities had specific procedures for common organizational needs, such as borrowing a college vehicle or throwing a party, the more than one hundred student organizations varied drastically in how often they met, how many people joined, and what kinds of activities they sponsored. Some had robust bureaucratic principles that allowed them to continue across generations of students, while others popped up for a year or two and then faded. For example, BUCRO (a civil rights group) was instrumental in recruiting students and scholarship funds for Black students in the mid-1960s. Yet by the early 1970s, the group had dissolved. Meanwhile, the Afro-American Society, founded in the late 1960s, has continued without interruption for decades, during this study known as AfAm and later as the Black Student Union.

Instead of arriving on campus with a prearranged and institutionally supported social life, students who were not athletes or in the Outing Club tended to collect friends from a variety of activities. Like many others, Luis (Latino man) got involved with one group at the urging of a floormate, "then from there, I made a few friends, and from there the friend groups just kind of started expanding, little through little." Extracurricular activities provided the structure for students to form friendships. Even if students did not have an enduring passion for the activity, the repetition of scheduled meetings created space for socialization and bonding, and finding new extracurricular interests often led students to find new friends. For some, this was a way out of peer groups they did not enjoy, for others it expanded their network. Isabella reported that during her first semester, "I was with these same seven girls almost all the time . . . that was definitely my scene. And then I . . . got into a [performance] group [second] semester, and that shifted my social scene." By sophomore year, she hit her stride: "Especially because my [one] group was predominantly seniors, I just felt like I had a real social 'in,' and also just loved that group a lot and loved those people and their friends." For Isabella, this group created a social circle akin to how many athletes felt about their teams. Yet just as extracurricular activities could create friendships, they could sometimes take them away. After studying abroad her junior year, a change to her extracurricular activities shook up Isabella's social networks. As a result, instead of a robust friend group, she bonded with a "select few" people her senior year.

The social advantage some white students gained from athletics was felt acutely by nonathletes. Annie (white woman) described her first year: "[My roommate] played [a sport], so that was probably the hardest transition. . . . I came in and she already had a group of friends, and I was like, 'What about me?' So, we didn't really spend time [together]. So, I had to get out of the room [to meet people], which . . . added a pressure that I might not have needed or wanted." Amy (white woman) explained, "If I were on an athletic team, I would have a lot more social options. They host a lot of the events. . . . People feel like the athletes are the cool people." Even white students who felt a strong sense of belonging on campus judged their experiences relative to classmates on varsity teams. Nonathletes, however, relished the relative diversity of their social groups. Isabella remarked, "My group of friends has been fairly diverse with regards to class. . . . But if you asked me if that was representative, I would say no. . . . Part of me feels like [it's] because I'm *not* an athlete [that I have a diverse friend group]." Because nonathletes had time and flexibility to try new activities, they had the leeway to change and diversify their social circles.

Affinity Groups. Some students found solidarity and socialization through groups catering to a particular racial or ethnic group. According to my campus survey, 87% of Black students, 62% of Asian/Asian American students, 58% of Latinx students, and about half of multiracial students reported being a member of an affinity group. Jasmine, after listing her two or three main extracurricular activities, was asked what she took away from each activity. She replied: "Friends! Obviously!" She continued, talking specifically about AfAm: "The African American Society gave me a community and then also a way [of] grappling with some of the stuff we have to deal with on campus as a Black person, and then all the stuff going on in the world." Cassie (Asian American woman) similarly reported that she "met good friends," through the Korean Students Association (KASA): "KASA wasn't really that much besides occasional events that they would have when they would bring a speaker. . . . It was just weekly dinners. And I think it was just nice to just have a set, standing dinner." For many students of color, affinity groups provided opportunities to form friendships with other students of the same race and stay informed. For some students, affinity groups also provided a much-needed respite from the pressures of being a person of color at a PWI.

Affinity groups did not feel welcoming, however, to all students who shared a broad racial or ethnic identity. Many students of color expressed frustration either that groups were cramming too many pan-ethnic and pan-racial identities under the same umbrella, or too few. For example, as a first-year student, Carlos (white and Latino man) remembered attending the activities fair, where clubs hosted tables and students milled about, visiting tables of interest. Carlos recalled: "I want[ed] to be involved with the Latino group on campus because I was like, 'This is a big part of my life!' . . . I didn't really know how you sign up, so I was just like [to the student at the table], 'Do you just . . . sign up?' And this girl was like 'Umm, yeah. That's great! It's okay, white people can join too.' . . . I didn't really know how to respond, so it was one of those things where you just laugh. And then I remember leaving and I was like, 'Why did that girl say that to me? She doesn't know me?' . . . I felt really excluded." Students' understandings and expectations of their co-ethnic or co-racial community varied widely. Yet because the number of students belonging to any given non-white racial or ethnic group was kept small (due to admissions practices), there were not enough co-racial or co-ethnic organizations to suit all potentially affiliated students.

Many students of color shared wanting different things from their affinity groups. For example, wanting to attend parties playing a specific kind of music versus needing to vent about microaggressions, racism, or the dissonance of supporting family members from their position of privilege. While

MULTICULTURALISM OR MONOCULTURALISM?

many of the pressures students of color faced originated from white people and institutionalized racism, some students also faced pressures from their co-ethnic peers. My campus-wide survey data show that about one-third of students of color and white students believed affinity groups were divisive, likely due to the reasons discussed earlier in this chapter.

Compared to athletic teams and the Outing Club, however, affinity groups received slim support from the college. Bowdoin had no theme or ethnic housing and only three buildings with spaces marked for minoritized students, each a renovated house centrally located on campus. The John Brown Russwurm House, a single-family home built in 1827 and renamed in honor of Bowdoin's first African American graduate after the creation of the Africana studies program in 1970, acted as a hub for AfAm. The other two houses were known only by their street addresses. One housed offices and meeting spaces for the Women's Resource Center and the Resource Center for Gender and Sexual Diversity. The other, dedicated in 2007 as the Multicultural Center,[51] included a kosher kitchen and a prayer room, and housed shared offices and meeting spaces for all other affinity groups. None of these groups had a dedicated advisor. It was not lost on minoritized students that these three modest houses were the only college-sanctioned counter-spaces to the normative white culture on campus, even though the students these houses served— everyone who was not straight, cis, white, Christian, men—comprised the numerical majority of the student population. The disproportionate allocation of resources to activities that served chiefly white and wealthy students scaffolded de facto segregation and resentment.

Sustaining White Monoculture: Housing Policies

Each of the three parties depicted in this book took place in a student residence on or very near campus. While admissions and extracurricular activities created and reinforced social divisions, those divisions became further cemented by the college's housing policies. The first-year housing policy was one of the few college-wide structures that attempted to disrupt de facto social segregation on campus. Unlike many universities, the college did not allow first-year students to request roommates. Instead, according to the website, "Students are asked about their sleeping habits, tidiness, interests, music likes/dislikes," and the Residential Life office (hereafter ResLife), "uses these answers to make pairs and groups of roommates." Besides accounting for personality, ResLife "takes a variety of other factors into account (such as high school and hometown) to make sure that floors are as diverse as possible." The college's attempt to disrupt segregation by curating "diverse" dorm floors created opportunities for individual friendships between roommates and floor mates. While some, like Margaret (Asian American), described it as "a nice concept . . . to help freshmen settle in," others made friends for life. Scott (white man) recalled, "[I] had a good freshman year, I really loved all my roommates. I lived with one of them for all four years." While the first-year housing policy seeded some lasting friendships, most had run their course by sophomore year.

Many students found the intentional diversity of first-year floors inconducive to making friends because athletes tended to set a tone by opting out of group activities. Weekly floor dinners (known as "flinners") were one way students got to know each other. Tyler described how his floor, "was not the most tight-knit," saying: "It was very rare to see people from all of the different aspects of our floor—like my roommate on the hockey team, for instance, would almost never show up to flinner stuff, there's another kid who's on the lacrosse team [and] football kids [who never showed up]. There were so many divergent interests and divergent social scenes that we would very rarely find cause to actually all get a meal together." Because athletic team bonding was so strong and often started before students even moved into their dorms, nonparticipation among athletes detracted from dorm bonding. As Evan (white man), an athlete, explained, "We used to do flinners and group activities and I thought those were mandatory at first. [*laughs*] And then [I] realized they weren't and stopped going." In short, first-year housing policies did little to disrupt segregation campus wide due to the pull of athletic teams.

After their first year, students could choose their own roommates, housemates, and residence hall. While most students remained on campus, juniors and seniors could opt to live off campus, primarily in nearby rental houses. Off-campus housing was often more expensive, but not subject to the college's meal plan or its policy prohibiting hard alcohol. Over the period of this study, the number of students living off campus increased dramatically. In fall 2014, 144 students lived off campus. The following fall, the count grew to 165. By the fall of 2016, the count rose to 217,[52] totaling nearly one-third of the senior class, and the highest of any NESCAC college.[53] That year, the college created a committee to reevaluate its amorphous off-campus policy. According to their report, 81% of students living off campus were white, 72% did not receive financial aid, and 61% were men. Furthermore, 55% were varsity athletes.[54] The chair of the committee reported to the *Orient*, "an increase in the number of students living off campus has implications for our sense of community on campus, our relationships with our neighbors and the town and for Bowdoin's operating budget."[55] As a result, the college implemented a cap on the number of students living off campus—two hundred students in 2017–18 and 185 in 2018–19.[56]

The disproportionate number of white, wealthy, athletes living off campus exacerbated de facto social segregation created by athletic teams and the Outing Club. Off-campus houses tended to become affiliated with an athletic team, inhabited by students who could afford the expense, and "handed down" to members of the team each year. Such houses also hosted many parties, including the Cracksgiving party described in the next chapter. As Rachel described of her house, "It's been handed down, so everyone who has lived there has picked the next people to live there and it's been juniors and seniors always and it's been a mix of people on the [sports] team and some [other athletes] and people in the Outing Club." Without a housing "lineage," students struggled to find off-campus options. Evan explained how he had always hoped to live with teammates and finding out about newly constructed units near campus allowed them to finally secure housing together. Because Evan's team did not have a house to "pass down," the students felt "stuck" on campus. New construction opened the door for Evan's team to finally have an off-campus house—not only for themselves but for future generations of teammates.

Parties at off-campus houses tended to be more exclusive (in part due to the added liability of serving hard alcohol). As Evan noted about moving off campus, "I was super excited because we were living off campus in a house. . . . That being said, I was kind of nervous just because any sort of trouble we got in was dealing with the [town] cops instead of [campus] security. My parents put a big emphasis on that." When asked whether he felt like he belonged socially, Evan elucidated how securing off-campus housing bolstered the sense of community among his teammates: "I definitely felt like I belonged—especially living off campus! I felt like it was on us to have our team over and have team bonding events at our house, just because freshman year that's what our seniors did." Housing lineages combined with athletic socialization to reinforce the racialized exclusivity of off-campus spaces.

By all accounts, team bonding came at the expense of racial integration. Evan admitted "the kids who come to our house are mostly white," and brushed it off, saying, "it hasn't affected me or anything. It's just the nature of the school." He continued, "It's definitely a problem, but I try and ignore [it]. Like when we have parties at our house, we definitely want everyone from campus who wants to come to come and we're not going to exclude anyone from coming. Definitely something that I'd like to see more of is more integration amongst groups, but I don't know how you change that." While Evan's intentions were to have everyone feel welcome, he and his teammates put no effort behind that colorblind ideal. Instead, they tried to ignore the issues—an example of systemic white ignorance manifested at the individual level. As a result, off-campus parties hosted by teams were rarely integrated spaces. After students' first year, the student-driven nature of the housing policy enabled de facto residential segregation, making it possible for socialization to occur in spaces that were divided along extracurricular, and thus demographic, lines.

In her undergraduate thesis, Bowdoin alumna Pamela Zabala characterized sports teams' off-campus houses, and men's houses in particular, as "hyper-cultural white spaces," building on sociologist Elijah Anderson's[57] conceptualization of "white spaces." Zabala argued that these hyper-cultural white spaces were being created by white students as an act of resistance against greater emphasis on diversity and inclusion in college policies.[58] Few students were willing to articulate this stance explicitly, but the timing of the upsurge in students moving off campus strongly supports this inference. This is another example of how students "inhabited" the college as a racialized organization; within the bounds of the "race neutral" housing policy, white students exercised agency to create racially exclusive spaces.

Students who were not athletes tended to room with friends, and often friends of friends. Without the structure of a team or preexisting roommate combination, deciding who to include or leave out of a housing block often became fraught. In my interviews, long-winded explanations of the roommate selection process were common among nonathletes, yet another example of the ways students' social lives became simpler when they were organized by athletics, and rife with uncertainty and complications in the absence of those structures. In the absence of athletics, however, uncertainty left room for students to maintain diverse connections from first-year dorms and make new connections through extracurricular activities. Policies allowing students' autonomy in housing choices thus accommodated the ways admissions and athletics enhanced feelings of ease, belonging, and personal agency among some students, particularly white and wealthy athletes, but not others.

In short, while other studies have focused on the ways diversity-related programming impacts racial equity on campuses, my data suggest that core structures matter significantly more. The unmarked whiteness of selective admissions, DIII athletics, and housing policies shaped dominant norms on campus by granting increased resources and agency to wealthy and white students, and particularly recruited athletes. Together these systems bolstered white supremacy and white ignorance. But how does the racialization of these structures remain unmarked? The next sections examine how students and administrators talk about race in ways that obscure the whiteness of core structures and thus sustain white dominance.

Diversity Discourse:
Scripting Race Talk

In the interviews conducted for this book, when asked about race and diversity, students responded with strikingly similar ideas in nearly identical language. Repetition was so common between interviews that I refer to these responses as "scripts." This approach draws on neo-institutional theory, where scripts refer to language individuals become socialized into using within an organization.[59] Organizational theorists argue that, at the macro level, scripts are influenced by racialized structures and support the development of narratives which reproduce social order.[60] At the micro level, scripts help individuals maximize positive emotions and minimize negative emotions.[61] Although prior studies have analyzed racialized scripts within and across organizational contexts,[62] this study adopts an inhabited institutionalist framework to highlight not only how scripts are shaped by the interplay of structures and agency, but to further examine the relationship between scripts and behaviors.

While overt racism and exclusion were, for many years, the norm on elite campuses, students have shifted to expressing racism in more covert ways. Landmark studies of integration at elite universities relying on data from the 1990s document the decline of outright racism and the rise of colorblind racism.[63] Colorblind racism is the belief we live in a post-racial society where race no longer matters. Colorblindness ignores historical and structural contributions to contemporary racial inequities. Sociologist Eduardo Bonilla-Silva conceptualized four tenets of colorblindness: naturalization (e.g., homophily happens naturally), minimization (e.g., racism no longer negatively impacts people of color), cultural racism (e.g., blaming culture rather than structure), and abstract liberalism (e.g., equal opportunity exists so group discrepancies must arise from individual's choices).[64] Scholars Subini Annamma, Darrell Jackson, and Deb Morrison argued more recently, however, that using the metaphor of disability (i.e., blindness) to convey purposeful avoidance not only perpetuates a profound misunderstanding of the ways disability is socially constructed but also implies that colorblind racism is individual and passive.[65] Instead, they propose "color-evasiveness" as an expanded term that emphasizes active refusals to recognize systems that perpetuate structural racism, without portraying people with disabilities as problematic.

Only a decade or two after the rise of colorblind racism, surveys again showed attitudes had shifted. Yet while most white Americans now outwardly agree racism is problematic,[66] color-evasiveness lives on. Drawing on interviews with undergraduates at Harvard and Brown, sociologist Natasha Warikoo argued that elite undergraduates' race-related attitudes form a limited menu of scripted remarks, identifying four frames: colorblindness, culture of poverty, power analysis, and diversity.[67] Frames were not mutually exclusive, and undergraduates employed multiple frames within an interview.[68] Students used colorblindness when they claimed to live in a post-racial society. Culture of poverty implied minorities' disadvantage stemmed from cultural norms. Power analysis recognized historical and contemporary power imbalances shaping racial inequities. Diversity portrayed racial differences as beneficial for learning, (superficially) acknowledging structural inequalities and highlighting race as one of many axes of difference.

Warikoo's diversity frame aligned with tenets of sociologist Sarah Mayorga's "diversity ideology."[69] Like color-evasiveness, diversity ideology "helps individuals who live within an increasingly multicultural environment reconcile a national value of egalitarianism with pervasive racial inequity."[70] Unlike color-evasiveness, however, diversity ideology highlights race as one of many axes of difference and acknowledges structural inequalities, at least superficially. Diversity ideology has four tenets: diversity as acceptance (i.e., tolerance and inclusion across all differences), diversity as intent (i.e., prioritizing intentions over structural change), diversity as commodity (i.e., people of color exist for the benefit of white people and institutions), and diversity as liability (i.e., threat to white American values).

As evidenced by these studies, overt racism and color-evasiveness seem to fit hand in hand. Using discourse analysis of media reports, court cases, and publicly released documents in the wake of racially charged incidents, researchers have shown how overtly racist acts give college administrators a platform to decry racism while delimiting the definition of racism to encompass only overt hostilities.[71] When administrators call out only overtly racist acts as reprehensible while maintaining everyday practices that systematically advantage white students, they simultaneously celebrate meritocratic ideals and protect systems of institutionalized racism.[72] The disconnect between how administrators talk about race, and the practices and structures operating within their colleges, thus sustains both color-evasiveness and overt racism. Sociologists Amanda Lewis and John Diamond documented a similar divergence between the ways white parents talk about supporting racial equity and their behaviors explicitly advantaging their (white) children within integrated public schools.[73]

At Bowdoin, two contradictory scripts dominated race talk: the naturalization script and diversity script. In the naturalization script, students tended to see their divisions as "natural human instinct." In the diversity script, students expressed the importance of learning from their diverse peers. While the diversity script is like the diversity frame Warikoo identified, the naturalization script maps more closely onto Bonilla-Silva's naturalization tenet of colorblind racism and does not appear in Warikoo's analysis.[74] My findings contradict Mayorga's claim that the diversity ideology has superseded colorblindness, instead showing that the naturalization of segregation (that comprises one tenet of colorblindness) serves to enable the "white-centering logic" of diversity ideology.[75] As Warikoo's study might predict, the power analysis and culture of poverty frames were not present in my data. Rather than suggesting that only color-evasive racism occurs on campus, the relative lack of overt racism and power analysis framing suggests either that students have been socialized (prior to or during their college years) to avoid talking about race using these frames, or they have not yet developed knowledge of and/or language for these frames. Together, the lack of explicitly racist language and lack of recognition of systemic racism offer evidence of the pervasiveness of color-evasiveness and diversity ideology.

As evidenced by their prevalence in prior studies, these scripts are not unique to Bowdoin. The fact that similar scripts pervade many elite campuses, and wider swaths of contemporary US society,[76] suggests social actors on elite campuses are not acting in a vacuum. Rather—as neo-institutional theory would suggest—elite campuses are responding to macro-level pressures to reproduce contemporary, white, elite norms for talking about race and diversity via organizational processes.[77] That a naturalization script emerged pervasively in this study but was absent from other recent analyses suggests that, as Ray argued, variation exists across organizations.[78]

DIVERSITY SCRIPT

The diversity script maintains that individuals are shaped in positive ways by exposure to racial diversity and is grounded in the objectification of students of color, neoliberal entitlement to unilateral consumption, and processes of white identity construction that give white people opportunities to appear "good" by benevolently associating with people of color.[79] The diversity script was employed by most of my interview sample, and support was even more overwhelming in my campus-wide survey. Nearly all students agreed that "interacting with students who are different from themselves with regard to race and class during college" would benefit them in their future career, and

90% agreed that it was an important component of their college education. While nearly all survey respondents agreed that "race matters in society because there are still unequal power relations between groups" and "individuals should actively work toward eliminating racial injustice," only 75% agreed that discrimination was an issue students of color faced on campus. My survey data offer support for Mayorga's argument that the diversity ideology is ubiquitous, as students uniformly recognized the existence of racism.[80]

Although the diversity script ultimately buttresses structural white supremacy, students of all racial backgrounds discussed their "diverse peers" as consumable resources. Taylor (white woman) argued diversity "is absolutely one of the most important parts of being [at college]. . . . This is the most powerful education you could possibly get . . . being able to learn from their [her diverse peers'] experience." Tristan (white man) stated, "People come from different cultures [and] have different ways of viewing the world. . . . I feel like I've learned a ton just by listening a little bit." José (Latino man) described how he had, "done a decent enough job of seeking out different people to kind of surround myself with and learn from," and that having an interracial friendship, "very much opened my mind and helped me see things from a different viewpoint." Maria (white and Hispanic woman) explained that diversity on campus allowed her to be "confronted with different realities . . . [which] challenged me to view things differently, question my experience, and then also acknowledge . . . where I am privileged." Some students went so far as to discuss their peers as objects curated to provide a stimulating environment. Tyler explained that socioeconomic and racial diversity are important because, if everyone's "backgrounds are the same . . . you're not going to have all that interesting of a collection." This objectification and consumption of diversity, however, negates the material consequences of structural inequities. As Mayorga wrote in her depiction of the diversity ideology, "A general ethos of acceptance that is not grounded in a discussion of inequitable power distribution becomes a tool of oppression for the powerful."[81]

As evidence of how the diversity script reinscribed racial hierarchies and magnified agency and resources available to the dominant racial group, white students generally did not acknowledge that students of color might experience "learning from diversity" differently. In this way, the diversity script was applied in a color-evasive manner, underscoring white ignorance.[82] Alexis (white woman) explained how the diverse student body had allowed her to, "learn from other people, which is how we get better as humans and learn from other people's experiences and be more inclusive." Tanner (white man) agreed: "The more diverse a body of people is, the more interaction you're going to get with different cultures, the more people are going to learn from

MULTICULTURALISM OR MONOCULTURALISM? 53

one another." Their use of general terms suggests that all people, regardless of identity, could access the commodity that is "diversity" on campus.

Studies have documented the crushing burden "racialized equity labor" places on faculty and students of color at PWIs,[83] yet only a few students acknowledged the color-evasiveness of the diversity script. Jasmine explained: "When we talk about diversity in the classroom, I feel like usually what we're saying is [it's] a way for white people to hear more sides. It's for their benefit. I don't really feel like I benefit from diversity that much." Paige agreed, "I think [diversity] affects different people differently. . . . I can say that it affects me in that it benefits me. I'm the recipient of being able to learn from other people and learn from other people's experience. . . . I'm the winner in the equation." Yet most students remained ignorant to this differentiation.[84]

Administrators normalized and promoted the diversity script in their public comments. In his first-year orientation address, the Dean of Students encouraged students to "prioritize meeting different people" because, "one conversation with someone who doesn't experience the world like you is when academic exercise becomes a moment of personal transformation." During the same event, the president boasted that the college would foster "skills, knowledge, and the emotional fortitude to deeply and effectively engage with the most challenging issues and problems." "Intellectual fearlessness," he noted, involved "being uncomfortable, at times rattled, and even offended." He stated that facing opposing viewpoints, or viewpoints that you find offensive, promotes learning. Similarly, the web page for the Student Center for Multicultural Life stated that they "bring together people of varying experiences and perspectives to learn and grow with the creative friction generated in contact with difference." Through the unmarked whiteness in these and other messages—including the homogenization of identities in the name of the center—the college promoted the color-evasive notion that diversity benefited all students equally, without recognizing the tax this expectation exacted on students of color.

NATURALIZATION SCRIPT

When employing the naturalization script, students explained de facto segregation as "natural human instinct" and claimed it brought "comfort" to all people to surround themselves with friends who are alike in background and appearance.[85] Paige reported, "I think people of color do group together. I group with white students, there's some degree of familiarity and comfort in sharing that same identity." Cassie agreed, "It's just something that happens because people feel comfortable around people that they're similar to." For the most part, however, when interviewees were asked why they felt more comfortable, they attributed it to human nature. Courtney explained, "It's natural humanistic instinct to be drawn to people that look like you and are homogenous to you." Jennifer (white woman) said, "People like to be around other people that appear in the same way. And I think there is an aspect of humanity in that." Explaining de facto social segregation through "comfort" and "natural tendency" disregards the role that historical and contemporary institutional practices and structures play in normalizing segregation.[86]

Students who used the naturalization script—more than two-thirds of the interview and survey samples—agreed campus felt racially segregated. Most students agreed that both white students and students of color encouraged self-segregation, usually referring to peer groups rather than physical spaces. Caleb stated, "I feel like there are diversities on campus, but people . . . turn them into cliques. . . . People tend to stay within their own groups, which makes sense to me because I do that too." When referencing spaces, students tended to ignore the unmarked whiteness of many off-campus residences and instead recognized counter-spaces, such as affinity group hubs.

Of the students employing the naturalization script, however, a minority argued that macro-level forces created a blueprint for campus divisions. For example, Anthony (white and Hispanic man) argued that self-segregation on campus had an obvious cause: "There's clearly a reason for it . . . there used to be forced segregation based on color. So, there's an historical reason for it." Few students explicitly stated that segregation on campus might result from many students being socialized in segregated schools and neighborhoods, but some implicitly acknowledged this fact while talking about segregation on campus. Annie said that she noticed a lack of racial mixing but said it was hard to expect that campus would be integrated because, our "society is so polarized [in terms of race]." Similarly, Danielle (white, Black, and Hispanic) posited, "the way that we as a society have lived for so long makes it a little bit challenging" to integrate.

No students attributed social segregation to college-specific structures— not surprising given Americans' ignorance of racialized social systems generally[87]—and several students stated overtly that divisions were not the college's doing. For example, Jasmine stated that while the social scene on campus was segregated, this was not a result of "the dominant culture [being] hostile to people of color," because "Bowdoin's a very friendly place." Students' inability to recognize structures and processes that encouraged social segregation shows how students bought into structural white supremacy—if segregation were "innate," the college could pretend its unmarked whiteness

MULTICULTURALISM OR MONOCULTURALISM? 55

was, instead, race neutrality and need not assume responsibility for structural change or resource redistribution.

The naturalization script was also espoused by administrators in speeches and campus-wide emails. For example, during first-year orientation, the Dean of Students addressed the class saying: "You will form a group of friends— they may be teammates, from your [pre-orientation trip], or your room- mates. This will be your crew. . . . Colleges are diverse, but students can spend their time on homogenous islands. . . . Students divulge into sameness . . . this is human nature." By disregarding organizational structures that encouraged social and physical segregation on campus, this remark promoted racial igno- rance, buttressing structural white supremacy. Instead, he cited "human na- ture," and placed the responsibility on individuals to overcome this instinct. While, later in the speech, his language encouraged students to interact with diverse classmates (i.e., diversity script), it simultaneously modeled and nor- malized the assertion that segregation on campus occurred "naturally" (i.e., naturalization script). This rhetoric shows how color-evasiveness—and spe- cifically the naturalization of segregation—contributes to the maintenance of white spaces.

Conclusion

Before delving into the controversial parties, this chapter has shown how ra- cialized organizational structures—namely admissions practices, DIII athlet- ics and other extracurricular activities, and housing policies—promoted and naturalized racial segregation on campus, while simultaneously endorsing scripts that evangelize the value of learning from diversity. Although students wanted to learn from their diverse peer cohort and the college prescribed first- year residential placements to facilitate interracial interactions, social net- works woven before and during college within socioeconomically and racially homogeneous athletic teams and prep schools overwhelmed the intent of in- tegrated first-year housing and created de facto social segregation. These find- ings introduce the mechanism by which an amorphous commitment to learn- ing from diversity ultimately undermines the possibility of structural change: racialized organizational structures enabling admissions, DIII athletics, and the Outing Club to further advantage wealthy, white students.[88] Having set the stage, the next chapters reveal how individual agency matters within this racialized organizational context. On a campus with such deep structural in- vestments in unmarked whiteness, at this moment in history, what happens when acts of bias, cultural appropriation, or racism become overt?

3

Racism as a Personal Problem

The costume parties that roiled campus during the four years the class of 2018 was in residence were—of course—not the first of their kind, at Bowdoin or elsewhere. A 2014 *Orient* article noted that, "According to Dean of Multicultural Affairs . . . at least one instance of cultural appropriation occurs each year, often by students who dress in 'native' costumes for Halloween or a themed party." The article went on to note that, "These instances are not always limited to Native American attire; [the dean] noted that earlier in the fall semester students wearing sombreros were brought to her attention." On a campus that had a student-acted minstrel show until at least 1905, the tradition of using costume parties to perpetuate pejorative stereotypes had not disappeared, only changed form.[1]

Prior to 2014, offending students were rarely punished or called out publicly. The deans would begin "a dialogue with students that focuses not on their intentions, but on the impact their actions had on fellow students." According to the Dean of Multicultural Affairs, "If the problem is ignorance, then the solution is education."[2] As this chapter will show, however, when administrators respond to racial transgressions by educating only the offending students, they reinforce false notions that racism is the product of individual actions. By circumscribing racism as the domain of ignorant individuals, this course of action strategically ignores the profound impacts of institutionalized racism. In other words, by calling out the students wearing costumes that perpetuated derogatory stereotypes, administrators signaled that *this* kind of racism was problematic; such messaging also implied that all other kinds of racism were, therefore, potentially acceptable. A few students got a slap on the wrist, while the unmarked whiteness of organizational structures—such as admissions, athletics, and housing—continued unchecked. But, as this

RACISM AS A PERSONAL PROBLEM   57

chapter will illustrate, white ignorance is not just an individual problem, it is also a structurally cast mandate. Just as the diversity script perpetuated notions that all kinds of difference were comparable and valuable, it also trained students to strategically ignore the very systems of oppression that feed white supremacy.

This chapter explores why treating racism as an individual problem encourages racially themed costume parties to recur using the example of a pilgrims and Indians–themed party that happened during the first semester the class of 2018 was on campus. In addition, this chapter shows why "dialogues across differences"—i.e., staged conversations between implicated students and students of color—do little to reduce the recurrence of racially themed parties. As prior studies have shown, students of color have historically borne the responsibility of educating their white peers and organizing against racialized campus structures.[3] While such conversations may aid some white students in better understanding the harms their costumes have inflicted and may help some students of color reclaim power via counter-storytelling, too often they also reinforce notions that racism is an individual problem and organizational structures are race neutral, ultimately bolstering systems of white supremacy.

"There's Only Three of Us, What Can We Do?":
A Tradition of Cultural Appropriation

As noted in previous chapters, the policies governing highly selective admissions play a starring role in maintaining the normative whiteness of campus culture. With every applicant considered in a "holistic" selection process, the demographics of each student cohort are in no way accidental. If the college's admissions process were based exclusively on merit, one might expect the demographic composition of each class to vary from year to year or, at least, to match the demographic composition of the US. It does neither. At elite colleges, changes in the demographic composition of each admitted cohort result only from intentional actions by administrators.

After decades of continuing to prioritize white students in admissions—including student athletes and the children of alumni—a change in leadership brought changes to Bowdoin's admissions regime starting in 2000. In the years between 2001 and 2009, Bowdoin lowered the number of athletic factor slots and began to racially diversify its student body by noticeable margins. In fall of 2001, there were fifty Bowdoin students who identified as Hispanic or Latino, making up 3% of the student body, and by fall of 2009, there were 181, 10% of the student body. Similarly, in fall 2001, there were fifty students who identified as Black or African American, and by 2009, there were 115. In fall of 2001, there were 113 students who identified as Asian, Asian American, and/or Pacific Islander (7% of the student body), by fall of 2009, there were 205 (12% of the student body). There was a short-lived increase in the number of American Indian and Native American students during this period, topping out at twenty-two in 2005, but by fall of 2010 there were again only two Native students enrolled.[4]

How did an institution with a conservative reputation make such significant demographic changes while largely avoiding cries of "reverse discrimination" from the wealthy white families that fill its coffers? Rather than reallocating admissions "slots" that had previously been awarded to white students to students of color, the college increased the size of its student body from roughly 1,600 to 1,800 undergraduates during this period, an increase comprised entirely of students of color.

Clearly, when an elite college makes changes to its enrollment numbers and demographics, those changes are intentional, strategic, and finite. Between the fall of 2010 and the fall of 2017, Bowdoin's demographic makeup remained mostly static. That the racial and ethnic composition of each cohort changed dramatically in one decade and then remained constant for most of the next is not a coincidence, a reflection of national demographic trends, or the product of innate differences between these groups. During the period that each Bowdoin cohort hovered at around 30% students of color, Swarthmore College's student body went from 55% to 61% students of color, and Colby College's student body went from 40% to 37% students of color. As seen in sociologists Lisa Stulberg and Anthony Chen's study of the disparate timelines of adopting affirmative action policies, each college navigated this puzzle differently—even among "peer" institutions.[5]

In short, isomorphism mattered, but each team of administrators also catered to an organizationally specific audience. In the case of diversifying incoming cohorts, as in the case of adopting affirmative action policies, Bowdoin lagged behind many of its peers. Although the college upheld a stated commitment to need-blind admissions and affirmative action, white and upper-class students remained the majority on campus. As seen in chapter 2, administrators were quite candid about striking this balance during the 1960s and early 1970s. But in more recent years, the college shifted its rhetoric to keep up with changing times, now loudly proclaiming the benefits of diversity while quietly attending to tuition payers and donors.

Indeed, although students often referred to campus as a "bubble," the college was not isolated from the broader social context. When Barack Obama was elected president in 2008, many wondered if electing our country's first

RACISM AS A PERSONAL PROBLEM   59

Black president would usher in a new post-racial era. But, as has happened in response to each monumental move toward greater racial equality in the US, the idealism of the moment was met with fierce backlash and retrenchment, with increasing numbers of white people defiantly claiming a white racial identity rooted in resentment and victimhood.[6] And, largely in response to that backlash and retrenchment, the Black Lives Matter (BLM) movement emerged. Many trace the founding of the BLM movement to a string of shootings that killed unarmed Black teenagers. In 2012, Trayvon Martin, an unarmed Black high school student was shot and killed on his way home from a convenience store. In 2013, shortly after George Zimmerman was acquitted of murder charges related to the shooting, a California-based activist, Alicia Garza, took to Facebook, writing, "I continue to be surprised at how little Black lives matter." Garza and fellow activists Opal Tometi and Patrisse Cullors helped popularize the phrase and hashtag #BlackLivesMatter on Twitter and Tumblr over the next year, building what became a global social movement.[7] Racialized organizations theory notes that changes to the racialization of an organization are often spurred by forces outside the organization, including social movements and macro-level policy shifts.[8] Fittingly, the launching of BLM ushered in a new era of campus activism and attention to issues of racial inequity in higher education.

As racialized organizations theory might predict, due in part to earlier demographic shifts in the student body and in part to this national context, conversations about race were already beginning to shift before the class of 2018 arrived on campus. For example, in the fall of 2013, the Bowdoin Student Government (BSG) president, a white woman, attended a party dressed in a stereotypical Native American costume. According to campus rumors, it was a "T" party, and she came dressed as the "Trail of Tears." Word of her costume spread around campus, and she was privately reprimanded by the Dean of Students' office. Based on this response, we can assume administrators viewed her actions as an individual transgression requiring no broad or continued attention. Neither the party nor the costume received mention in the *Orient* or any other media outlet. Up to this point, the events played out as expected based on precedent. But, against the odds and inspired by national events, one student activist mounted a response ensuring the BSG president's transgression would not be quickly forgotten.

At the time, Native American students recalled feeling powerless due to their small numbers on campus. According to an *Orient* interview with a Native American student, "I was so surprised that nothing was being done about [the party] because I was really offended, but there was only me and two other girls on campus who were Native," she said. "And they were like, well,

60   CHAPTER THREE

this has been happening [for years] and like there's only three of us, what can we do?"[9] Native students felt helpless and outnumbered, an example of how organizational structures surrounding admissions curtailed agency for some racial and ethnic groups.

Despite the small number of Native American students and faculty on campus, one concerned student of color exercised personal agency and worked to change the narrative. Contesting the individualized nature of the college's response, he worked to cultivate a more public reconciliation. He compelled the BSG president to be one of the featured speakers at a "teach-in" where she would take responsibility for her actions. The event took months to plan, but in late April 2014, the BSG president took the stage of a small but crowded auditorium and addressed her peers, saying: "When I met with the dean's office [after the party] and heard how hurtful my actions had been to some of my peers, I was embarrassed, horrified and surprised." She continued, "That I had owned a costume for six years and was so ignorant to the fact that it was a misappropriation of someone else's culture—someone else's identity—terrified me." She concluded by asking the crowd to do better, saying: "I hope that, in listening to my story about a time when I made a serious error, everyone here will be more willing to talk to their peers, especially their peers of different races and ethnicities, about where the holes in our understandings of each other's identities lie."[10] Her testimony was followed by a speaker from the Native American Students Association and two faculty members, introducing the audience to the scope and impacts of systemic racism. Overall, this event contested racialized norms on campus by seeding the idea that students (and particularly those in symbolic leadership positions) who dressed up in offensive costumes should not only be subject to private admonishment but could also be held publicly accountable.

While the act of holding a white student publicly accountable for racist actions held bold symbolic power—at least momentarily—the offending student's narrative reinforced familiar themes. She lamented that her actions had caused hurt feelings, and she implored her peers to lean hard into the notion that conversations across difference would make the world a better place. The event was grounded, in part, on the premise that education could change hearts and minds. But as would be obvious in the years that followed, racism is about more than hurt feelings, and conversations about differences that ignore the role of power and oppression rarely serve to upend systems of exploitation.

This was most immediately evident in the fact that the entire event, including the brokering required to coerce the BSG president to participate, was organized and executed by students of color, uncompensated for their labor. When white students have the agency to spend their time as they

RACISM AS A PERSONAL PROBLEM   61

wish—studying, working for wages, engaging in extracurricular pursuits that bring joy or strengthen their résumés, cultivating stronger bonds with friends and family—they can choose activities that bolster their stores of economic, social, or cultural capital. They may personally benefit in ways that potentially have lifelong dividends. Because their humanity is affirmed—not questioned or threatened—by the racialized systems they are embedded within, they have the luxury of increased agency. As codified in racialized organizations theory, when students of color feel marginalized, oppressed, or exploited by their social context, they not only have less access to resources, but they also have less agency. They are, of course, not obligated to engage in activities with hopes of furthering social justice. The alternative, however, is accepting their marginalized status—an uneasy bargain by any measure.

What is most interesting about the parties that happened on this campus in subsequent years then, is not that students dressed up to play Indian, wear sombreros, and reinforce derogatory stereotypes as they had been doing for generations, but rather the advent of public outcry and a heated campus response. How was it that bias incidents and acts of cultural appropriation that were once celebrated or swept under the rug would soon become newsworthy? The answer to this question offers a window into how racialized norms become contested within organizations.

"A Plastic Smile and a Plastic Hello": Starting College in the Black Lives Matter Era

In summer 2014, BLM played a leading role in drawing attention to the disproportionate number of Black Americans killed by police officers and other symptoms of systemic racism. In July 2014 in New York, Eric Garner, a Black man, was killed by Daniel Pantaleo, a white police officer, after being held in a choke hold. His death was filmed by a friend with a cellphone and Garner's last words—"I can't breathe"—were replayed by millions, sparking #ICantBreathe.[11] Less than a month later, Darren Wilson, a white police officer in Ferguson, Missouri shot and killed Michael Brown, another unarmed Black teenager, and the BLM movement continued to mobilize. Protests began the morning after the shooting and engulfed the city for weeks.[12] People across the nation gathered for vigils. Even though police officers across the US have been killing Black men at disproportionately high rates for generations, the summer before the class of 2018 started college, racialized social systems dominated news headlines.

Even though the class of 2018 arrived on campus just days after the Ferguson protests began to simmer, conversations about racism and cultural appropriation from the prior year had faded. Administrators started an Intergroup Dialogue (IGD) program—where interested students gathered to discuss race—and student affinity groups struggled for visibility, including a whiteboard campaign sponsored by the Asian Students Association. The big issues on campus, however, as presented in the *Orient* (at that point still drafted by an almost entirely white team of student volunteers) were back to stereotypical college fare: hazing, alcohol transports, and whether women should have to pass a "pretty test" to get into a keg party.

Although the class of 2018 set the record for the largest number of students who "self-identify as multicultural," making up 32% of the class,[13] students were still subjected to racialized messaging regarding normative whiteness even before they slept a single night in the dorms. All students were required to embark on a multiday wilderness excursion with a small group of classmates prior to orientation. Given that legacies of slavery and violence have racialized American's perceptions of "the great outdoors," the idea of camping as a leisure activity has been associated with whiteness, as have many of the other activities students participated in during these "Pre-O" trips, such as kayaking and rafting.[14] While administrators positioned Pre-O trips as an equalizer, varying degrees of comfort in the wilderness due to racialized exclusion, prior experiences, and socioeconomic status meant that rather than level the playing field, Pre-O trips began the process of indoctrinating students into the myriad ways that whiteness has been both dominant and unspoken on campus.

After returning from their trips, the class reunited on the quad for a formal welcome from administrators, where the process of indoctrination continued. In his remarks, the president encouraged students to explore the breadth of course offerings, forge relationships with professors, and learn from their peers. He also introduced the diversity script: "You are all very different people, so if you're open-minded, kind, and respectful, you'll learn an immense amount from your new friends about their customs, the way they think, what they believe and what's important to them." The president continued, "Respectful disagreement, respectful questioning and challenging, respectful listening and communication are what we're about. . . . This means real engagement with each other—not politically correct platitudes."[15] While the president eschewed political correctness, he mentioned nothing about structural racism or enduring inequities on campus. As students continued through the subsequent days of orientation programming and onto the start of the academic year, similar remarks would be repeated on various occasions, encouraging all students to challenge one another and learn from these interactions. This is where norms of the naturalization and diversity scripts began to take hold.

As sociologists Elizabeth Lee and Mitchell Stevens have both described in their studies of elite liberal arts colleges, administrators must constantly engage in a delicate dance—trying to accentuate their carefully cultivated diversity enough to retain their high position in college rankings, while amplifying the college's elite character enough to attract the wealthy students, alumni, and donors who pay the bills. The framing and rhetoric offered by college leaders implicitly and explicitly delineates what kinds of people, activities, and professions are valued, and for what purposes.[16] As students were welcomed into the campus community, messaging from college leaders was one of the ways they were inculcated with its norms and traditions.

Peer socialization promoting normative whiteness began early as well; Pre-O trips were led exclusively by trained students (often Outing Club leaders) and dorms were likewise supervised by student staffers. In one of the first issues of the *Orient* that fall, two juniors (one of whom would be elected BSG president the following year) wrote an op-ed directed at first-year students. In the column they described the excitement of a new academic year, "Reuniting with friends, exchanging tales of absurd shenanigans from the summer, and let's be real, going to the lobster bake—all these things make for a delightful cocktail of fun times and cute outfits." The authors called out first-years and, in their admonition, revealed the nature of the campus to new students:

> We have a habit of choosing the easy conversations and ignoring the difficult or more interesting ones in an effort to appear put-together. Bowdoin students don't do "disheveled"—we leave that to kids at Colby and Bates. Even the kids who do look disheveled spent a lot of time digging around "Salvo" [Salvation Army] looking for that perfect owl shirt and hand knit sweater. We look nice every day, get to class, offer politically correct statements in difficult discussions, smile fabulously on the quad, rant online, and then silently cry in our showers. We hope that the new first-year class will break this culture—we hope first-years choose the difficult conversations, attack the issues they are passionate about with energy and unashamed intellectualism, and realize that they will learn more about (and from) their peers when they say provocative and thought-provoking things.[17]

As Jennifer (white woman) would say in our interview, "A plastic smile and a plastic hello, those are the things that make people successful at Bowdoin." While students recognized and lamented the campus culture that valued image over mental health and seeming smart over challenging preconceived notions, they echoed the president's distaste for political correctness and urged

64   CHAPTER THREE

incoming students to break away from the mold cemented by generations past. The events that would transpire over the next four years would put this charge to the test. What would happen if students began to truly speak their minds on a small elite campus plagued by unmarked whiteness?

"Because I Didn't Have to Wear a Shirt to the Party": Individualism and White Ignorance

Despite the growing BLM movement, racially themed costume parties were still a tradition that fall at Bowdoin, as they were (or still are) on many historically and predominantly white (PWI) campuses. One of the more infamous happened every year, sometime between Halloween and Thanksgiving, and was dubbed Cracksgiving—a combination referring to the "Pilgrims and Indians" Thanksgiving theme and the fact that it took place at "Crack House." While my research did not reveal the origins of the house's name, it is likely a reference to the racialized stereotype of drug users and unkempt houses. Crack House was a slovenly off-campus rental, handed down from year to year to (predominantly or exclusively white) members of the men's lacrosse team, and known for its raucous parties. As Tristan (white man) reported in our interview, "I had never gone to Crack, but I heard a lot about it. It was like a myth on campus." The invitation lists for Crack House parties were often exclusive and most students had never been inside, which only served to build its legendary status.

In November of 2014, in the middle of the second annual No Hate November campaign, the Cracksgiving party took place as usual. Ben (white man), a member of the lacrosse team, described: "Our team threw a Thanksgiving party or a party around Thanksgiving and a bunch of us dressed up— some of us as Native Americans, some of us as pilgrims." Because seasoned team members had been privately reprimanded for the same party theme in prior years, returning students knew administrators did not consider the theme appropriate. But they carried on with the tradition because the college's individualistic response led them to believe that only players wearing offensive costumes would get in trouble. In other words, the individualistic nature of the college's reprimands gave upperclassmen a loophole to continue their tradition, an example of the kinds of agency individuals possess within organizational mandates and of how rules become decoupled from practices in a racialized manner.

Upperclassmen who had been previously reprimanded for offensive costumes did not dress up, but, at their urging, the same party and the same costumes recurred. Instead of educating their peers on the harmful impacts of

RACISM AS A PERSONAL PROBLEM   65

the costumes, upperclassmen deliberately encouraged their impressionable teammates to perpetuate the practice while staying silent about the potential repercussions. Trevor (white man), also a member of the lacrosse team, recalled the power dynamics underpinning how the costume party played out: "I was not one of the people who dressed up, but . . . I very easily could have been. . . . Upperclassmen—who knew the repercussions for it—would tell [underclassmen] to dress up. . . . A lot of times they would tell freshmen [to] dress up and [we] would—having no idea we weren't supposed to or ever thinking how it could affect some other people." Anticipating only minor disciplinary consequences (if any), upperclassmen reframed getting reprimanded for cultural appropriation into a rite of passage for new teammates. Since administrators had only ever punished students who actually wore offensive costumes, the upperclassmen knew they could continue to throw and attend the party without getting in trouble themselves. For the predominantly white men's lacrosse team, individualistic consequences did not act as a deterrent, but instead as a perverse incentive.

Many of the freshmen who dressed up for the party were, in fact, clueless. Ben, who dressed up and attended the party, reported: "I wasn't acting with any sort of intention or malice or anything like that. I remember telling the deans [when they asked], 'Why did you choose to dress up as a Native American as opposed to a pilgrim?' And to me the answer was so clear, I was like, 'Because it was way cheaper and I didn't have to wear a shirt at the party!' And [the dean] was kind of taken aback by it at first, but I guess it was so candid that she was like, 'Oh, I guess I can't really not believe you.' That was my whole thought process." Because of the ways the racial contract is buttressed by white ignorance, Ben's ignorance was entirely believable to the dean.

Arguing that ignorance, like knowledge, is a social product grounded in both explicit and tacit practices, sociologist Jennifer Mueller's work shows how racial ignorance works as a core process that helps "maintain white supremacy by allowing white people to experience their inequitable and unjust power, status, and wealth as legitimate."[18] Dominant groups hold a rational investment in not understanding racism and racial domination; the "possessive investment in whiteness" creates real material and psychic benefits.[19] All major US institutions have been formed as white institutions and structured to normalize white interests as common interests. As a result, as philosopher Charles Mills argued, white people act ignorantly because they can trust that societal institutions will approve of their racialized not-knowing.[20] As in Sarah Mayorga's conceptualization of the diversity ideology, in the eyes of white administrators, Ben's lack of *intent* to harm mattered more than the impact of his actions.[21] Thus, in Ben's recounting of his disciplinary hearing,

66   CHAPTER THREE

his straightforward revelation of his own racialized ignorance was met with sincere belief and acceptance. Through the lens of racialized organizations theory, this example shows how whiteness acted as a beneficial credential to enhance the agency of white students.

"I Want My College to Implement Policies": Individualism versus Structure

In addition to legitimating white ignorance, the college continued to treat racism as an individual transgression. Administrators met with the implicated students and doled out consequences behind closed doors. The week after the party, the Dean of Students sent an email to the campus that was broadcast on the *Orient* web page and—because of the national attention to racial justice at that moment—picked up by news outlets around the state. The email reported that fourteen of the lacrosse teams' fifty members were being disciplined for wearing Native American costumes at the party. The email referenced the fact that similar parties had happened in prior years and that students should have known better. "For some, wearing a headdress and 'war paint' on one's face and bare chest is just harmless fun. For others, it is cultural appropriation that demonstrates poor judgment and insensitivity. And for others still, it is a racist act that perpetuates prejudice, promotes hurtful stereotypes, and demeans others. Especially disturbing is that the hosts of this event knew—or should have known—that their actions would offend; yet they went ahead with their plans nonetheless." Given the shifting racial climate, the team not only engaged in educational programming, but the fourteen students who wore Native American costumes were punished for their actions. The email continued, "While I'm glad the team has begun productive conversations about this matter, we must continue to educate about these issues and the impact this behavior has on members of our community. We will take disciplinary action against those who recently dressed in Native American attire since this is 'conduct unbecoming of a Bowdoin student.'"[22] Exactly what those punishments were, however, was never publicly disclosed.

With this missive, administrators maintained their commitment to indoctrinating students to the belief that racism is only an individual act, failing to address the historicity of whiteness.[23] They entertained multiple different interpretations of how people might have viewed the party—a validation that all differences matter. Ultimately, they blamed the older students on the team, saying they should have known better, but again only formally punished students who wore "Native American" costumes. Locating the fault narrowly in the actions of those fourteen individuals—and this form of cultural appropriation—administrators strategically defined which racial transgressions would be counted as problematic. Yet staying silent on the ways core organizational structures promoted ignorance and white supremacy allowed the college itself to remain blameless.

The secrecy of the punishments for those fourteen students marks a further manifestation of this individualistic approach. My interviewees revealed that for some students on the team, the fallout felt severe. Evan (white man) recalled, "A few kids quit lacrosse because of it. Some kids actually moved out of the house and then the house shut down after this event. This pretty much is what closed Crack in some sense. Besides all the partying that went on there, I feel like this was the final straw for that house and the school took action to shut it down." While Crack House was not on college property and administrators never publicly claimed responsibility for shutting down the house, this party indeed marked the end of an era. Although closing Crack House and forcing its residents to relocate may have been more successful at breaking up the locus of the Cracksgiving party than prior disciplinary attempts, through the lens of racialized organizations theory this micro-level structural shift had little impact on the campus more broadly.

Even while one of the front-page stories in the *Orient* the next week was about the non-indictment of Darren Wilson (the white officer who killed Michael Brown in Ferguson), the responding campus protest vigil, and other questions of race and justice, the Cracksgiving party did not make the campus paper. Buried in the opinion section, however, one student of color called out administrators for their lack of action: "Some of my closest friends left crying from Crack House because it was too hard to see students dressed up like Native Americans right in their faces. I want students to continue connecting with each other and the community around them about issues of race, but more than that, I want my college to implement policies that won't allow the same things to keep happening over and over again."[24] The author continued, "What does it mean when a student can dress up as a Native American or 'dirty Mexican' and just get a stern talk, while plagiarism can get a student kicked out of school?" This student's call to action and commitment to activism sparked more and more visible conversations about racial justice on campus—another example of students exercising agency within the bounds of existing organizational structures.

As had been the case in prior generations, students would lead the charge and administrators would be slow to follow. For example, in the years leading up to Bowdoin's adoption of affirmative action policies in 1969, a small cadre of student activists began calling for a structural response long before administrators got on board. In the fall of 1963, students began a program with the goal of recruiting at least sixty-five Black applicants by the fall of 1965. The first iteration was "a partial success"—without any college funding, about sixty students returned to their hometowns over the winter holiday to promote the college among guidance counselors and high school students— but student leaders soon realized that, to achieve its goal, the program would need a wider reach and better organization.[25] Perhaps predictably, given the status of higher education as a tuition-dependent industry, scholarship funding for Black applicants proved a significant obstacle to their recruiting efforts, and student organizers began encouraging administrators commit to financial aid for Black matriculants. While administrators dragged their feet, students worked tirelessly and, in the spring of 1967, earned Bowdoin a $150,000 grant from the Rockefeller Foundation. With this grant, the college could double—from five to ten—the number of scholarships for Black students, with the understanding that the college would eventually agree to take over funding these scholarships.[26] Even though nearly every administrator went on record supporting the proposals put forth by student activists, action was slow to follow. Similarly, the administration was slow to adopt structural changes in the wake of the Cracksgiving debacle.

When students returned to campus after the long winter break, the party finally appeared on the front page of the *Orient* under the headline, "Administration Falls Silent on 'Cracksgiving' Appropriation Incident." The article reported that the party had developed into "an embarrassing news story for the college, with dozens of news outlets reporting on it."[27] Given the national attention to racial injustice in the US, the perceived silence of the administration was finally newsworthy—to students and outside journalists alike. But administrators opted to narrowly identify the harmful act, gently condemn it, and swiftly move on. Through this course of action, they sent a clear message about what kinds of racism they would respond to and how, and what kinds of racism they would allow to continue.

"I Don't Ever Want to Hurt Anyone's Feelings": Pros and Cons of Civilized Diversity Discourse

Prior studies have argued that because small, elite campuses engender a strong sense of community and lack of anonymity, activism most often takes the form of deliberation and dialogue—what Amy Binder and Kate Wood, in their study of conservative undergrads, dubbed "civilized discourse."[28] Following suit, this book develops the concept of "civilized diversity discourse."[29] Applying this notion to conversations about race may seem farfetched, but in fact the small, elite campus environment in this case applied the same

RACISM AS A PERSONAL PROBLEM 69

pressures, leading students to favor dialogue over disruptive forms of activism. By placing all students' experiences on a level playing field and centering individuals' feelings, rather than structural inequities and oppression, civilized diversity discourse maintains racialized organizational processes that benefit white people and institutions. While the diversity and naturalization scripts described in the last chapter characterize what students say when asked how diversity matters for campus life, civilized diversity discourse describes the rules of engagement for talking about race and other kinds of diversity on campus.

On the surface, civilized diversity discourse has pros and cons. The stated purpose is to educate students—as the dean quoted earlier stated, if racism is a product of ignorance, education is the solution. In fact, my interviews suggest that some white students did become more racially aware from participating in civilized diversity discourse. When it works well, this is one perk. However, this benefit impacts only a small number of students and comes at a steep cost to many of the students of color on the other side of the table.[30] Although dialogues of this sort are often conceived of as "safe spaces," the reality is that, for participants of color, conversations about race that include white people are seldom safe.[31] Drawing on the work of philosopher Frantz Fanon,[32] scholar Zeus Leonardo posits that such dialogues act "as a negotiating table that seeks peaceful compromise without engaging in the violence necessary to both explore and undo racism,"[33] where violence is operationalized as a liberating and life affirming force. In this framework, white narcissism and color-evasiveness supersede creativity and transformation. In addition, such conversations reinforce the notion that the main problem with cultural appropriation and racism is that they hurt people's feelings. While this is certainly one impact, focusing on hurt feelings reinforces white ignorance by erasing the structural impacts of white supremacy.

In the aftermath of the Cracksgiving party many members of the men's lacrosse team were asked by the dean to take part in a formal conversation with representatives from the Native American Students Association. For some members of the lacrosse team, this process was educational. Trevor attested, "I . . . learned a lot from that and [it was] a very impactful, serious, issue that happened." As Ben detailed, "The Native American student group actually was really nice and really understanding and they just said they wanted to talk with us and let us know why what happened could be taken in the wrong way and was offensive and that was the most productive conversation we had." Ben continued, "I didn't really think twice about it—going into the party [it] never once crossed my mind that . . . dressing up as a Native American could really offend. . . . I definitely felt bad that I *did* offend people.

I don't ever want to hurt anyone's feelings. If I could do it all over again, I wouldn't have done it." Ben was profoundly impacted by the experience, "It was a really interesting learning experience . . . it actually has shaped a lot of decisions that I have made and conversations that I have had, and our team has had, and I think the campus has had since then." Thanks to the efforts of Native American students and the willingness of the lacrosse players to engage, some of those who participated in this conversation repented for their transgressions. Trevor and Ben began to understand why making someone else's culture into a costume transformed something sacred into a joke. They felt sorry for offending their peers.

Similarly, some students who were not implicated in the party chose to learn more in the wake of the controversy by participating in civilized diversity discourse through other venues on campus. Many of these students had never heard of cultural appropriation and were ignorant as to why white lacrosse players dressing up as Native American stereotypes could be hurtful. Cindy (white woman) recalled, "I remember talking to my roommate [who] had been at that party . . . and being like, 'I don't get what happened. The school's being very ambiguous about what this issue is.' I had never heard of cultural appropriation before. I think I called it cultural *innapropriation* for a while because it was a term I wasn't familiar with." Cindy continued, "I was frustrated that, to me, it struck me that that event was a big deal, but I felt like it wasn't treated like it was a big deal—[there] was just this cryptic email [from the dean]." Cindy took it upon herself to "opt in" and learn more but was careful to adhere to the norms for civilized diversity discourse: reading books, talking calmly, and attending organized educational events. She recalled, "I definitely pushed myself into situations because I wanted to learn about this and didn't really know. . . . All of a sudden, I was like, 'All right! There are some things that aren't going to automatically come as a part of my Bowdoin education, and I have to take care of that myself!'" She continued, "I did some book discussion group my freshman spring where we really went into [cultural appropriation] and we were just sitting with a professor and a bunch of other students, and we talked about it." As evidenced in Cindy's response, there were ample opportunities on campus for motivated students to "opt in" and learn more.

Cindy and other students who chose to take part in these educational opportunities were, like Ben, grateful to learn more and newly aware of their own ignorance. Many remarked on how similar parties had happened at their high schools, without reproach. Evan remarked, "[Dressing up] is probably something that I would have done in high school and not seen why that's so bad. I guess that's one way that Bowdoin changed me. I've become more aware

RACISM AS A PERSONAL PROBLEM 71

of how certain things can hurt people from such diverse backgrounds." Riley (white woman) talked about changing social norms and what she learned from the aftermath of the party:

> When I was in preschool, I dressed up as a Native American for a school event. So, seeing how times have changed and people have been made more aware of what's right and what's wrong. . . . It was something I had never considered— that putting a feather on my head and putting paint under my eyes could be offensive to anyone. I honestly probably didn't even think that it was offensive, which goes to show how sheltered I guess you could say I have been most of my life. . . . Then realizing it does matter, it offends a certain group of people and that holds merit . . . it's not something to just be pushed aside.

Many students remarked on how social norms diverged on campus from their hometown or their high school and that Cracksgiving gave them a window into these different norms. These students credited activities that fit the mold of "civilized diversity discourse" with shifting their understandings.

Even so, individual-level interventions did little to alter the dominant campus culture. Instead, such powerful testimonies reinforced the characterization of racial ignorance as an individual problem that can be improved through educational programming. Shifting understandings did not necessarily shift students' behaviors because the unmarked whiteness of core organizational structures still offered broad protection for white ignorance. What are the alternatives to individual-level interventions? Racialized organizations theory suggests systems-level change that reassesses how resources are distributed, how agency is constrained or magnified for different racial and ethnic groups, and how whiteness acts as a credential. Stakeholders would need to first acknowledge the unmarked whiteness of many of the college's structures and policies, then begin the work of rebuilding and reallocating in ways that decenter whiteness.

"They Didn't Do Anything Wrong": Perpetuating a Culture of Ignorance

While some students were learning new things by "opting in" to civilized diversity discourse, others chose to "opt out." Research has shown that, in many organizational contexts, mandatory anti-racism trainings can backfire.[34] But swinging to the other end of the spectrum—nurturing organizational norms that prioritize white racial comfort by avoiding conversations about race altogether—is also not ideal. Students like Jacob and Adrian thought the party was problematic but stayed quiet because they worried conversations might become confrontational. Jacob (white and Hispanic man) recalled, "Because my roommate was a lacrosse player, and also my teammate who lived on my floor—he lived with a lacrosse player . . . we got a pretty inside look at that whole situation . . . seeing some of their reactions and how some of the people [on the team] didn't think it was a big deal." Adrian (white man) also had a roommate who was involved, "I didn't see his costume. One of my [other] roommates said it was horrible." After the party, Adrian avoided conversations with the implicated roommate, "I avoided talking to my roommate about it because he didn't—from what I heard—he didn't seem that apologetic about it. I didn't want to get mad at him. Because I definitely felt like it was bad, and [the team] didn't respond that well to it." In the examples of Jacob and Adrian, to avoid confrontation and abide by the norms of civilized diversity discourse, they avoided talking about their grievances with implicated players.

A larger body of research documents how many white Americans strive to avoid being perceived as racist, primarily for moral reasons.[35] In the case of elite liberal arts colleges, because students stand to earn individual dividends (both social and economic)—on campus and postgraduation—from preserving their reputations, all students—but especially those who were not already embedded in resource-rich networks—strived to maintain respectability when discussing "sensitive topics" like race. Like Ben, Jacob and Adrian did not want to offend anyone or pick a fight. But because their roommates or floormates did not share their views, this meant not talking about race at all. By sustaining an organizational context wherein many students—and particularly white students—could easily "opt out" of race talk, the college enabled white ignorance to continue and reinscribed its campus as a white space.[36]

Indeed, while some students took the critiques of the party to heart, other students did not. Many of those students bemoaned the way white students were being punished for merely wanting to have a good time. Alexis (white woman) remembered conversations about the party among upper-class students on the women's lacrosse team. She recalled, "In hindsight, they probably weren't productive conversations at all because it was more like, 'Why did this have to shut down [Crack House]? They didn't do anything wrong!'" Brooke (white woman) echoed this sentiment saying, "The upperclassmen kind of made it a big deal, because they were like, 'This is where we always go when we go out! I'm not sure what we're going to do now!'" On a campus rife with white spaces, the demise of Crack House—what Zabala described as a hyper-cultural white space[37]—still came as a loss to many members of the lacrosse team and their friends. Even with conversations about racial justice escalating nationally and on campus, many students could not see the extent to which campus structures privileged white students. Instead, they echoed

RACISM AS A PERSONAL PROBLEM   73

broader claims of white grievance, painting themselves as victims of an unjust system. In line with the diversity script, which encouraged students to learn from all kinds of diversity without attending to any kind of structural inequity, claims from white students insisting they too had been wronged offered a counterclaim to those highlighting the harm done to Native American students in the aftermath of the party. These counterclaims served to perpetuate white ignorance on campus.

Collective Action for Structural Change

Yet tracking national attention to racial justice, student activists' claims continued to gather momentum. Ben reported that it felt like the Cracksgiving controversy, "opened the Pandora's box of all this stuff that happened later at school." In the short term, one dorm canceled their annual "Inappropriate party," out of fear the theme might prompt students to wear problematic costumes. And, exemplifying the norms of civilized diversity discourse, many columns in the *Orient* debated the merits of free speech, political correctness, and racial justice. But, as some of those articles noted, BSG and college administrators remained silent. Their silence, in part, prompted students to undertake a broader movement for structural change on campus.

In the winter of 2015, student activists spearheaded an open letter to the college community discussing issues of race and diversity on campus, and then held a meeting in the student union to discuss the demands of the letter. In a direct rebuke of the president's bidding for students to eschew political correctness, the preamble to their demands stated: "We aim to illuminate the difference between political correctness and that which is morally imperative: equality, inclusiveness, and authentic mutual respect."[38] The demands included programming in first-year orientation about race; training for Residential Life staff about race; changes to support equity in the student disciplinary system; support for increasing diversity in athletics, the Outing Club, and the Women's Resource Center; hiring and supporting faculty of color; training for all faculty about race; an explicit statement from the administration supporting students of color; a better system for reporting acts of bias; making Martin Luther King Jr. Day a college holiday; and many more. For the most part, the demands were specific and concrete—in addition to platitudes, students advocated for structures and resources.

The college responded by creating a working group to address the students' demands. That group gradually implemented changes to policies and practices in many divisions of the college, which are noted in later chapters as they came to fruition. But the list of demands, the Meeting in the Union, and their impacts were rarely mentioned in my interviews. Perhaps that is because, as first-year students, very few members of the class of 2018 were networked into activist circles and invited to sign the letter. Or perhaps it is because the events of the following year did more to illustrate the costs of white ignorance than a cogently worded petition and a peaceful indoor rally ever could. As coming chapters will describe, one year later, the *Orient* revisited the list of demands to update the community on benchmarks of progress, but by that time the campus climate had taken a dramatic turn.

What Students Learned

Most respondents in my interview sample were not directly asked about the Cracksgiving party, but instead were asked about any events or controversies they remembered for each of their four years on campus. When asked about any events or controversies their first year, more than half the sample made no mention of the Cracksgiving party. Others vaguely remembered the event or were prompted about it by the interviewer and were not impacted by it in any way. Anthony (white and Latino man) summed up the general sentiment, saying, "Now that you say 'Cracksgiving' I remember it, but the fact that I didn't remember it, I think, is a statement to how much it's impacted me: not very much." Because the college chose to only reprimand the students directly involved with the party and to otherwise condone a model for civilized diversity discourse that allowed students to opt in or out of conversations about racism and cultural appropriation, the Cracksgiving controversy did not reverberate into the social or academic circles of most first-year students.

By design, only a small number of students were impacted by the Cracksgiving party. A handful of lacrosse players felt newly enlightened because of their conversations with the Native American Students Association, while another handful begrudged their loss of a legendary (white) party venue. Other students took it upon themselves to attend campus events, write columns for the *Orient*, and participate in nondisruptive collective action—forms of engaging with diversity that fit the mold of civilized diversity discourse. In general, these events reinscribed the campus culture whereby racist actions were treated as individual transgressions and conversations about difference were enacted in ways that protected white ignorance and white supremacy.

4

The Pros and Cons of Civilized Diversity Discourse

The last chapter introduced "civilized diversity discourse" as the norm for conversations about race on this small, elite campus. This chapter depicts the exacting cost of civilized diversity discourse for students of color, relative to the discrete benefit for a small number of white students, and the broad benefit for the college in sustaining white ignorance and white dominance. Through the detailed retelling of the Gangster party that happened on campus in fall of 2015, we again see white ignorance on full display. But as the national spotlight on racial justice grew more intense that year, so did organized responses to incidents on campus. Events that had previously drawn no attention or garnered quiet reprimand, were now becoming the subject of fiery public debate and agitation. Even as student activists turned up the heat, however, administrators found ways to reinforce whiteness not only through what they said and did, but also through what they neglected to say and do.

The Next Fall

By the next fall, more than a year had passed since the Ferguson protests and the Black Lives Matter (BLM) movement was continuing to gather strength, size, and sophistication. On campuses around the nation, issues of race and inequity were demanding center stage and garnering media attention. The protests at the University of Missouri (Mizzou) were some of the most notorious. In mid-September 2015, people riding in the back of a pickup truck screamed racial slurs at Mizzou Student Government President Payton Head. Head, who is Black, broadcast his outrage in a widely shared Facebook post: "For those of you who wonder why I'm always talking about the importance of inclusion and respect, it's because I've experienced moments like this multiple times at *this* university, making me not feel included here." While the chancellor issued a statement calling recent "incidents of bias and discrimination" "totally unacceptable," students protested, saying university officials had done nothing to address Head's concerns. Protest rallies were held in late September and again in early October. But it was only after another racist incident on campus that the chancellor ordered diversity and inclusion training for all students and faculty. Even as student activists acknowledged the trainings as a "step in the right direction," they continued protests calling for broader recognition and change.[1] While how people talk is part of the problem, they argued, systems structuring campus interactions and resource distribution also needed to shift to better support students of color.

On October 10, in an incident that captured national headlines, protesters blocked Missouri University System President Tim Wolfe's vehicle during the homecoming parade. Wolfe did not respond to protesters. On October 20, student group Concerned Student 1950—named for the year African American students were first admitted to Mizzou—issued a list of demands that included, among other things, an apology from Wolfe and his removal from office. Wolfe met with the student group the following week but did not agree to their demands. By November 6, Wolfe finally issued an apology to Concerned Student 1950. But that night when protesters asked him if he knew what systematic oppression was, Wolfe responded: "It's—systematic oppression is because you don't believe that you have the equal opportunity for success."[2] Shocked and outraged, protesters found this limited understanding of how institutional structures shape inequality unacceptable. Two days later, Black football players announced what many agreed was the fatal blow—they would not practice or play until Wolfe was removed from office. Many white players and coaches announced support for the boycott. The prospect of a strike by a team in the country's most dominant college football league drew national attention. Officials estimated that forfeiting one game would cost the university one million dollars. The following day, the chancellor and president both stepped down.[3]

Protests taking place at Mizzou in the fall of 2015 became a lightning rod for racialized activism nationwide. In an analysis of Black student activists' demands on seventy-three campuses throughout the US since 2015, scholar Michael Ndemanu found striking similarities among the movements. The most common demands, expressed by more than half of the sample, included increasing the number of faculty of color, increasing the number of students of color, mandating diversity training for faculty and staff, and requiring a social/racial justice course for all students.[4] These demands came in response to centuries of exclusion of people of color from the campuses and curricula of most US institutions of higher education. Nationwide, in 2018, only 5.5% of all full-time postsecondary faculty—and only 3.7% of full professors—identified as Black[5] compared to the 15% of undergraduates who identified as Black.[6] Student demands aimed to not only increase the presence of students of color, but also shift how those students were treated on campus.

That fall, Bowdoin welcomed a new president. Introducing his vision at the annual convocation ceremony, Bowdoin's new president offered a model of how to talk openly about racism while undercutting its impacts: "Since the end of the last academic year, much has happened in America with regard to the issue of race—the massacre in Charleston, debates about the Confederate flag, and the shooting death in Cincinnati of Samuel Dubose, among them. These events are stark reminders that race can create different opportunities and experiences for those of color, different from those of white Americans."[7] He acknowledged horrific, racially motivated violence, but described those acts as "different experiences."

He then modeled how to talk about race, without acknowledging whiteness. The president highlighted positive aspects of the college's history, but made no mention of the Cracksgiving controversy, the plaque in the auditorium commemorating alumni who fought for the Confederacy, or the Jefferson Davis prize awarded for scholarly excellence each spring. He also made no mention of the fact that he was fifteenth in a line of cis, white men to lead the college since its founding. Instead, he appealed to his predominantly white audience, reinforcing false notions that race does not impact them: "For those of us not of color, we can understand that race still does matter, not just as the social phenomenon we read about or watch on the news, but in the life experiences of our friends, classmates, and colleagues." Rather than recognizing white privilege—or the conditions of white supremacy that make white privilege possible[8]—he celebrated diversity, "We can strive to understand what makes us each unique, help others understand who we are, and celebrate our differences." Here he individualized the issue, putting everyone on an even playing field to talk about our differences, while evading mention of structural oppression.

Finally, he underlined the implicit point that racism is only overt and individual, rather than also omnipresent and structural. The president called on white people to, "rally around and support those in our community when their race becomes an issue because of some national event or a personal attack." He concluded, "Sadly, vexingly, race remains an issue in America. It is well within our ability, and part of who we are at Bowdoin, to make some difference, quite personally, for those classmates, colleagues and friends where race affects their experience." Again, he underlined the notion that white people do not experience race, let alone benefit from racialized social systems.

As prior studies have documented, school size and status matter for how students engage politically.[9] At massive public universities like Mizzou, student activists mobilized to attract media attention to racial injustice on campus that fall. But at Bowdoin, conflicts were handled primarily through civilized diversity discourse.[10] Race talk was relegated to the back pages of the student newspaper. Would-be activists debated in club meetings and organized shuttle vans to protests in the nearest city, twenty-five miles away. On this small elite campus, disagreements tended to be fodder for dialogue wherein all differences were held on an even playing field, rather than outright upheaval. Nearly a year after the final Cracksgiving party, however, this would begin to change.

The Next Party

One year after Cracksgiving, another predominantly white team decided to host a costume party at Bowdoin. This one was thrown by the sailing team which, that year, had about twenty-five members. Although those with extensive precollege sailing experience tended to come from upper-class families, the team was open to newcomers and thus cultivated some racial and socioeconomic diversity. For example, Ella (Asian American woman) attended an East Coast prep school but had never sailed. She joined the team because she saw a poster and thought sailing sounded fun. Scott (white man), on the other hand, had been sailing competitively for many years. He had attended a large public high school and was recruited to Bowdoin by the sailing coach.

As was tradition, each Thursday the sailing team's social chairs hosted a themed party. As Ella explained, "Basically the way the parties work is they're on Thursdays, the entire team gets an email that's sent out, and then you either show up or not." She continued, "There always is a theme and [the emails] say like, 'Join us tonight!' and are always some funny—I don't know—like joke . . . they're meant to be lighthearted." As Scott foreshadowed, however, "Sophomore year is a weird year, especially on an athletic team, because you transition from a super junior role to a leadership role that you might not be fully aware of yet or fully comfortable with. I think sophomores on the sailing team shape a lot of the social culture on the team. . . . Juniors and seniors are starting to pick up academically and they're more preoccupied with other things." Indeed, sophomores on the team had an outsized influence on its social culture.

Thursday, October 22 was no different from any other Thursday that autumn. Scott recalled, "There was an email that was sent out by another team member basically inviting everybody to this [Gangster] party. It was a party [theme] that [had] happened the year before also." Seeing the theme, one team member—a white man—asked on the group chat for his dorm if anyone could give him cornrows. A housemate quickly volunteered. As Ella pointed out, "Prior to the party, nobody from the team or outside of the team brought up any concerns about the theme, and people in [that student's dorm] helped to put cornrows in [his] hair." The party was not advertised outside the team email list nor intended to draw crowds, yet even among residents in one entire dorm, no one questioned the fact that a white guy was asking for help with cornrows.

The party was small, maybe twenty-five people, and held in an on-campus apartment. Most of the costumes were unremarkable. Scott observed, "I think particularly because of [one person's] actions—you know wearing cornrows—the team was sort of lumped into 'Everybody was wearing that degree [of costume],' but it was really for the most part people wearing sweatpants." The team's costumes were later described in the *Orient* as including, "baggy pants, jerseys, gold chains, and 80's style LL Cool J hats."[11] Despite most team members putting little effort into their costumes, they were nonetheless recognizable as exactly the gangster stereotypes they were trying to portray.

After the party, the team went to Super Snacks (a.k.a. Supers), a fourth meal (consisting of jalapeño poppers, grilled cheese, pizza, and the like) provided in the larger dining hall on weekend nights. Still dressed in costume and intoxicated, the team went in, sat down, and proceeded to eat and hang out. Team members who were there remember being "pretty drunk." Most of the rest of the dining hall was oblivious to their costumes initially.

But soon, recognition rippled through the crowd. Specifically, a member of Black Girl Brunch (BGB) group chat—a robust communication network among Black women on campus—posted something to the group. Lauren (Black woman) explained, "Per usual, something goes on [and] somebody puts into BGB: 'Do you see these people wearing baggy clothes and chains in Super Snacks?' And some other Black women were in there and said 'No, I don't see them. I'm not there.' Somebody says, 'Yeah, I see them I am going to go talk to them,' because they knew somebody that was sitting at that table." Through this chain of messages, Black women in BGB were alerted to the situation. Because campus is small, Mena, an upper-class student and leader in various capacities around campus, had a personal connection with one of the sailors and took it upon herself to confront them.

According to multiple observers, Mena walked over to the team and calmly asked them to leave. Scott recalled, "Mena comes and she sits down at our table, and really I don't know how, but she remained incredibly calm and just explained that there were people who were not incredibly calm a couple tables over, and who were really, really angry and really, really hurt in this moment. And that we probably should leave and that we should probably be ready to talk about [it] in the morning." He continued, "Everyone was really drunk, but I just remember sitting there and looking around and I became hyperaware of that space that I was in." After being approached, the team left without further incident.

In that moment, civilized diversity discourse prevailed. Black students took it upon themselves to confront their peers, even while diffusing the tension. They were calm, respectful, and articulate—even while they were furious and hurt. They invited their peers into conversation, without provoking an altercation. Mena returned to her table and diplomatically reported back to BGB. A few members of the group chat who were "very close with [the dean]," vowed to bring the matter to the attention of the Dean of Students the next day. Everything about the encounter was orderly, an incredible testament to the hegemonic power of the norms surrounding civilized diversity discourse on campus.

Some students outside of the sailing team and BGB witnessed or heard about what happened at Supers that evening. Many acknowledged the problematic nature of the costumes but remained nonchalant. Xavier (African American man) remembered hosting a group of high school students and wrestling with the puzzle of what and how to tell them: "[My friend and I] were talking to some prospective students who were at Super Snacks with us, and then we heard a lot of noise going on and two tables over from us were some members of the sailing team who had come from the party, and one of them was wearing the cornrows, and there were some other Black students who were older that were really reacting to it. . . . I was like, 'Okay this is racist,' but I did not think it was the worst thing ever." Similarly, Luis (Latino man) recalled, "One of my friends texted me who was at [the dining hall] during Super Snacks when people had walked in with what they were wearing, and I know some of my friends were saying that people were annoyed and kind of confused, but other than that I didn't think much about it at that moment." Word of mouth and social media gradually spread news of the encounter across campus, but still everyone remained calm and civilized—at least in public spaces.

"A Weak-Ass Email": The Administration Responds

The administration's response to the Gangster party began like its response to other similar events. As per the pattern, by the next afternoon, the team captains and coach had been called in to meet with the Dean of Students privately. Some team members who had not attended the party or Super Snacks were just learning about the incident. Ella recalled, "I remember getting in the van [to practice] on Friday and people were talking about it and they were like, 'Oh, did you hear? There was some trouble at Supers.' And they were like, 'People talked to us.'" Ella continued, "I remember at some point the captains at the time being like, 'This is what happened, and this was wrong.' . . . I don't exactly remember ever having a discussion as a team, but I viscerally remember being like, 'Holy crap! We did something terrible.'" Every member of the sailing team interviewed for this study came quickly to that same conclusion. Students were uniformly apologetic, regretful, and willingly engaged in doing the work to know more and do better. Administrators accepted their contrition, as it fit comfortably with the college's established norms for addressing and then dismissing racialized transgressions.

The same afternoon, a small group of Black women brought their concerns to the Dean of Students. Lauren reported, "The women in the class above me were very close to [the dean]. And so, because they were close to him and this seemed like something he should do as Dean of Student Affairs, [they decided] that it would just be the easiest to go talk to him." Students who attended that meeting remember having the opportunity to share their "thoughts and feelings." Lauren described the dean's response as "This is a problem and we're going to handle it." In the moment, these students felt listened to and assured that action would be taken. They continued to play along with established norms for dealing with racist acts on campus by adhering to the rules of civilized diversity discourse. Even in their fury, they did not riot or demand structural change, they scheduled a meeting with authority figures to calmly discuss. Administrators, for their part, accepted the last-minute meeting and agreed to handle the problem. But then the waiting game began.

Grounded in their commitment to treating racism as an individual problem, administrators' method of dealing with the partygoers was to hold a series of private meetings with individual students. Because these meetings were happening behind closed doors, campus was relatively quiet that weekend, with no further public words or action from the administration until the following week.

Six days after the party, the Dean of Students sent out a campus-wide email admonishing the partygoers and proclaiming the value of civilized discourse. His email first emphasized that the main problem with racialized costume parties is the hurt feelings they cause, saying that "students were justifiably offended by this narrow, stereotypical representation of African American culture," and calling the "insensitivity" of the party participants "disappointing and disheartening." Then, the dean iterated the college's commitment to celebrating all kinds of diversity, while ignoring institutionalized racism: "Let me be clear: racial and ethnic stereotyping is not acceptable at Bowdoin." He recalled the president's convocation speech which, "challenged us all to do what we can to learn about one another, and to strive to understand our differences and the unique ways we see and experience the world." He noted that he and his administrative colleagues were, "deeply disturbed by this incident and what it says about the work we must do on our campus around race, racism, and issues of difference." While he acknowledged there was work to be done, based on the way he homogenized all kinds of differences and avoided mentioning whiteness, the work he was referring to was educational rather than structural.

He continued, explicitly reifying a model of civilized diversity discourse where students of color bear the brunt of the burden. He wrote, "In our view, the most powerful and effective response is an honest, open discussion between the students who dressed as they did, those who were stereotyped, and the larger student community." He then detailed the steps for moving forward: "We will work with students to facilitate these direct, honest, and constructive conversations, recognizing that, for some of our students of color, having to engage in this discussion—to explain and represent their race—carries an additional burden and poses a regrettable additional cost of this incident. This work is about our community and our obligations to one another. That's why it is incumbent upon all of us to engage these issues, to exchange different points of view openly, and to gain the insights necessary to influence better understanding and behavior." The dean pointed again and again to the need for civilized conversation, dialogue, and discussion. And, although administrators claimed to recognize the "regrettable additional cost" to students of color, their response was, nonetheless, to ask students of color to help "facilitate these direct, honest, and constructive conversations" with the mostly white sailing team.

While Black students continued to publicly adhere to the conventions of civilized diversity discourse, they also recognized how that email protected white supremacy on campus. To students hurt and outraged by the Gangster party, this "weak-ass email" sidestepped the real issues. Some students wanted to see the perpetrators disciplined, or at least feel the pain and lose as much time as the students both victimized and then tapped by administrators to educate their peers. These students wanted to see the administration make a stronger statement. Lauren recalled, "I started to get frustrated with how much time I was really spending on trying to educate my peers. And it didn't feel like the administration was backing us up. I mean that email was not! It was not clear, it wasn't specific, it didn't talk about what we as a community should care about—our standards. . . . Where is it condemning [the students who threw the party] at all? I think the email talked about our feelings were hurt, what is that going to do?" Lauren and others noted that the email made no mention of white privilege or structural racism. The focus on hurt feelings individualized the issue, revealing administrators' hopes that educating the implicated individuals would pass as an acceptable response.

"Attempting to Offer Generosity":
Students of Color Trying to Educate Their Peers

Although many students were outraged, student activists continued to turn to dialogue and education, rather than rallies or riots—again playing by the rules of civilized diversity discourse promoted by this small, elite college. While administrators had to craft statements that would please wealthy, white parents and donors, students were free to address racism more directly. On Tuesday, October 27, an opinion piece, written by a weekly columnist, was published online by the *Orient* ahead of its Friday issue.[12] The author, a Black woman, encouraged students to learn from the debacle: "I am naturally tempted to embark on a furious rant, but I have decided to instead rein in my frustration and attempt to offer generosity. To those who do not yet understand why the sailing team's party theme is unacceptable: I am perplexed by you, but I do not resent you. In the aftermath of this incident, however, you need to learn." In accordance with the norms of campus culture, white ignorance would be addressed educationally; the need for the uninitiated to learn was so urgent, it could not wait until the Friday printing.

The author used her column to explain why some Black students were offended by a group of predominantly white students using gangster tropes as costumes. The author defined cultural appropriation as, "the adoption of one culture's aspects by members of another culture," and proceeded to explain how individual's donning costumes from cultures that are not their own misrepresent other's cultures and traditions, draw out negative stereotypes, and reinforce systems of oppression by making fun of marginalized groups. Good intentions, the author noted, did not blunt the sting of the offense. "Cornrows, braids, twists—they are not just hairstyles. The earliest depiction of African cornrow braiding dates back to 500 BC. Intricate hair designs have long been an integral part of African culture and that tradition came to America on the slave ships. . . . Not only are these hairstyles a part of Black culture, but they are also a source of discrimination. Many workplaces ban these hairstyles and some even ban Afro-textured hair as a whole." The column continued: "Whether the involved members of this team realized it or not, their theme directly took negative stereotypes of the Black race and made them into a costume . . . one of the most dangerous Black stereotypes is that of the 'thug.' . . . A Black boy, such as Trayvon Martin, cannot even walk home with his life intact because his 'gangster clothing' (i.e., hoodie and brown skin) signified his criminal intent. Members of the dominant culture cannot try on these stereotypes for fun then stand idly by while these same harmful stereotypes end lives." To what extent the column reached its target audience is unknown, but what is clear from the events that followed is that the column instigated a major uptick in columns and op-eds in the *Orient* about race, equity, and PC culture. To the extent that students were outraged about the party, they remained civilized, channeling their grief, anger, and confusion into sternly worded public statements.

Bowdoin Student Government (BSG) also joined the conversation, addressing the incident directly. At the regularly scheduled meeting on the same evening the dean sent his campus-wide email, public comment time centered on the Gangster party. Students of color used the time to unload their anger and concern. The sailing team (including athletes who had not attended the party) attended together and were seated in the front of the room. Scott described, "Our captains [sat] directly at the [head] table [and] the team sat behind them, and then there was the entirety of BSG. And students said how they were feeling, and it was really raw—there were a lot of tears, a lot of anger." Ella agreed, "That was particularly difficult to listen to what people were saying and how [the party] had affected them. And the last thing I want to do in this world is to hurt someone else, and to listen to what the actions of my team had done and how much it had affected people and hurt them was really hard." Scott continued, "I think public comment time needed to happen, I don't know [that] public shaming necessarily had to happen, but there needed to be a space and venue for people to share their emotions and think." The team largely agreed that public comment time was a cathartic and important step in taking responsibility for their actions. Contrary to the model of "safe space" dialogues that center whiteness, public comment time featured counter-storytelling by students of color that invited the team to take ownership of their racialized discomfort.[13] The team was not defensive or dismissive, yet still the onus fell on students of color to educate their white peers.

At that meeting, the General Assembly of BSG voted on and unanimously agreed to issue a Statement of Solidarity, symbolically asserting their moral claim but not enacting structural change. In the statement, released publicly the next day, they condemned the party as an "incident of cultural appropriation,"[14] stating: "The assembly asserts that issuing a Statement of Solidarity is the right action that should be taken by student leaders. . . . The assembly is resolved to help educate all students on the inappropriateness of these acts and their inherently racist nature." As student activists had the winter before in their letter listing demands, the statement specifically addressed the issue of political correctness, saying "cultural appropriation is distinctly different from and not to be conflated with issues of political correctness or freedom of expression (in that cultural appropriation perpetuates the exploitation of certain cultural aspects of marginalized groups in American society, allowing the identity of marginalized groups to be trivialized in the name of freedom of expression, when in reality individuals identifying with these groups are treated poorly due to said stereotypes)." The statement concluded, "It is the hope of the assembly to move forward with a restorative vision and progress with the help of all parties." To those involved, the statement felt like an important way to articulate their morality by explicitly standing against racism. Although the statement diverged from administrative communications by calling out racism and rejecting anti-PC rhetoric, it acted as a way for student leaders to pacify the demands of their constituents. Future events would reveal that the statement had little impact on students' behaviors, however, even those who helped write it.

Meanwhile, two more articles posted to the *Orient*'s online platform ahead of the Friday print release revealed the paper's commitment to hearing "both sides," part of the civilized diversity discourse package. One, written by a member of the sailing team who did not attend the party, continued the trend of students of color educating their peers and explored why even someone who self-identified as a "half-Mexican person from Los Angeles" did not anticipate the problematic nature of the party's theme. This student pointed toward structural issues and solutions. "It's about this being one of a huge number of incidents that contribute to US society—all of us, not just ignorant white people—associating poor Black people with violence, crime and bad behavior. I don't think 'offense' is something that we will ever be able to agree on, but statistically proven institutional bias is! I'm sorry that my team's actions offended my friends and classmates, but I'm more sorry that we added one more thing to the list of news reports, TV shows, and fads that focus on the part of Black culture that institutional poverty has forced into gangs and criminality."[15] This student pointed out the macro-level structural factors that shaped the team's micro-scale actions, and the utter disconnect between classroom learning and everyday behaviors.

But the other, written by a self-identified "white guy," argued that the dean's call for "open and honest" exchanges was contradictory to his convictions that the Gangster party was, "narrow, stereotypical," and "deeply disturb[ing]." The author asserted, "How can we have an open exchange of ideas when we've already decided that one side is right and the other is wrong?"[16] Isabella (white woman) recalled that, in the dorm where the cornrows were braided, the controversy made the building feel divided and uncomfortable. "I know that [the person who braided the cornrows] issued a formal statement of apology in one of our [dorm] meetings, but I think also—if I remember correctly—our [dorm] vice president gave a speech essentially being like, 'Let it be known that not everyone thinks that you did something wrong.' So there was a lot of mixed politics in one room, and in one house—which made it very fragmented and difficult." While some students seized the moral high ground by disavowing the party, others defended the diversity script arguing that all viewpoints should be granted equal airtime.

The *Orient*'s editorial board, however, sided with BSG and others who were coming to the defense of students of color. They pushed back against the ways civilized diversity discourse promoted white supremacy in their column: "As is often the case with incidents of this nature, administrators and many students are calling for a renewed focus on conversation and dialogue. Dialogue is happening, but it's not the kind they're hoping for. . . . There is still a population here unwilling to participate in the public dialogue so many of us are asking for. Moving forward, we must consider how to break this cycle of asymmetrical dialogue in which students putting themselves on the line are made to feel unsafe."[17] As long as explicitly racist viewpoints were seen as deserving of equal footing in campus dialogues—as the rules of civilized diversity discourse would dictate—such conversations were harmful rather than generative.

Still much of the campus felt only the ripples of an uncomfortable confrontation. As in the wake of Cracksgiving, some students did not understand why the party was problematic, and, out of fear of offending anyone—or being labeled racist—they had trouble finding ways to learn more. Caleb (white and Asian American) attended events to try and improve his understanding. "When we had the [BSG public comment time], I was like, I'm going to go and like learn a lot about this, because I wanted to know why people were upset. And it just seemed like everybody was yelling at each other. And they were like 'I'm upset that you did this!' and the sailing team was there." But Caleb did not gain any understanding from the student-led events. "I didn't really feel like the town hall event at all was useful. . . . It was advertised as like, we're going to have conversation about this, and come engage with us. And then it was just people yelling at each other. And then at the end, some of the sailing team was like, 'We're sorry.' And like, 'We're going to try to be better,' I

PROS AND CONS OF CIVILIZED DIVERSITY DISCOURSE 87

don't remember what they said. But I was just like, that didn't help me at all."
Instead, seeing the discord made him reticent to engage any further, "After
that I was just scared to ask people, because I asked my roommates and they
were like, 'Yeah I don't really understand what's going on either.' Everybody
in my friend group, we all thought a big portion of the campus was just being
sensitive and we didn't understand why people were so upset about it. And
we were all too scared to ask people why they were upset about it, because all
we had seen was angry Facebook posts and yelling at the meeting." Racialized
ignorance thus prevailed because students feared being seen as racist for not
already understanding the crux of the controversy. After checking in with
his close circle of friends, Caleb grew wary of extending himself any further.

Meanwhile, given the national political climate, such events were now
newsworthy. Local media outlets picked up the story, and the *Bangor Daily
News* ran an article that led with: "Less than a year after members of Bowdoin College's lacrosse team were disciplined by the college for dressing as
Native Americans at a 'Cracksgiving' party, members of the college's sailing
team held a 'gangster-themed' party."[18] The college now not only had to contend with discontent on campus, but watchful eyes from off campus as well.
Thanks largely to social media, what might have been a casual night with
friends had now begun to go viral.

Civilized Discourse Meets Uncivilized Discourse:
Anti-PC Backlash Couched in Anonymity

While face-to-face meetings and volleys on the pages of the *Orient* remained
largely civilized, the anonymous users of Yik Yak were anything but. In Yik
Yak, a localized messaging app, users post anonymous messages visible only
within a limited geographic radius. The app became popular with both high
school and college students, "who used the app to share gossip on campus
without their names attached."[19] In 2014, its founders raised $73 million in
venture capital funding and downloads hit an all-time high. By early 2015,
downloads were beginning to decline overall, but the app was still widely
used.

Some students first learned about the Gangster party via Yik Yak. Genesis
(African American woman) said, "My friend [was] like, 'Did you see that
thing on Yik Yak?' And I was like, 'What are you talking about?' and she said,
'Did you see that kid who put his hair in cornrows and [was] wearing a jersey
and was coming from this thing called the Gangster party?' And I was like,
'What are you saying? That really happened?'" Yik Yak spread news of the
events wider and faster than word of mouth alone.

Others took to Yik Yak to air grievances campus norms prohibited them from saying out loud. Xavier explained, "[The dean] sent out this weak-ass email like, 'You guys should talk more about these tough issues,' to the whole campus, which [was] not inherently a bad email—we should do those things—but Yik Yak blew up in reaction to his email. But the anger wasn't really directed at [the dean], it was directed at 'PC rats' and 'soft POC students,' and all of that language, who I guess provoked [the dean] to write that email." Lauren reported, "[Yik Yak] probably incited more feelings for me, more than the party itself. Because people were like, 'If a Black girl straightens her hair isn't that cultural appropriation?' And I was like, 'So wait, we're here now?! I know that that's wrong. Why don't you know that that's wrong?'" Lauren continued, "I thought people cared about diverse issues! . . . It felt very pressing for me to do something because it was clear that people didn't understand the issue through Yik Yak." Scott agreed, "Yik Yak was this whole different thing because it was just really factionalized and that was just so incendiary." Comments that would never be shared in forums, class discussions, the student newspaper, or club meetings, were shared openly via the app. While the social norms on campus made it clear that such comments would not be tolerated in public, the anonymous platform gave airtime to overt racism.

Students of color who had made themselves vulnerable speaking out against the Gangster party began to question their place on campus. Lauren remembered, "It just became this tense environment because I was thinking, 'So which one of y'all is writing this in Yik Yak—because it's anonymous. Is this just me? Is it my previous roommates? Is it people who say hi to me every day? Or is it the anonymous white male athlete I don't know who was never going to talk to me in the first place?' It just became this anxious feeling of who can I trust? Who sees me as a human being and not as a stereotype?" Luis agreed, "I know a lot of people who deleted [Yik Yak] from their phones because [they felt] this is too much for me to constantly keep engaging in this way that could be a little counterproductive. But I constantly kept looking at stuff, kept looking at what people were saying. It could be either amazing or it could be super frustrating. So, that was always a really hard thing [trying] to know: What are my peers around me really thinking about what's going on on campus? Am I over exaggerating?" Regardless of their views on the party, students of color felt increasingly more unsafe because of the anonymous vitriol spewed via Yik Yak.

Members of the sailing team were also resentful of what was being posted on Yik Yak, but for different reasons. One of the team's leaders recalled, "[Before the party] I was so proud to be on the sailing team, but then [after the party] I wasn't proud to be on the sailing team and didn't want to be associated with the team and stopped wearing my Bowdoin Sailing gear. I felt like I had this giant target on my back. Particularly with all the Yik Yak stuff that was happening and making arguments like defending our actions and we, as a team, were like, 'Do not defend our actions—we admit this was wrong and we're trying to learn from it.'" Having the controversy explode online took control of narrative away from the perpetrators and those championing resistance, who were together earnestly working at reconciliation.

Online commentary gave a platform to students who were not participating in face-to-face dialogue, shifting the focus away from building community and making amends—work that was occupying a tremendous amount of time for Black students and students on the sailing team—to a larger conversation about PC culture. In a later email the college president would agree: "There is no place for the cesspool that is created by Yik Yak and other forms of anonymous postings. Apart from the content, the anonymity of these postings erodes trust and creates considerable distress within our community."[20] Shifting the focus away from students of color and toward the grievances of white students, students acting via Yik Yak reestablished the centrality and dominance of whiteness on campus. Their actions worked outside the college's purview and beyond the bounds of civilized diversity discourse. Even as the college, as an organization, constrained students' agency through campus norms regarding acceptable forms of expression, some students exercised their agency by turning elsewhere to express themselves. Although Ray's articulation of racialized organizations theory recognizes that both external (e.g., social movements and state policies) and internal (e.g., hiring practices and diversity programs) factors can change the racialization of an organization,[21] this example shows how social actors can mobilize external forces, such as social media, in ways that impact organizational processes. Technology, then, is not only renegotiating the rules of racial discourse,[22] but also the process of racialized contestation within organizations.

Unmarked Whiteness Sets the Terms for Civilized Discourse: The Administration Responds

In the continued turmoil surrounding the dean's email, the BSG meeting, and the budding media coverage, administrators made a point of meeting with students of color in person. On Saturday, October 31, the president, Dean of Students, and newly hired director of the Student Center for Multicultural Life were scheduled to meet with students at Russwurm African American Center. African American Society (AfAm) leaders were initially excited for the meeting and planned carefully. One of the AfAm leaders remembered,

"I spent hours the night before planning. . . . We wanted this to be a small conversation of us briefly talking about our problems, but then trying to work with [administrators] and how they can make this less of an issue, so it doesn't happen again." At this point, the students still trusted administrators to have their best interests in mind.

Instead, something unexpected happened—the Director of the Student Center for Multicultural Life invited members of all campus multicultural groups to join the meeting. AfAm leaders were irate that administrators were again homogenizing racial differences. Lauren recounted:

> We were supposed to have this one event where AfAm met with the administrators . . . to share some of the things that go on in our lives—about microaggressions and other students telling us that we don't belong here—so that they have a sense of: "These are our personal testimonies. Please hear us and understand this is larger than just this one party!" But instead, [the Director of the Student Center for Multicultural Life] suggested or invited the entire Multicultural Coalition which included a lot of other student groups that were not involved . . . in a lot of the aftermath of the Gangster party.

Lauren continued, "I remember some [AfAm] board members being really frustrated by that because maybe our message of wanting to work with [the administrators] isn't going to come through. It might just come through as a venting session to them. . . . The meeting was very emotional with the administration, but it didn't feel like it was productive in the way we wanted it to be." While AfAm leaders went into the meeting proud of their preparations and hopeful, they left utterly discouraged. Xavier was livid, "I went off on [the Director of the Student Center for Multicultural Life] and was like, 'You invited all these people into our space without consulting us!' It was just an attempt to water down our voices." Even though the party theme most directly played on deadly stereotypes of African Americans, administrators chose to homogenize all students of color in their meeting with students.

This strategy caused frustration and confusion within and between racial and ethnic affinity groups on campus. Elijah (Asian and Hispanic woman), not a member of AfAm, remembered:

> It was like the Oppression Olympics of which culture does the culture fall under—is it only Black culture? Is it only Hispanic? But no, Asians [are] like, "There's a yakuza too!" I'm like, "Oh no, there's something from El Salvador!" It felt like there was this big debate amongst who gets to voice their opinion on a certain incident. Like what minority has access to these issues and which ones don't? And it was really frustrating. I was like, "Well everyone does!"

PROS AND CONS OF CIVILIZED DIVERSITY DISCOURSE 91

> But I think, relevantly so, [our peers] are not dressing up as a yakuza, they're dressing up as Black rappers, so maybe we should let [Black students] talk.

Even some Black students felt excluded. Xavier gave an example of how intersectional identities complicated AfAm's process, "There was this other camp of people that was more privileged and Black, that was like, '[The partiers] should be suspended because I am so, so, so hurt!' But this doesn't really apply to you as much as you're making it apply to you, because you grew up in the suburbs, and you're not really on financial aid, and you're just being hurt for the sake of being hurt." The strategy of inviting all minoritized groups to the meeting perpetuated the ways the diversity script plays into white supremacy; not only were racial and ethnic differences flattened into a single non-white conglomerate, class and gender differences were also ignored. While this study did not investigate administrators' motivations, their actions successfully upended AfAm's carefully strategized agenda and began to pit students of color against each other.

"Our Ignorance Is No Excuse": When Civilized Discourse Works

Around the same time as the email went out from the Dean of Students, the sailing team began drafting its own email; while the dean's email promoted dialogue, the team sought to apologize and distance itself from the diversity ideology being evangelized by administrators. On Sunday November 1, they issued a joint apology, sent from the coach's email to the entire student body. It read, in part: "We are sorry. In choosing to host a Gangster party, our team marginalized members of our community and made many individuals feel unsafe and excluded. We sparked anger and divisiveness on campus. . . . The party also reinforced existing negative stereotypes in our society as a whole." The email continued, explicitly diverging from the diversity ideology: "Our ignorance regarding how our behavior would impact our peers and our community is no excuse," and listed how the team would take responsibility and move forward including attending the BSG meeting, engaging in a session with Intergroup Dialogue (IGD), having discussions with members of AfAm, and potentially a conversation with all members of the campus. This group of predominantly white students apologized not only for causing hurt feelings, but also for perpetuating harmful stereotypes. They also worked to disrupt what they newly recognized as white ignorance.

In the subsequent weeks, the sailing team made good on their commitment and team members lauded the educational value of those experiences. Scott recalled, "We engaged in all sorts of IGDs with AfAm and [one of the student leaders] was actually in my group for that and I became pretty good friends with her just through that process and conversations after." Ella recalled, "We also had a meeting with a sociology professor—or two professors—and we talked about cultural appropriation, and they basically told us, 'What you did was racist.' In not the typical way you think of racism but promoting institutional racism. And I think that changed our understanding of it. . . . I think [that] made us really think about [what we'd done] more head on than we had been." The meetings and educational offerings were offered only to members of the sailing team—a bold choice by administrators, given the scope of the hate speech on Yik Yak. Sailing team members (even those who did not attend the party) participated willingly and were effusive about the transformative impact of these sessions. Scott confessed, "I probably have grown more from that event as a person than any other event in my life," evidence that in some cases educating transgressors can increase understanding and reduce the likelihood such events will be repeated—at least by those individuals.

The sailing team's response was indeed a beacon of hope for how colleges might stem the recurrence of racially themed costume parties. Scott spoke to how the events of that fall were not forgotten by the sailing team: "I'll probably get a lot of eye rolls saying it was tough being a member of the team then, because we were the ones inflicting the hurt for a lot of people. But it was tough . . . [we had] lot of shame and a lot of regret." Scott also emphasized the good: "It's really changed . . . how I perceive things and look at things . . . and I think it's absolutely for the better. I wish [the party] had never happened, but in a way, I've learned so much and I think a lot of dialogue was brought up on campus as a result of the Gangster party." For the team, "We're incredibly engaged in dialogue about race ever since then . . . we have one [IGD] at least once a semester. We try to stay constantly engaged in these things and, as freshmen come in, we just tell them what happened and impart what we've gained and learned. [We] drive the legacy in a certain direction, because we could be the team that had the Gangster party and that's it, or the team that had the Gangster party and learned a bunch from it and try to make positive change from using the things that we learned from it." By introducing new team norms, such as regularly scheduled conversations about race, the sailing team worked to change the racialization within its organizational structures in ways that could be carried on by continuing cohorts of athletes. Such changes implicitly recognized the takeaway from racialized organizations theory: without intentional and fundamental disruption, structural racism would perpetually reproduce white ignorance.

To achieve those gains, however, AfAm members had to give freely of their time and energy. Even though administrators rallied around the value of dialogue and the offending team learned and grew as a result, Black students did not reap similar benefits. Lauren remembered, "We were asked to meet with the sailing team to have a conversation as the [AfAm] board [with] their captains. And then we also had this . . . IGD facilitation of AfAm students and then also members of the sailing team and then they put us in small groups and [we] kind of shared our feelings and talked about it. It was still tense—it didn't feel like it was resolved in any way." While they sincerely wanted to help and their efforts were appreciated, Black students were repaid with only exhaustion and burnout.

Scholars have dubbed this cycle "racialized equity labor," wherein students of color identify problems in the racial environment of their organizations and work to solve them, then administrators appropriate their labor, and in doing so convert it into a diluted diversity initiative.[23] As sociologist James Thomas argued, "multicultural transactions do not benefit whites and non-whites equally. Instead, the discursive representation of all that is non-white as an investment opportunity converts ethnoracial difference into embodied human capital."[24] While civilized diversity discourse began to fracture the ignorance of a small cohort of teammates, the labor required came at a direct cost to a small cohort of Black students. This exchange was both acknowledged and encouraged by administrators, an example of the college as a racialized organization legitimizing the unequal distribution of resources.

Some other students also gave freely to help the cause. Jesse (white, Latinx, and nonbinary) remembers being both frustrated by how little their friends knew about matters related to racism and appropriation and inspired by the women of AfAm. Like many other students of color, Jesse spent a lot of time teaching their peers, "[My roommates] were looking at it like, 'Oh these people were just dressing up, it wasn't a big deal.' Like, 'What does it really matter?! You should be able to dress up how you want,' and hadn't really thought it from a Black person's perspective." Relaying their Black friends' experiences, Jesse set to work: "I remember having—over the following three weeks or something—many 'til-four-a.m. conversations with [my roommates] just trying to explain that other side of the coin." The silver lining for Jesse was that "[my roommates] really did want to know the other side of it. They just had a lot of trouble grasping it, but that's why conversations lasted until four a.m.—because they were curious." Rather than see the controversy as a defeat, Jesse became inspired, saying: "I had never been part of a community, either small or larger, like campus community, where people of color had such a strong voice. And that was really cool to see that the administration and the general campus population was able to rally behind students of color." Instead of responding with cynicism to the ways the administration used labor from

94   CHAPTER FOUR

students of color to respond to the controversy, some students viewed the effort as a sign that Black students' voices were valued by campus leaders. Scholars have described how many students of color disengage from white-centering conversations about race as a survival mechanism, arguing disengagement itself is a "symptom of structural racism."[25] For other students, their willingness to engage serves as an act of resistance, a refusal to surrender to the "enormity of whiteness."[26]

The President Responds: Focus on the Feelings

When the president publicly weighed in, he maintained the college's commitment to portraying racism as an individual problem and civilized diversity discourse as the solution. On Monday morning, November 2, the president issued an email stating that he and the Dean of Students had met with students from the African American Society and leaders of other multicultural student organizations to discuss the Gangster party and its aftermath. He expressed his gratitude "for their candor," and stated that "the party and the dress adopted by partygoers—the ugly racial stereotyping—were wrong and deeply hurtful to our students of color." Such language reiterated that the team's actions were wrong but not racist, and that the incident was deeply hurtful, but only to students of color. By framing the impact as a matter of hurt feelings, he paved the way for individual redemption rather than structural change.

The remainder of the email echoed similar themes—individual accountability for the students involved, but no ownership of the organizational context that had allowed parties like this to continue happening on campus. He employed passive voice when speaking about accountability, "There needs to be accountability by those responsible, and the note to campus by the sailing team and their presence at the BSG meeting is a good beginning," but did not take responsibility for his role in creating or sustaining organizational structures. Although he newly noted, "The failure by many—in the moment and in the days that followed, to understand why this party and its aftermath were offensive and hostile experiences—points to the larger problem of recognizing clearly that race is an issue for us all, one that transcends the actions of a single group," he failed to call out normative whiteness on campus. He referenced his convocation speech, "I spoke about the challenges faced by our students and other members of our community who are of color, and our collective need to support them and to understand these issues. We have fallen short in doing so." In addition, he too called for dialogue—"honest, thoughtful, and at times deeply uncomfortable dialogue is one critical element to progress"—but made no mention of the toll this dialogue exacted from students of color.

Students, writing in the *Orient*, lambasted the emails from the dean and the president. As one frequent columnist noted: "They both focus on people being offended and hurt and mention no concrete steps to address white privilege on this campus. In fact, they don't explicitly acknowledge that racism and white privilege exist on our campus. Focusing on 'feelings' makes it seem like the problem is simply people's feelings, specifically the feelings of people of color." She continued, tongue in cheek, "Thank you . . . for coming to protect people of colors' feelings, minimizing the historical context and current ramifications of racist acts, and failing to actually take any proactive steps."[27] These exchanges used the framework of civilized diversity discourse to call out the ways that lively public debate had not yet yielded structural change.

The president, for his part, began to make good on his pledge to participate in uncomfortable dialogue. More than a month after his college-wide email, the president hosted an evening town hall titled, "Why Do Issues of Race Matter If I'm White?" The event was well attended, with more than five hundred students, faculty and staff packing all three levels of the student union. In an interview with the *Orient*, the president said that "The meeting and the question . . . came directly from meeting and a discussion that I had with the leaders of the multicultural groups," noting specifically that "out of that came a discussion about the necessity . . . to engage the white majority on campus."[28] At the event, the president committed, "I'm going to weigh into this thing, deeply. I'm not going anywhere. And I will definitely make mistakes, and I will get called out for them, and I will feel horrible about them, but it's not going to deter me."[29] Even as he leaned into dialogue as a lever for redemption, the president hoped his white ignorance would be forgiven. Although the town hall was a one-time affair, the president followed up with concrete actions.

Later that week the president committed resources to better understanding the issues students of color were facing on campus. He announced plans to hire an outside research team to study how students of color experienced campus life, what policies and practices contributed to these differences, and what strategies the college could pursue to improve the experiences of students of color.[30] The researchers, sociologists from prestigious universities whose expertise centered on higher education, were to visit campus in the spring to speak with students, faculty, and staff. They would also have access to relevant administrative data. The president's stated hope was that this would be the beginning of a carefully measured journey toward structural

96   CHAPTER FOUR

change. By first gathering and then examining data before committing to any course of action, the president also bought himself time to assess what kinds of changes donors and parents might support.

Opting In and Opting Out: Civilized Diversity Discourse through a Wider Lens

In the weeks that followed, issues brought up by the Gangster party remained in the public eye. Unlike in years past, the aftermath of the party did not just evaporate. Concerned students largely adhered to norms of civilized diversity discourse—staging peaceful protests, writing columns and letters in the *Orient*, and crafting an exhibition in the student union—but their resistance was growing louder. In November, student activists organized a peaceful protest addressing the experiences of students of color on campus. Students, faculty, and staff members wore black, placed pieces of tape that read "We will not be silenced" over their mouths, and marched through the student union chanting.[31] The next night, signs containing the hashtag #AStatementIsNotEnough were posted throughout campus.[32] The editorial and other columns in the *Orient* critiqued the expectation that students of color had been "asked to devote long hours on top of their usual course load and activities to facilitating dialogue," and urged the college to recognize the imperative to hire more diverse faculty.[33] The presidents of the Asian Student Association and AfAm called off their respective fashion show and party during admitted students' weekend, refusing to advertise false notions of campus diversity to prospective first-year students.[34] The long-standing Bias Incident Group worked to outline specific procedures for how the college could most appropriately respond to different types of bias incidents in the future.[35] In the same week that Black football players at Mizzou were refusing to play until their president resigned, students at Bowdoin continued with structured dialogues, pleading opinion columns, and exhibitions.[36] These students "opted in" to conversations about race, but their demands remained modest and their methods remained civilized. Nothing in their repertoire came close to threatening to cost the college a million dollars, as the Mizzou football strike did. While their actions created pressure on the organization to enact structural changes, the college bought itself time by acknowledging the issues (to a certain extent) and hiring outside consultants. Meanwhile, student activists marched wearily toward total exhaustion and little else changed.

Before long, students were buried in final papers and exams. The five-week lull between semesters, when students scattered to their homes around the globe, dulled the urgency of the work on campus. Rebecca (white woman) recalled, "I remember feeling disappointed in the administration because we were all really invested in [the aftermath of the party] and good conversations were beginning to happen, but then winter break happened, and we totally forgot about it! And I still think people refer to [the Gangster party] now and don't have any conclusion to it. It was just like, 'People apologized and now we're done.'" For many, the tale of the Gangster party was wrapped up neatly. Black students respectfully called out their peers, the sailing team apologized and worked to reform, administrators straddled the fine line of admonishing the team's transgressions without taking a stand against the systems of white supremacy that ensured the college's solvency and legitimacy, students engaged in rigorous debate publicly, while uncivilized discourse remained in the sordid realm of social media.

For students with the privilege to "totally forget about it" the urgency of the catastrophe passed, just as in the case of Cracksgiving. Many students did not remember the party as seniors or felt like their social status allowed them to opt out. For Riley (white woman), the Gangster party "didn't affect me directly because I honestly don't know anyone on the sailing team and I'm a white girl and I've never really thought about cornrows and how they're used." For Jaden (Black man) the reasons to not be involved were different: "Growing up [abroad], sometimes I don't really feel like an African American native, because I'm not. But since I've been [in the US] so long, I've learned the culture, and I feel like I'm a part of [the Black community]. So, I was like, 'Oh, this is how they see the Black community. It's a problem.' And then, in another sense, I was like, 'I didn't come here [to college] to worry about stuff like this. I just want to go to school, go to classes.'" Both students mentioned the party in their interview senior year as something they remembered, but not as something that impacted their attitudes or behaviors. The pervasive hold of white ignorance and civilized diversity discourse again permitted most students to simply "opt out" of conversations about race.

To some, after a racially charged incident like the Gangster party, what happened at Bowdoin that fall was a textbook example of repentance and recovery done right. Administrators created platforms for counter-storytelling, educational programming, community conversations, and intellectual engagement.[37] Yet all these actions continued to center whiteness and prioritize the needs of white students, while extracting labor from Black students and diluting their voices. At this point, what played out exemplified Williams, Squire, and Tuitt's notion of plantation politics—where Black people are consumed for the benefit of the institution.[38] While, for many white people, critical learning and deep self-reflection—akin to what some students began in the wake of the Gangster party—pave the way for future action, such transformational work does not have to come at the expense of their peers of color.[39] To imagine how a college might respond differently, racialized organizations theory calls for recognizing the ways whiteness is baked into structures, policies, and norms—then working to dismantle or shift the racialization of those systems.[40]

5

Campus Is Not a Bubble

Students often talked about campus as a "bubble," removed from the outside world. In some ways this was true; students would eat, sleep, work, study, and play, all without leaving the grounds. To persuade students to buy into the all-inclusive residential experience, first-year students were not even allowed to have a vehicle on campus. While students could often be seen strolling into the local village for gelato or sushi or carpooling to Walmart for personal supplies, off-campus excursions were novel but unnecessary. This all-inclusive residential model encouraged students to invest in the kinds of relationships and traditions that would cultivate a robust alumni network and promote broad ignorance to the ways the college was embedded within and dependent upon other social institutions. Yet, as the events of the subsequent months would reveal, the fantasy of the bubble was a facade. Through the example of the Tequila party, which happened less than four months after the Gangster party, this chapter illustrates what can happen when implicated students decide not to play along with the norms of civilized diversity discourse and instead draw on norms and resources from outside the campus bubble.

In the study of organizations, neo-institutional theorists have long recognized that organizational change can be spurred by factors both within and outside the organization—ranging from pressures to keep pace with or stand out from peer institutions to the ways social actors inhabit their organizational roles. For colleges, external factors include macro-level policy changes, such as Supreme Court rulings on affirmative action, and field-based isomorphic pressures (i.e., pressures to keep up with peer schools). Social movements also push for organizational change, both from outside and from within; for example, the institutionalization of Black studies departments emerged from a national movement in the 1960s but took root on individual campuses via local actors.[1] In the winter of 2015, student activists built on the momentum of the Black Lives Matter (BLM) movement to contest the racialization of campus policies and processes in the wake of the Cracksgiving party through a formal list of demands. That fall, the impact of national social movements was again visible in collective actions happening on campus in the wake of the Gangster party. Just as racialized organizations theory suggests, in response to both external social movements and internal actions, activists drawing attention to the college's "tacit refusal to name whiteness" stirred up racialized contestation.[2] But, as we see in this chapter, students were also drawing on outside resources to resist these racialized contestations—borrowing not only movement tactics, but also social, cultural, and economic capital.

Return to Campus

When winter break ended and classes resumed, ripples of the Gangster party remained in motion. A representative from the Multicultural Coalition—a coalition of twenty-two affinity groups on campus—joined Bowdoin Student Government (BSG) for the first time.[3] Although BSG already had representation from the coalition of college houses, the coalition of varsity teams, the public service hub, and the entertainment board, multicultural groups had not previously been represented. In addition, the consultants hired by the president to evaluate racial climate on campus began planning for their mid-February visit, and columns and opinion pieces in the *Orient* kept debates about racism and political correctness alive.[4] Yet the intensity of the fervor had quieted since the break.

On February 12, a front-page article in the *Orient* highlighted the one-year anniversary of the "Meeting in the Union"—a reckoning of sorts regarding race, diversity, and justice on campus in the wake of the final Cracksgiving party, wherein student activists presented a letter to the president and campus community that included eighteen calls to action. The article detailed how much progress had been made on each of the eighteen calls; while most had been acknowledged and directly addressed by administrators, some were in progress or unaddressed. The article cogently summarized, "An overarching sentiment exists among administrators and students that while progress is being made, it will be made slowly and there is still work to be done."[5]

The truth in this statement was evidenced by administrators' divergent comments for the feature. The Director of Athletics commented on how his department now addressed incidents such as the recent parties: "thinking about it along the lines of apologizing, educating and trying to leverage the learning opportunities associated with people making mistakes, then

CAMPUS IS NOT A BUBBLE

thinking about the ways in which we are able to positively impact the community." Although he recognized the need for recruiting more coaches and athletes of color, he failed to acknowledge the outsized role of white athletic culture on campus and the structural racism endemic to social systems that produced "recruitable athletes."[6]

In contrast, the associate dean for diversity and inclusion addressed broad structural concerns, saying: "We're asking institutions that were built 200 years ago for a very different population to reimagine themselves, and that takes a lot of intentionality and examination of where are our traditions, where are our policies, where are our practices not meeting the needs of students today, where are they not reflecting the diversity of our world, where are they creating barriers to inclusion and equity." This focus on policies and traditions had been the driver of some of the progress the college had seen over the past year, like developing programming about race for first-year orientation and expanding the Intergroup Dialogue (IGD) program.

In addition, that issue of the *Orient* highlighted a panel discussion titled, "Why Do College Houses Feel So White?"[7] College houses were created by administrators when they disbanded fraternities in the late 1990s. Sophomores applied to live in houses and provide programming for first-year students and the campus at large. While the demographics of the residents mirrored the demographics of the student body (because residents were hand-picked by staff based on an application process), students talked about the unmarked whiteness of these spaces, as exemplified by aspects of the vibe and decor. According to one student, the application process tokenized students of color; having a student of color in your roommate "block" apparently raised your odds of getting to live in a house: "Maybe this wasn't my friends' intention[s], but I felt like I was always being singled out as someone who would make the block better because I'm Puerto Rican," she said. "That felt uncomfortable to me because I didn't want to be living with people who saw me as just someone that would help them get in [to a house]." Another student pointed to music played at parties, commonly held in house basements, as another example of the unmarked whiteness: "There's no denying 'Stacy's Mom' is a white, suburban song," she said. "It's a fun song, but now as a senior every time I hear that song I think 'that wasn't my life experience.' So just knowing now that every time it plays in a college house it's just a reminder that this is the culture I'm in, and I can't forget that." Events like this panel signaled more openness toward discussing unmarked whiteness on campus, but as evidenced in the small crowd size, the conversations were not yet reaching broad audiences.

By the next week, the *Orient*'s top stories focused on the Outing Club, the board of trustees, and a group of students searching for bears in the frozen

Maine wilderness for their advanced winter field ecology course. Perhaps no one could have predicted from these features what would happen that weekend—that a small dorm room birthday party would reignite the embers of racialized discord. Or perhaps turning the spotlight away from racialized exclusion and white ignorance is exactly what opened the door for the events that followed.

The Party: "It's Not *Not* a Fiesta"

That weekend in February, Vanessa (white and Hispanic woman)—a self-described "rule tester"—was busy collaborating with her friends to plan a surprise birthday party for their mutual friend, Aubree. They selected a tequila theme for the party because that was Aubree's favorite drink, even though hard alcohol was prohibited in campus dorms and nearly all of the invitees were underage. Vanessa recounted the fun they had planning the party: "We wanted it to be a surprise party and I remember . . . being like, 'Oh my god it'd be so fun if it was a Hawaiian theme, Mexican theme, it'd be so fun!' Then, we were like, 'Yes! Yes! Yes!' So, we went to the party store, got a piñata, streamers, birthday signs, pack of mustaches to play pin the mustache on Aubree. I blew up this huge picture of her and put it on my door. That was a party game. Then I bought this big banner that was like 'Fiesta,' and I was like, 'Ha ha! The perfect party!'" Vanessa and her friends furnished food, decorations, and, of course, tequila. Notably, however, they did not furnish any sombreros. The emailed invitation advertised games, music, and "other things that are conducive to a fun night." Then, in its most infamous line, the invitation read: "The theme is tequila so do with that what you may. We're not saying it's a fiesta but we're also not *not* saying that."

The guest list had about forty names, as the gathering was meant as a "pregame" for a larger party everyone would head to later that night. All four residents of the room hosting the party were invited (even though they were not all involved in planning), as were other residents of their floor—it was easier to invite the neighbors than deal with noise complaints—and friends from across campus.

Preparing for the party, Megan (white woman) and her friends also went to a party supply store. Megan recalled, "The party was themed as a fiesta, and it was called the Tequila party because my friend Aubree's favorite drink is tequila. So, because the email said, 'It's not a fiesta, it's not *not* a fiesta,' we got sombreros. Honestly, I told a bunch of people this." Megan admitted to furnishing the sombreros, but also wanted it on record that—as with the white student who sought out cornrows for the Gangster party—no one objected

CAMPUS IS NOT A BUBBLE

to her plan either before or during the party. In retrospect, Megan admitted she should have known better, "I'm totally willing to own that what we did was hurtful for a lot of people. But I didn't think twice about purchasing the sombrero even after . . . being present when students of color were crying at BSG meetings because of the sailing team's actions." Due to different degrees of racial and socioeconomic privilege, Vanessa tried to ride the line of acceptability—using her savvy and privilege to mock PC culture in her invite—while Megan did not even see the line she was crossing.

Attendees all agreed it was a great party. Jennifer (white woman) described how the dorm room "was decorated and there were different beads hanging and there was a piñata." There were games, like "pin the mustache on the donkey" and "little party hat sombreros and then actual sombreros," and fresh snacks, including "pineapples, produce everywhere, [and] avocados." She summarized: "It was a really fun party and that was actually one of— until I woke up the next morning and saw the aftermath—that was one of my favorite nights sophomore year."

In retrospect, some partiers recalled a hint of hesitation, but at the time no one expressed concern over the sombreros, decor, or presence of hard alcohol—they were there to have a good time. Vanessa described, "These girls . . . brought the sombreros and the mini party hats and started passing them out to people and that was sort of the moment when I was like, uhh. And then other people came with big sombreros, and I was like, uhh. And then it was like whatever and we went to another party and the night was over." Jennifer similarly recalled, "I wore a sombrero, and I remember thinking, 'Wow, this might not be okay,' but I also thought, 'That's silly! Why would it not be okay?'" Their hesitation lines up with the ambiguity many felt afterward about whether people who were not Mexican wearing sombreros at a party that was "not *not* a fiesta" could be considered cultural appropriation—after all, as another white-presenting Latinx student would later point out, "They didn't mean it in a mocking way, it's not like they did blackface or something." Sure, it did not feel quite right—but was there really anything wrong with it?

Prep Schools, Privilege, and Chevy's: Importing White Supremacy

Although Vanessa, Megan, and Jennifer were all affiliated with similar social circles on campus by midway through their sophomore year, they came from different regions, high schools, and class backgrounds. While to the average American, they would all be considered upper class and all benefited from the kinds of racialized segregation and wealth accumulation that enabled them to play on Division III (DIII) varsity teams, because Bowdoin's demographics skewed toward the uber-affluent, there were stark differences between upper-class kids and the ultra-wealthy. When each arrived on campus, she brought with her the norms of the culture in which she had been raised.

Vanessa grew up in a wealthy suburb of a major East Coast city with the kind of father who "schmoozed his way" to securing her a last-minute spot in one of the most prestigious boarding schools in the country. Citing her family's international ties, Vanessa described her racial identity as complicated, "I just don't even know what my racial identity is. I think on paper when I do the bubble things, I do white and then Hispanic." Like many of her prep school peers, she became a competitive athlete while also garnering academic successes, making her a strong candidate for admission to New England Small College Athletic Conference (NESCAC) schools. Although she was not recruited to her Bowdoin sports team, she applied early decision with the coach's blessing and was admitted.

When Vanessa first arrived on campus, she felt comfortable in part because she already had good friends, including a handful of other students from her private high school. She did not struggle academically—like many prep school students she wagered the academics her first year were less rigorous than her high school courses—hung out with her friends "every single night," listening to music and watching TV, and went out drinking every weekend. Because she already had friends on campus from high school and garnered additional connections from her team, she was "pretty removed" from the community Residential Life (ResLife) staff were trying to build in her first-year dorm. When Cracksgiving happened, she was already friends with guys on the team. She heard firsthand accounts of the aftermath of the party and knew it "was definitely a traumatic thing," for the seniors on the team especially.

During sophomore year, Vanessa ended up blocking with a group of girls from her "larger friend group" and, in the housing lottery, they managed to score an entire floor in a dorm close to the center of campus. The floor mates were mostly athletes or former athletes like Vanessa, who had decided not to return to her team sophomore year. When asked how they met, Vanessa explained their web of athletic and boarding school ties in detail before summarizing with: "Pretty girls unite, I guess!" She laughed, then specified, "Pretty girls who hang around athletes!" Comments like this reveal how the athlete crowd was not strictly limited to current players but expanded selectively to include students from similar prep schools who may or may not have joined (or stayed with) their college team.

Jennifer was part of Vanessa's larger friend group. She grew up in the suburbs of a major West Coast city, attending racially diverse private schools where "people's first cars were BMWs." Differentiating herself from the uber-wealthy, Jennifer described herself as a "normal person" whose first car was a used Honda. She was recruited to play on a sports team and was excited to attend a college with strong academics and "a big outdoor culture." Despite her racial and socioeconomic privilege, like other students from outside New England, she did not feel like an insider on campus. When pressed to explain, she reflected: "I feel like I speak more straightly [at home] and I'm not necessarily as genuine [when I'm here] in the sense that I feel there are more norms. I don't know if that's a Bowdoin thing, but Bowdoin is a lot of who you know and what you wear. It's old money—versus [the] West Coast, which is new money." As previous chapters have shown, institutional history and admissions priorities informed dominant norms on campus; such norms were so tailored that even students with sufficient race and class privilege felt marginalized due to regional cultural differences.

That said, Jennifer was quickly networked into the social circles of elite athletes upon arriving on campus. Jennifer remembered attending Cracksgiving with her teammates during her first year, agreeing that the costumes were inappropriate, but not being impacted by the fallout. Sophomore year, Jennifer returned to campus with a bright outlook. She had different roommates from her first year and ended up living down the hall from Vanessa, although they were not close friends. She described the floor as "a sorority house," that was "so fun!" She believes she was only invited to the Tequila party, however, due to proximity: "I don't know if I would've been invited if I wasn't [living in] the room [down the hall]."

Megan grew up in a rural town about a half-hour drive from a mid-sized western city. She had professional parents but attended public schools where about two-thirds of the students were white, and the rest were Hispanic. Like Jennifer, she distanced herself from the uber-wealthy (but also from the Hispanic component of her hometown), saying she came "from a tight-knit community of white people—but middle class, my family is middle class." After a Bowdoin coach recruited her, Megan was admitted early decision. She remembers feeling "out of sorts" when she first arrived on campus because the academics were more challenging than her high school and the students were more diverse. But her teammates were "a huge godsend," who became some of her "best friends," and she stayed with her sport through all four years. Unlike Vanessa and Jennifer, she bonded with her floormates during her first year and, as a result, she was not yet connected with higher-status athletes when Cracksgiving happened. Sophomore year, Megan opted to stay with her first-year roommate. Until the night of the Tequila party, her year was uneventful.

When invited to the Tequila party, Megan purchased and brought sombreros without a second thought. Unlike Vanessa, whose international social networks and access to extreme wealth gave her a more nuanced understanding of elite norms, Megan's upper-middle-class public school upbringing meant she arrived on campus steeped in mass market, white American culture. As she argued based on her experiences at a national restaurant chain featuring "fresh-mex" cuisine, "I'm from [the West], I can go to Chevy's anytime I want, and they will literally put a sombrero on my head while singing 'Happy Birthday' to me." In this way and others, each student arrived with differing norms from outside the bubble. In the case of Vanessa, Jennifer, and Megan, each brought racialized norms characteristic of their disparate upper-class backgrounds and regions of origin.

After the Party: The Role of Social Media

Word of the party spread that night on campus via social media. Luis (Latino man) recalled, "I was doing [home]work in the pub and then I was scrolling through Instagram, wasting time like I always have, and I saw a picture of a group of girls that were wearing sombreros. . . . Me and my friends had a conversation about it and were like, 'Okay, this is weird. Don't people have anything better to do today?'" A few other respondents also remembered seeing the post on Instagram, but it was not up for long. Although Luis and his friends did not immediately respond with outrage, their disdain festered with time.

When Vanessa and her friends saw the posts the next day, they asked that they be taken down. Vanessa recalled, "I remember waking up the next morning and looking at my phone and seeing other girls that had gone to the party . . . were Instagramming and making the captions like, 'Super fiesta'—Mexican-themed or whatever. And I was like, 'Oh, that is like . . .' So, [my friend] sent an email to the group being like . . . 'You don't need to put pictures on social media. We all know we had a good time, but it wasn't a Mexican-themed event.'" But it was too little, too late—someone had already taken a screenshot of the post, merged it with the email invitation, and shared it anonymously in other venues. True to form, Yik Yak was already alive with vitriol and debate. Since the invitation and photo were now posted in the public domain, they began to take on a life of their own.

Because the Yik Yak conversation stayed live after the original Instagram posts were removed, most students learned everything they knew about the party from Yik Yak. One partygoer reported it felt like "everyone was talking about it." Others paraphrased the posts, "It was like, 'The witch hunt begins,

CAMPUS IS NOT A BUBBLE

these stupid white bitches!'" Hateful rhetoric targeting the partygoers and those who were hurt by the party's theme both boiled over in the anonymous app. Much like in the aftermath of the Gangster party, Yik Yak played an outsized role in stirring up tension and distrust on campus.

While students could feel the controversy quickly escalating, many could also tell that, outside the bubble, things would be seen differently. Seeing how the posts blew up online, Vanessa knew the party would have consequences on campus. In her mind, "alarms were going off everywhere." She reached out to her family for support, "I remember calling my [family] and being like, 'I think I did something bad' and told [them] about it and then sent [them] the invitation and [they] were like, 'What are you talking about? This is insane if you think something is going to happen.'" In the coming days many of the other partiers would also reach out to their parents for support, most getting similar, incredulous replies. In fact, almost no students—on any side of the issue—reported that their parents found the sombreros problematic. To those outside "the bubble," the issue seemed trivial and passing. José (Latino man) who was not involved, described his mixed views when first hearing about the party:

> I saw a friend of mine, who's also Latino, and I went up to them . . . and we were just chatting, and then other people came up to us and they were like, "Yo, have you all heard about Tequila-gate?" And I just laughed and was like, "What?!" And they were like, "Some people have posted some pictures. They took them down, but we got screenshots." And I was like . . . "Oh, just look at the photos!" And I felt like such an asshole . . . [when] I found out how other people felt about this. But I saw it and I just laughed because it seemed kind of silly to me, because it was a group of people with a whole bunch of sombreros on and . . . I'm surprised they would put that on social media. . . . It seems so goofy to me, and they should know better. I was like, "Guys, do you know where you go [to college]?! You guys are going to get shit on so hard!"

While José was not personally impacted by the party or its aftermath, he articulated the disconnect between outside perceptions and the storm of controversy that would follow on campus based on his own observations of prior parties.

By Monday, the Dean of Students had set up individual meetings with the students they believed to have attended the party. Unlike the students accused in the Gangster party who were called out and took responsibility for their transgressions, students who attended the Tequila party sought to share the blame. One partygoer bemoaned, "The reason why this thing became a thing was because girls posted it on social media." Another agreed,

"One of my friends that posted has a private account and the girl that turned it into the deans happened to be following her and saw it." According to her logic, if no one had posted photos to Instagram or if the post had remained among a specific friend group as it was intended, there would not have been a problem. As in generations past, without social media (or with more tightly controlled access to social media postings), racialized transgressions would have remained "backstage,"[8] fodder for private entertainment and reification of racialized attitudes among like-minded friends. Revealingly, years later when asked what she learned from the whole debacle, Vanessa's first joking response was still: "Don't invite girls you don't like to your party." At the time, these students did not regret throwing the party or wearing sombreros—they only regretted getting caught.

"Getting All Their Information from Yik Yak": The Administration Responds

In the case of Cracksgiving and the Gangster party, the structures surrounding DIII athletics created white spaces that nurtured white ignorance. Those structures sustained generations of exclusion, but they also fostered team cohesion. And when it came time for administrators to respond to those parties, they took advantage of preexisting hierarchies within each team. Coaches acted as conduits between athletes and administrators, athletes used practice times to craft their apologies, and upperclassmen exerted pressure on underclassmen using the combined threats of lost playing time and social ostracization. The structures of DIII athletics gave the college leverage to produce an outcome that would satisfy the needs of all consequential parties—just enough reprimand to keep students of color from rioting, not enough disruption to inflame major donors and tuition-paying families.

But because this party had been thrown by a group of friends, rather than a team, the partiers were more difficult to identify, pin down, and coax into compliance. Many students who attended the party vividly recalled clumsy meetings with the deans in the days after the party. They agreed it seemed as though the deans, like everyone else, "were getting all the information from Yik Yak." Jennifer recalled, "I just remember getting an email that said, 'Come meet with us,' from my dean and it was like [the Dean of Students] and three different [associate] deans and all the girls in my room and not [the girls who threw the party]. And [the deans] were like, 'We know you threw the party!' And we were like, 'Well wait, we didn't.' They didn't even have proper information. And they were asking us all these questions and I remember thinking, 'Is this even allowed?' Like getting interrogated about a situation."

Vanessa was also called in with her roommates: "I remember meeting with the deans and . . . I was the only one that was talking because . . . my roommates didn't have anything to do with [the party]. But [the deans] . . . didn't understand that. It was me and my *other* friends who had thrown the party." By multiple accounts, at least one of Vanessa's roommates had not even attended the party, but that fact seemed irrelevant to administrators.

Chase (white man) attended the party with friends and was also called into the dean's office. He corroborated other students' accounts, "I remember having been there and thinking that, at the time, nothing of the party really seemed to warrant the way [the administration] handled us, and the way they brought us in, questioned us." He continued, "The dean that interviewed me, questioned me in a tone that . . . made me feel overtly guilty for something that I thought wasn't so [bad]." He argued it should have been, "more a matter of like, 'Let's talk about this and engage with the real problems at hand and have some dialogue,' rather than him enforcing guilt upon me that I didn't feel personally. . . . That was not a proper way to conduct that sort of discussion or that sort of conversation." Unlike the sailors who expressed remorse, the accused expressed indignation—complaining about the lack of information retained by administrators and the tone of their questioning, insisting their actions were not deserving of such pejorative treatment.

Implicitly, these partygoers expected systems of white ignorance to protect them, as they had protected their peers in the past. Recall Ben (white man) who, in the aftermath of Cracksgiving, was granted leniency by administrators because he claimed he chose a Native American costume simply to avoid having to wear a shirt. White people feel comfortable acting ignorantly because they have been taught to trust that societal institutions will approve of their racialized not-knowing.[9] In Ben's recounting of his disciplinary hearing, as in the sailing team's apology tour, their disclosures of racialized ignorance were met with acceptance. But in the immediate aftermath of the Tequila party, partygoers bemoaned not being granted the same benevolence.

Yet unlike the students implicated by the Gangster party, many who attended the Tequila party took a defensive stance—mobilizing racialized emotions. White innocence—the insistence that white people are not responsible for or complicit in systemic racism—is often accompanied by emotions such as anger, defensiveness, and guilt.[10] Building on the work of scholar Cheryl Matias, sociologist Eduardo Bonilla-Silva argued that racialized emotions are group-based relational phenomena, central in the production of subjectivity and racial domination, that levy material consequences.[11] Rather than claiming they meant no harm and apologizing, these students challenged administrators' authority, indignant that they were subject to reproach. Sensing that their race and class privilege were being threatened, even slightly, students responded by mobilizing first their emotions—anger, contempt, denial[12]— and then their networks. Much like the members of the lacrosse team who mourned the closing of their party house—albeit in that case among friends and in private—the response of Tequila partiers to being called out for their actions exemplifies how people with race and class privilege can reframe controversies to paint themselves as victims. In doing so, they bolstered systems that supported their privilege.

Because administrators continued to pin the blame on a few bad apples rather than racialized organizational structures, participants' lack of cooperation in the investigation forced administrators into somewhat unfamiliar territory. That evening, the Dean of Students emailed the entire campus, encouraging students to come forward with additional information. The email made clear that administrators were aware that "an act of ethnic stereotyping may have occurred at the college over the weekend," that they were investigating "what we have learned from students and from posts on social media," and that they did not have a full picture. On Wednesday, the president sent a campus-wide email as well.

In their confusion about what had happened and lack of streamlining in how to talk about the incident, administrators set the tone for the rest of the campus. An article in the *Orient* that week would note that, "administrators have largely moved away from the language of 'cultural appropriation,' which was used in official emails after the Cracksgiving incident and has still been a common topic of debate on Yik Yak. [The Dean of Students'] email referred to 'ethnic stereotyping,' while [the president's] referenced an 'act of bias.'"[13] Their lack of agreement on language implicitly communicated uncertainty about the extent to which the party might be considered problematic.

Given this muddled messaging, most students reported that the weeks following the Tequila party were a time of intense conversation and debate among friends. For example, after receiving the president's email, José thought back on his conversation the day before:

> I found out the next day this exploded and there are serious repercussions and there are people who are extremely upset by this. And I was like [breathes in deeply], "Wow. Okay. I understand." Just because I find it silly . . . I understand it doesn't take away from the hurt it can actually cause to people who find major offense to that. I was like, "Okay, that's a little bit on me that I kind of goofed off [and] found it a lot more sillier than I probably should have." I remember going to talk to the person I was there with [when I first found out]. . . . We both met back up and were talking about it. We had conversations with different people and a lot of people are finding this really offensive, and

CAMPUS IS NOT A BUBBLE 111

[it was] making a lot of them feel really alienated, and I was like, "Yeah, I can see how that can happen."

Like many students who were not directly involved in the party, José initiated conversations with friends to learn more about what had happened and how people were thinking about the controversy. But, on a campus segregated by extracurricular affiliations and thus by race and class, the content of those conversations varied dramatically from one peer group to the next. As many scholars have shown, students' public reactions concerning race and racism often diverge from what comes out in more private settings.[14]

"The Pain in the Room Was Palpable": Students of Color Trying to Educate Their Peers, Again

As administrators went silent, student activists rose to fill the void. As per the precedent established in the wake of the Gangster party, the usual Wednesday meeting of BSG had time set aside for open dialogue. The meeting was well attended, primarily by students of color and their allies. Megan recalled, "A bunch of students had come in and were really upset about what had happened. In that meeting, they expressed how hurt they were and upset they were, and they knew that members of the BSG that had attended the party." Luis concurred, "A lot of people came in and voiced a lot of their concerns and voiced how they felt that they were super invalidated at Bowdoin and how two people who were on our board . . . were at the party." The front-page *Orient* article reported, "Of the students who spoke at the meeting, none defended the party's theme or said that they had attended. Several members of LASO [Latin American Student Organization] discussed meetings that they had held with administrators."[15] As Friday's editorial would state, "The pain in the room was palpable."

By the end of the meeting, BSG had unanimously adopted a "Statement of Solidarity re: 'Tequila' Party"[16] that was emailed to the entire campus the next morning. As with the BSG response to the Gangster party, the statement defined cultural appropriation as, "the manifestation of racism where there exists a power dynamic in which members of a dominant culture take elements from a culture of people who have been systemically oppressed by that dominant group, perpetuate racist stereotypes, and/or misrepresent a people's culture," and asserted that "such behavior will not and should not be tolerated by the Bowdoin community." The statement pushed to "move forward with a restorative vision" and use this as a "teaching and learning moment." BSG recommended that the administration make supportive spaces available for targeted students (i.e., students to whom sombreros were meaningful), separate spaces for other students to process, mandate academic experiences and punitive measures for those involved, and support students of color who were responding to the incident. BSG also formed an ad hoc committee to "draft an amendment to either the BSG's bylaws or its constitution to address situations when members of the assembly break the social code."[17] BSG and the *Orient* sided with those offended by the party, calling for continuing civilized diversity discourse but now also seeking individual accountability and structural changes.

The rage and exhaustion of students of color, particularly those who had spent countless hours engaging with and educating their peers after the Gangster party, pulsated through campus. The day after the BSG meeting, the *Orient* published a piece online ahead of its regular Friday edition by the same columnist who had patiently educated readers about the problematic nature of the Gangster party that autumn. This time, however, her column began: "The following piece is a work of satire. I chose to use this approach to address this issue because I have explained and re-explained cultural appropriation and its effects and I am exhausted. I said everything I had to say last semester."[18] The Friday edition was packed with articles and columns about the party. One student reflected on her roots as "a Southern Californian Mexican American,"[19] saying, "To those who threw this party: your intentions were very clear as to what kind of 'fiesta' you were going to have and what Mexican stereotypes you were going to display." She continued, "My family wears sombreros, not as ridiculous props but as a sign of a proud heritage. . . . I didn't appreciate someone making my home into a theme. You cannot take my culture for your own entertainment."

The editorial voiced a similar sentiment, additionally calling out the partiers for their defensiveness: "The fallout from the Tequila party isn't about breaking rules or your relationship with the administration. It's about basic empathy. It's not about finding a loophole in the college's codes of conduct, and it's not about a debate over political correctness. It's about respecting your peers as human beings and acknowledging what makes them feel unwelcome in our community." The editorial board repeated, "If you're confused about why people are mad, take the time to figure it out. Listen to what your peers are saying, learn from past mistakes, recognize that this behavior has a historic and political context and stop throwing these parties."[20] The refrain was now familiar—we, as a campus, have done this before and we have agreed it is not okay because one person's right to throw a theme party should not trump another person's right have their humanity recognized and affirmed.

The method was familiar, too: respectful and eloquent writings through normative channels.

Others adopted a more personal approach, still within the bounds of civilized diversity discourse. Luis, for example, recalled seeking out a conversation with one of the partiers, an educational olive branch he chose to extend in service to his friends who were deeply hurt by the party. To Luis, having a one-on-one conversation with an acquaintance who had attended the party seemed like a tangible action toward making campus a better place—a mentality informed by the pervasive culture of civilized diversity discourse. Afterward, however, Luis felt disillusioned: "I told her my entire life story and why that was important to me," detailing what it was like to grow up in Mexican American communities with undocumented parents. "After those two hours, she didn't get it." As the inadequacy of civilized discourse caused feelings of anger and fatigue to flourish, Luis and others began to hope for more public accountability. Lacking other options, they continued to agitate through established structures within the campus bubble.

Tipping Off the Media: Involving Outside Bloggers

The partygoers, their racial privileged threatened by the conversations with the deans and campus outcry condemning their actions, still largely refused to publicly apologize. The weekend passed with few developments, but Yik Yak continued to roil to the point that many implicated students felt the public scrutiny acutely. One student who attended the party recalled, "I couldn't go into the dining halls without thinking that everyone was staring at me and talking shit and thinking all these mean things. Everyone had an opinion about it!" Some opted to leave campus for a few days. Over time, other partygoers would report they had received death threats and were victims of hurtful acts, such as receiving a pile of poop in their campus mailbox. While formal consequences remained in limbo, partygoers and their allies sought to turn the tide of public opinion in their favor. Unlike many students of color and low-income students, however, they had options outside of campus norms.

That week, an anonymous student tipped off two "xenophobic, sexist and racist"[21] blogs, and the bloggers stepped in to defend the partygoers. *Barstool Sports* printed a "reader email," along with screenshots of the party invitation, a photo of partiers wearing sombreros, and the emails from the dean and the president.[22] The reader email from sophomores who found themselves "in the middle of an authoritarian takeover by PC culture and its crooked army," drew heavily on established anti-PC rhetoric to claim that, "the majority of students on campus disagree with what's going on here, but as soon as anyone disagrees they are declared a bigot and a racist, so this speech is quickly suppressed." The sophomores pleaded, "I hope you find our situation as ridiculous as we find it, and we would really appreciate it if you could help us get our story out there." Students whose white innocence felt threatened on campus used these blogs to unleash their emotions and co-opt reinforcements from the internet. Taking a page from the broader anti-PC campaign rampant at the time, white students unironically used outsized media platforms to claim they were being silenced.

Turtleboy Sports also posted to their blog, under the title, "Tequila-Themed Party Deemed Racist by Bowdoin Students Who Had Their Feelings Hurt."[23] The write-up quoted the *Orient* and featured screenshots of the party invitation and an Instagram photo of partiers wearing sombreros. This post pointed out that the party hosts must have known they were riding a thin line: "I love how they have to write, 'we're not saying fiesta' because they can already tell that the PC police will be out in full force to call a 'fiesta' racist. Preexisting butthurt insurance." The post went on to ridicule activist students of color, singling out individuals and pulling photos from their social media feeds and previous *Orient* articles, stooping so low as to insult their clothes and their families. While this level of public humiliation did not cause those students to back down, it greatly impacted their mental health and sense of safety on campus. By going outside the "campus bubble," the partiers piggybacked on national narratives to paint themselves as victims rather than as perpetrators of symbolic violence. This is how racialized emotions, such as anger and contempt,[24] feed white supremacy. But this is also an example of how individuals can shift their impact within an organization by bringing outside actors and organizations into the fray. In this moment of racialized contestation, white emotions fused with movement strategies to shift the organizational terrain.

For many students of color who bought into the premise of the diversity script and civilized diversity discourse, that was a turning point. Victor (Latino man) summarized: "I encourage healthy dialogue, but not getting aggressive. . . . The other side of the argument [i.e., the partiers] took it too seriously and that's when it spread out on social media and then on news sources and stuff like that. It was at that point where I was like, 'Woah, this got blown way out of proportion!' And the comments that were released by [the partiers] were like, 'I feel unsafe with the Latino members of the community!' Like, 'They're aggressive! They're hostile! They're all this stuff.' And I was like, 'I could be sitting in class with these people.'" When the blog posts emerged, Victor and other students of color—even those who were not involved in the controversy—began to feel even more unsafe on campus. Unlike most face-to-face encounters at the college, racism in the blogs was overt, anonymous, and targeted. Intentionally bringing in outside media sources not only violated the norms of civilized diversity discourse, it escalated the scope and scale of the controversy in ways that recentered white grievances and amplified claims of white innocence.

When Civilized Discourse Breaks Down: Impeachment

In the wake of such hateful attacks on their friends and in the absence of clear action by administrators, student activists began to pursue public accountability for the partiers through other channels. Namely, a small coalition of BSG members wrote articles of impeachment for the two members of BSG who had attended the Tequila party. One member recalled, "We felt like we needed to listen to other people who were around us who were already talking about [impeachment] and felt like that was a process that we needed to go through, for our campus." Two members were "held under articles of impeachment for alleged violation of the spirit of the Statement of Solidarity issued by BSG in October, violating the nondiscrimination policy of BSG and for 'injurious actions towards other members of the General Assembly.'"[25] In short, the articles called out these students because their words had not aligned with their actions, and their public positions meant that, as in the case of the teach-in more than two years prior, their peers wanted to hold them to their word. According to the *Orient*, this marked the first time BSG had moved to "indefinitely remove" any member from its assembly.

While the coalition intended to pursue the impeachment process quietly, that plan evaporated when word leaked out via the *Orient*. One BSG member explained, "To file impeachments . . . you have to first write out a proposal to impeach and then you introduce it at the next meeting . . . behind closed doors . . . so [BSG] would know but nobody else would [know]." But, as another BSG member clarified, "We send out meeting minutes every single week, in the mornings, and they weren't supposed to include [the impeachment proposal] in the meeting minutes, but they did." *Orient* writers, who were always included on the BSG distribution list, spread the story, and attendance at that evening's BSG meeting ballooned to nearly two hundred students—more than the usual meeting room could comfortably hold.

This time, instead of ceding the floor to students of color, white students refused to stand down. Although the articles of impeachment targeted only two of the roughly forty students who attended the party, their friends and teammates swiftly rallied. While this party was not formally linked to any athletic team, the partiers were able to activate structures undergirding boarding school and athletic social networks to pack the chamber with students who would speak in their defense. The implicated members of BSG finally publicly apologized. They repented for "misrepresenting the BSG and the principles that we stand for," and for failing "to connect tequila and sombreros with their deeper cultural implications," in "an inexcusable act of ignorance and negligence."[26] They called out their own racial ignorance. But still, the partiers and their friends employed racialized emotions to push back against the notion that these "inexcusable" actions warranted consequences.

In part because of the partygoers' defensiveness, other students present began to question whether educational consequences were sufficient. Because this party happened so close after the Gangster party, students newly debated, "whether campus conversations and 'safe spaces' can effectively educate students who commit acts of bias, or if more punitive measures are necessary."[27] Even while the debate grew heated, the coercive power of campus culture became clear: the two options—educate or punish—were both still grounded in the portrayal of what had happened as an individualized problem.

To those who believed in the power of civilized diversity discourse, the premise of that BSG meeting was hopeful; students came together across their differences for real conversation. Because the college had largely maintained its norm of civilized discourse by allowing students to "opt in" or "opt out" of conversations about race, most white athletes had not previously opted to engage. Luis and other student activists felt validated that white athletes were finally showing up for a conversation about diversity: "That was the first time that students of color and white students were in the same space having—I don't want to call it a discussion, because I don't feel like it was actually productive—but we were there just sitting for like half an hour having students of color voice similar things that they had voiced the week before and had always voiced, but now this time having a group of white students— mostly white student athletes—come in and talk." On the surface, just getting white athletes to sit in a room where students of color were sharing their experiences felt like a small win.

In reality, however, the meeting was unproductive at best. No one had come to listen and learn. The dialogue was not civilized. Megan described it as a "screaming match." Up until this point, "opting out" had come without risk—saying nothing had always been better than saying the wrong thing and being labeled racist. Now that two of their own were "under attack," white athletes felt they had something to lose if activists were to become successful

CAMPUS IS NOT A BUBBLE

at wielding power on campus, even if that power was largely symbolic. Ben described the scene:

> I'll never forget this, literally all the minorities were on one side of the room, and it was all white people on the other side of the room. It was like something out of the 1950s. I will literally never forget that moment. And I walked in late . . . and everyone just sort of looked at the door and I looked at one side of the room which was all my friends for the most part and a lot of other people on the other side of the room that I didn't necessarily know. It was super awkward because I feel like everyone was waiting for me to choose a side.

Crystal (white and Hispanic woman) similarly described, "It was so divisive. . . . It was literally students of color and white students, and every time a white student would speak then the white students would clap and every time a student of color would speak then the students of color would clap. It was so tense and terrible." Never had the impacts of the de facto segregation of student athletes been more obvious, visceral, and contentious.

Many attendees noted with shock and disappointment how little that crowd of athletes had learned from persistent activism in the wake of prior parties. One of the students who helped write the articles of impeachment recalled, "There was a lot of tension in that meeting because it was just a lot of students of color who came in—it was kind of like what happened the semester before after the Gangster rap party—that similar group of people once again showed up to vocalize how they felt, like how people were viewing them or talking about Latinos and people of color just generally on Yik Yak." Based on his eye-opening Gangster party experience, Scott (white man) agreed: "The first thing I noticed [was that] it was the exact same people that were speaking at the Gangster party public comment, and they were saying the exact same things at the Tequila party public comment." Scott and others were fed up:

> That was sort of a light bulb moment—the same people are saying the same thing over and over again and that's got to be exhausting. I guess all these different connecting groups [i.e., athletic teams] that had people represented at the party came and attended and . . . they were like, "Oh, we just had no idea. We had never heard of this experience." And I was like . . . "You had to have experienced some effects of the Gangster party in the fall." I sort of empathize with the frustration that I feel a lot of students of color on campus had been feeling for a long time because there was also . . . the Cracksgiving party at the beginning of the year earlier. . . . People claiming that they had never heard of any of this stuff before, it just really demonstrated the lack of engagement on campus from white students specifically.

Following the Gangster party open comment time, the sailing team had apologized, participated in an IGD, and worked with peers and staff members to educate themselves. But the aftermath of this public comment time played out differently. The implicated members of BSG publicly apologized, but many of the other partygoers did not. The fact that, according to many students and especially student activists, the partiers should have known better by this time, added anguish, rage, exhaustion, and sadness to an already scorching fire.

In retrospect, Megan recognized that the condemnation of the party emerged from forces both within and outside of the campus bubble: "I think [the BSG members who attended the party] just became scapegoats for a lot of students who had suffered racial discrimination and been marginalized the entirety of their life, and this was the straw that broke the camel's back. And I also think a lot of anger had been pent up from the Gangster party." Yet even while recognizing the extent of racial discrimination more broadly, Megan also echoed anti-PC claims that she was being discriminated against because of her race, "I remember feeling like I couldn't speak because I was a white female on this campus who wore a sombrero and exercised white privilege." Even though the national media would largely come to her defense, Megan and other white athletes continued to play the victim.

While gender is not a primary focus of my analysis, it is worth noting here the ways white women wielded power at the intersections of gender and race. At historically and predominantly white institutions (PWIs), white students tend to create a more hospitable social environment for themselves by avoiding engaging with their own role in structural and interpersonal racism, even during conversations about race.[28] By evading the realities of contemporary racism, white students gain not only what scholars have called "racial comfort,"[29] but also access to the often capital-rich spaces, networks, and relationships that also prize normative whiteness.[30] White women, like Megan, tend to use outward displays of emotion to recenter whiteness and maintain racial comfort—a phenomenon highlighted by the now infamous "Karen" memes.[31] By crying or otherwise making an emotional spectacle—of guilt, grief, helplessness, or self-victimization—white women feign weakness to activate white dominance, often by calling on authority figures or institutions to enact their will.[32]

Gathering White Defenses: The Conservative Media

Prior studies have shown that small, elite campuses tend to encourage civilized discourse because students have a material investment in maintaining

CAMPUS IS NOT A BUBBLE

a respectable reputation.[33] Because all but the wealthiest students were banking on benefiting from the social and economic capital embedded in alumni networks, maintaining one's reputation on campus could carry lifelong consequences, and students worried any transgression might cause their peers to push them out of the fold. For this reason, the uptick in outside media coverage stirred major anxiety on campus. Luis remembered, "I wasn't expecting national news sites to start getting involved and trying to interview me and other people about our opinions and what our thoughts were. I didn't think it would go that far." Dealing with the intense scrutiny on campus was challenging, but the added stress of national media attention was more than any students were prepared for. While the other recent parties had been noted briefly in regional newspapers, the tenor of this coverage was notably different.

Quickly, the conservative media rallied to the defense of the partygoers. An article in the *National Review Online*, informed by the same student who would later take credit for writing to *Barstool Sports*, ridiculed students who were hurt by the party claiming that: "Some students wore sombreros to a tequila-themed birthday party at Bowdoin College—and others were so offended that the school had to provide them with safe spaces and counseling to deal with it."[34] Because of the ideological leanings of the *National Review*, the piece was published in their "Politics and Policy" section. An article in the UK news outlet *The Independent* stated, "A university offered counseling to students 'injured and affected' by a group of classmates who wore small sombrero hats to a tequila-themed birthday party. The row, which erupted at Bowdoin College, a private liberal arts college in the US state of Maine, is being seen as the latest instance of a new mood of censorious political correctness sweeping university campuses on both sides of the Atlantic."[35] A similar article in the UK online publication *The Telegraph* followed.[36] That Snopes.com deemed the salacious claims mostly false[37] did not dampen the fact that the stories continued to garner international media attention—albeit biased—keeping the attention on the perceived injustices thrust upon white partiers rather than the symbolic and emotional violence perpetually inflicted on students of color.

The next day, an opinion article with similar themes was published in the *Washington Post* online and reprinted in regional newspapers across the country.[38] It began, "On Saturday, two members of Bowdoin College's student government will face impeachment proceedings. What heinous transgression did they commit? Theft, plagiarism, sexual assault? Nope. They attended a party where some guests wore tiny sombreros." The article argued that while blackface is "generally outside the accepted bounds of taste, civility, and human decency," there does not "seem to be any sort of settled social norm about the offensiveness or inoffensiveness of sombreros. Go to Chili's, Chevy's, or other Mexican and Tex-Mex restaurants, and you'll likely find similar decor and garb." Neither administrators nor the students directly involved commented for the article, but it was clearly informed by inside sources because it correctly noted that, "on the very same night of the 'Tequila party,' just across campus—Bowdoin held its annual, administration-sanctioned 'Cold War' party. Students arrived dressed in fur hats and coats to represent Soviet culture; one referred to herself as 'Stalin,' making light of a particularly painful era in Slavic history." The author questioned why it would be okay to dress up as Stalin but not okay to wear a sombrero, raising a point that would be echoed by students on campus in the weeks ahead. The article clearly garnered interest, as the author continued with two more installments.

In a follow-up the next day, the author defended her choice to write about the controversy and pointed out the underlying fear gripping many students. The article quoted, "'I'm really afraid to have a discussion about it anymore with people here,' one student, a self-identified political moderate, told me, on condition that I not use the student's name. 'Getting labeled a racist, or a bigot, or intolerant or insulting toward other cultures, that can stick.' People often say talk is cheap; on these campuses, students have learned, talk can be very, very expensive. Claims of offense, witch hunts, a new and seemingly arbitrary litmus test of who is sufficiently dedicated to the cause or ideologically impure, chilling effects on public debate."[39] The author reiterated a familiar conservative punch line that the left stifles healthy debate with PC culture. Yet one aspect of her argument is well supported in my data—students were heavily invested in preserving their reputations on campus. Contrary to the author's claim, however, the pressure to conform to the norms of civilized diversity discourse did not further a woke anti-racist agenda. Instead, students' fears reinforced racialized organizational practices that protected the unmarked whiteness of core organizational structures. The reason why "talk can be very, very expensive" is because one of the key payouts of attending a small, elite college is the (predominantly white) alumni network students can draw on down the road.[40]

The media attention continued with a column by Pulitzer Prize–winning journalist and humorist Gene Weingarten in the *Washington Post* lifestyle magazine. He applauded students' convictions in jest, "After social media photos surfaced of students at your Maine campus wearing festive mini sombreros at a tequila-themed party, you did not merely chide the participants for possible insensitivity. You issued a denunciatory manifesto that contained about as many words as the Declaration of Independence, and with many more 'whereases' and 'be-it-resolveds.'"[41] The column poked fun at the

CAMPUS IS NOT A BUBBLE

seriousness of the impeachment proceedings and the characterization of elite students as snowflakes. "If you ask me, it's simply activism, and activism is good. I fondly remember my own college years, the turbulent 1960s and 1970s, when we, too, protested against the actions of the entrenched and powerful against those who were poorer and weaker. We were protesting the Vietnam War, mostly, but the War on Hurt Feelings is a valid theater of combat, too." His satirical take surfaced how civilized diversity discourse furthers white supremacy—if the problem is hurt feelings, it is by virtue an individual problem that might be resolved with an apology and a hug. If we instead located the problem in the unmarked systems and structures that privilege white and wealthy students, the solution must now involve restructuring institutions and reallocating resources. Hugs and apologies allow white ignorance and white supremacy to continue—invisible and unchallenged. As these examples show, the outside media attention was largely one-sided.

"Such a Lack of Respect": The Administration Responds

While the media firestorm continued, the deans' office began handing out disciplinary consequences to those involved in the party. Like in prior instances, the consequences were assigned to individuals in accordance with the perceived severity of their offense. Rather than shifting their approach given the rapid recurrence of racially charged controversies, administrators doubled down, continuing to treat racism as an individual act. Megan explained, "There were varying degrees of punishment for . . . purchasing, being photographed, or donning a sombrero. . . . I had friends who got [a] reprimand which was basically just a slap on the wrist. Then social probation was the most severe." Jennifer described social probation as, "basically the step below getting suspended . . . it means if you get in trouble again then you get suspended . . . and it stays on your record for seven years." Underlining their commitment to individualism, punishments were again handed down behind closed doors.

The bumbling nature of administrators' investigation, lack of ongoing communication or cooperation with implicated students, and legal obligation to maintain confidentiality led students to question exactly what administrators hoped to achieve with their punishments. To some extent, the deans were eventually able to sort out who hosted and attended the party, but students agreed there were some attendees who "slid through the cracks and didn't get in trouble even though they were there," and some students who were punished disproportionately to their involvement. For example, according to students' reports, all students who lived in the room where the party was held received the same consequences even though only one of them had helped plan and host the party and at least one of the others did not even attend. Jennifer summed it up, "The deans were doing what they thought they were supposed to do, but they didn't know if it was right." Administrative fumbling only contributed to privileged students' claims of victimization and injustice. Jennifer added, "It was so disorganized. It was [administrators] trying to cover their asses. And this distracted from . . . this institutional problem that actually happened, you know?" Jennifer was right. In part because of the way the students who threw the party drew attention to the lack of transparency in the investigation and appeals process, the main story was about their perceived injustices rather than the students who were hurt by the party's theme or the institutionalization of racialized practices and structures. Racialized emotions, again, bolstered white supremacy.[42]

All told, about twenty students were reprimanded in connection to the party. Drawing on elite white norms, these students shared profound outrage at not being treated as equals during the investigative process. Jennifer recalled, "They told us [initially], 'We're going to contact you again to have individual interviews.' And then next time they contacted me was in two weeks and they were like, 'Come in.' And there was a stack of letters, and they were like, 'Here you go,' and it was my social probation letter." Jennifer continued, "The reason why that event is so traumatizing for people is that it just represented such a lack of respect [for the students accused]." Megan remembered, "I came in and sat down and expressed everything that had happened, and they were like, 'Okay, got it. Here's your punishment.' There was no explanation, no previous discussions, I was just given social probation." Megan continued, "That week the deans doled out punishment to everyone that they could find." She mused, "It was kind of strange because a lot of people who hadn't even talked to the deans yet just got this message and sat down and received punishment before even being talked to." In some ways, these actions suggested that administrators had changed their approach, and unlike in prior cases where education took center stage, in this case disciplinary consequences came first. Even though administrators had not undertaken significant educational initiatives, they seemed to implicitly side with students who believed everyone should have somehow already learned their lesson.

While, through an organizational lens, it makes sense to view administrators' motives according to their structural positions, their individual positionalities likely also matter. As officers of the college, they must engage in the campaign for solvency and legitimacy. They must put the college in a position to accrue status among its peers and donations from its patrons. For this college, that meant appealing to elite white norms for talking (or more often not

CAMPUS IS NOT A BUBBLE

talking) about race. But because administrators were intimately familiar with elite white norms and deeply embedded and benefiting from systems of white ignorance, it is possible they may have been as ignorant as many of their students regarding structural racism and cultural appropriation, leaving them unable to educate students on matters they knew little about.

Vanessa and her roommates shared feelings of entitlement, outrage, and disrespect. According to Vanessa, "[The deans] just chose a side and ran with it. I think they dug themselves so deep into this hole, in our meetings I just felt like no one was hearing what I was saying." Vanessa described:

> [My roommates each] had individual meetings [with the dean] and I remember I was the [next] one to go in and my roommates had texted saying what the punishment was and I remember hearing it and being like, "Okay." And I walked in [to the dean's office] and he handed me the letter saying all these things and he was like, "You can take as much as you need to read it over and really have it sink in." And I remember opening the letter and staring at it and flipping it over and being like, "Okay." Then he was like, "Do you have any questions?" And I was like, "No, and I'm done," and walked out of the room being really bratty.

Vanessa listed off the punishments she had been given in that meeting: "We had to move from our room in [one dorm] to [another dorm]. Which was just like, what? You're having me move 150 feet away just to inconvenience me? Okay, thank you. Also, you're putting us all in the same dorm. If your logic is to split us up, you're literally dumb. I was on social probation for a year which meant that if I got in trouble again, I would go to the [judicial] board. I couldn't go to [two campus-wide parties]. I had to attend active bystander training and I had to talk to LASO." Vanessa pushed back against the formal declaration of consequences, foregrounding her own emotions and intentions over the impact of her actions. She recalled, "In retrospect, those are all just such punitive measures of reprimand. . . . I was just so angry!" But when asked if she ever got an explanation of why she was being punished, Vanessa articulated concisely: "The official explanation was that it was 'conduct unbecoming of a Bowdoin student.' I performed an act of bias by putting all of these different elements of Mexican culture together and using it as a way to have fun. . . . That hurt people." She understood perfectly.

Yet instead of regret or remorse, Vanessa insisted she had not meant any harm and therefore should not be held accountable for her actions. Like Megan, she argued, "They used me as a scapegoat for racism. . . . I was accused of this terrible, terrible crime when in reality I hadn't meant to commit to the crime. . . . They told me the impact and intention were off." In other words, administrators made clear to Vanessa that her intent with the party (to have fun) did not matter because the impact (hurting students' feelings and perpetuating racialized stereotypes) was damaging. But Vanessa, not knowing what to do with that information, crumbled: "I was like, 'Okay? I guess I'm a bad person?' [*starting to cry*] I don't know." Vanessa was a good student and a competitive athlete from a wealthy family; she was not accustomed to the rules not working in her favor. Tangible consequences violated tenets of the diversity ideology, where privileged people's intentions matter more than their impacts.[43] For those reasons, this fight was not over.

Reinforcing the notion that campus was not the "bubble" students often believed it to be, Vanessa and other partygoers' families and friends stoked their outrage and confusion. Vanessa's family was "super, super upset," and her friends rallied to her defense. Vanessa described, "I definitely was so confused. The administration and the school [were] telling me that I was an awful person and then it was my parents being like, 'You're fine! The school is dumb! You need to transfer! Stop! You're right! You did not do anything wrong!' Also, all of my friends being like, 'You didn't do anything wrong.'" Because any meaningful repair work after previous parties had occurred behind closed doors, Vanessa had no clue how to move forward. While she genuinely regretted causing pain to her classmates, she felt stuck between administrators' official claims of wrongdoing and her family's insistence otherwise.

In the first issue of the *Orient* after spring break, articles continued to document the aftermath of the Tequila party. One front-page story again focused (belatedly) on the BSG meeting, while another reported on the national news coverage and alumni backlash. According to that article, "In the weeks following the party, [the Office of Development and Alumni Affairs] has received over 400 formal comments from alumni and parents," noting that, "the 'overwhelming majority' of these complaints expressed disapproval of how the incident was handled."[44] Activating the conservative national media had successfully spread word of the controversy beyond campus. Clearly, Vanessa's friends and family were not the only people who disagreed with how things were being handled.

What Students Learned

Even though liberal arts colleges were founded in idyllic rural hamlets to ward off the corrupting influences of urbanization, no campus is a world unto itself. Colleges, as institutions, have always been subject to the influences of other social institutions and vulnerable to the same social conflicts playing out broadly in society. As colleges cater to peer schools for status and donors for solvency, each college develops racialized organizational structures that indoctrinate and reward students in accordance with the priorities of those audiences. Yet as students increasingly matriculate from around the country and the world, bringing their own histories of socialization, campuses have become racially contested terrains.

Cracksgiving and the Gangster party were handled within the campus bubble largely because administrators treated racism as an individual act and the students involved, squeezed by the cultish enticements of their DIII teams, abided by established norms for white ignorance and civilized diversity discourse. But in the case of the Tequila party, student activists contesting their peers' costumes were tired and angry from volunteering their labor and seeing little payout. In addition, the implicated students were not incentivized by athletic consequences, and therefore acted as free agents striving to maintain their race and class privilege. Doing so, they drew from a familiar playbook that included activating their own racialized emotions as well as friends, relatives, and the anti-PC foot soldiers of the national media. As a result, what students on all sides learned in the early days following the Tequila party were cynicism and retrenchment.

6

Money Talks

In the weeks following the Tequila party, the drama continued. Despite their public apology at the Bowdoin Student Government (BSG) meeting, the partiers pushed back against the formal consequences issued by the deans, insisting their racialized ignorance and entitlement should be excused. They cried. They refused to engage in anything resembling civilized diversity discourse. They turned inward, confiding only in their closest friends. And, at times, even turned against each other. Without the norms and structures of an athletic team to bond them together, the partygoers were free agents, each navigating the specter of punishment in their own way.

Except, as we know, these students were not actually on their own. This cadre of partiers had access to highly resourced social networks and now, the sympathies of the right-wing media. Even as student activists worked through established channels—like BSG and the *Orient*—to challenge the premise of white ignorance and hold the partiers accountable, their arguments held little sway outside the campus bubble. As this chapter will show, their relative lack of resourced networks outside the bubble and lack of resonance within those outside networks with resources would ultimately render their defeat. This chapter will also show that, because elite colleges are financially dependent on wealthy donors, white wealth has the power to tip the scales of justice in its favor. Just as the unmarked whiteness of core organizational structures conveyed advantages to white students, so too does the market dependency of higher education more broadly.

You might find yourself asking whether the Tequila party was actually that bad, and whether students' behavior really warranted the firestorm that followed. As important and nuanced as those questions are, they are not the main focus of this book. Instead, this book is the study of how a college, as an

MONEY TALKS   127

organization, navigated the demands of multiple stakeholders in a moment
of racialized contestation. To that end, this chapter explores how, after outside
actors used their social and economic capital to protect and defend the partygoers, the college returned to its norm of civilized diversity discourse. Administrators and students alike utilized established channels to promote programming and push for dialogue. Students either "opted in" or "opted out" of
conversations about race. Those who "opted in" chose to discuss race, diversity, and cultural appropriation with their close friends, much as they usually
would. Students of color felt more pressured to "opt in," due to the ways the
diversity script presented them as resources for their white peers to consume.
Yet by sustaining an organizational context wherein many students—and
particularly white students—could easily "opt out" of race talk, the college
enabled white ignorance and white racial comfort. Keeping the spotlight on
these civilized debates also helped the college promote the myth of meritocracy by working to obscure the true power major donors possessed.

Lawyers and Donors: Drawing on Outside Connections

After administrators handed out their punishments, the students implicated
in the Tequila party quickly appealed to their social networks—bringing in
parents, family, friends, and anyone else they thought might have favor with
the dean or the president. Although the students had also appealed their
punishments through the formal disciplinary appeals process, they knew
that this action alone was unlikely to produce a favorable outcome. Because
the partygoers came from many different strata of the upper class, each was
able to summon different constellations of resources; even so, all had been
similarly socialized to advocate for their continued advantage—a hallmark of
contemporary middle- and upper-class parenting.[1] The implicated students
maintained their stance of innocence, ignorance, and injustice. They clung
to their class and race privilege, secure in the knowledge that because the
system was not working in their favor, they were entitled to work outside
formal channels.

For their part, rather than leaving their children—in fact, all legally
adults—to fend for themselves, students' families hurried to their rescue,
marshaling resources to bolster white supremacy by defending white ignorance. Jennifer recalled, "Everyone brought their parents into the equation,
everyone was trying to contact [the president]. . . . My dad left two voice-
mails, [the president] never emailed or called back." For Vanessa: "My dad
sent letters to [the dean] and was trying to call them and they wouldn't return his phone calls—at all." Other students reported having lawyers in their

family write letters on their behalf. Based on this initial lack of response from administrators, it is easy to imagine that, given a different combination of partygoers, efforts to work outside the system may have fallen flat. After all, recall from the last chapter that the college was up to this point unmoved by correspondence from more than four hundred concerned alumni.[2]

While some students exerted their privilege by having family members call or write to administrators, others took it to a different level. At least one student hired a top-tier lawyer, and at least one other reported that their parents started working their connections on the board of trustees. Because of the ways boarding schools and athletic teams intersected to shape the formation of friend groups on campus, all or nearly all the students reprimanded for the party were from professional upper- or upper-middle-class families, and white or white presenting. Although these students all experienced some degree of socioeconomic and racial privilege, at this moment the distinction between those who were well-off and those whose money wielded influence became abundantly obvious. While, in many cases, these students could be lumped together as "wealthy white kids," in this case the difference between "professional parents who sent their kids to good schools and poured money into elite high school athletics," and "parents with the kind of wealth and connections that can land their child in an elite prep school on short notice," stood in sharp relief. Somewhere in their midst, the convicted partiers had access to something even more powerful than the smear campaign machine of the conservative media: a major donor and a major lawyer.

How could it be possible that the judgments of such a small number of people—largely outside of the day-to-day operations of the college—could hold such influence? Following the financial deregulation of the late 1970s, bankers and financiers built new financial organizations that transformed higher education. As a result, starting in the 1980s and continuing today, the number of private equity and hedge fund managers on the boards of elite universities has skyrocketed.[3] As sociologists Megan Neely and Charlie Eaton have documented, financiers' success depends on the trade of private information and thus an incredible degree of trust. So elites' social ties—like those forged by prestigious colleges—convey an unusually high premium in this industry, helping investment funds secure initial capital and stimulating continued gains.[4] It follows that prestigious colleges are one of the largest beneficiaries of philanthropic giving among the very wealthy; through what Eaton calls "philanthropic homophily"—giving to the same organizations—financiers reinforce their already cloistered and insular social networks.[5] Given the intimate ties between elite college endowments and densely woven networks of superrich financiers, a small number of people, positioned at the nexus of these networks, could quietly wield a significant influence over the college.

But, for their part, most students were unaware of the behind-the-scenes workings of the financial sector. In part because many of them lived in close proximity on campus, the implicated students shared with one another some news about their meetings with the deans and their plans to appeal. Yet many students also strategically concealed the extent of their parents' involvement, leading to rampant rumors and speculation, even among those most implicated in the party. Jennifer (white woman) recalled that when word got out that "lawyers started helping people write appeals," "the term[s] 'white money' and 'white privilege' started getting thrown around Bowdoin really strongly." Jennifer elaborated, "Some parents were doing worse things and people didn't want to let that be known." When I asked what she meant by "worse things," Jennifer clarified, "like threatening their donations and stuff like that. . . . People would be like, 'Did you hear this person's dad did this?' . . . I would say about at least five to ten of the attendees have parents who donate full scholarships." Students pointedly learned the power of extreme wealth to work covertly, outside of formal rules and structures—an example of what racialized organizations theory would call the decoupling of formal rules from organizational practices.[6] Such speculation created lasting divisions among students who had previously been friends, neighbors, teammates, or at least friendly acquaintances.

Even the most privileged students, however, did not want to let it be known that they were calling in outside reinforcements. Why not flaunt it? As Shamus Khan argued in his ethnography of an elite boarding school, while the children of wealthy families once openly leveraged their upper-class connections and entitlements, contemporary elite norms dictate that even the wealthiest of students should strive to appear as though they earned their privilege in a purportedly class-neutral meritocratic system.[7] The ways the highly selective admissions process continues to privilege wealthy applicants while masking the ways that privilege matters, plays heavily into this charade.[8] Elite colleges thus provide the credentials that facilitate social reproduction while helping maintain the myth of meritocracy. On campus, the charade is enacted in the ways students talk about each other as "smart," and in the diversity and naturalization scripts. Through these scripts, students reinforce false notions that all kinds of diversity matter equally and that de facto segregation is merely the product of human nature. As chapter 2 showed, these scripts strategically render structural inequities invisible. Because wealth still conveys coveted power but flaunting one's wealth in mixed company violates the elite code of conduct, students seeking to escape reprimand tried not to call attention to their methods.

Perhaps unsurprisingly, administrators soon buckled under the pressure from parents and donors. While only a few of my respondents knew the details of what had happened, the partygoers were all largely aware of the generalities. When asked if her appeal had worked, Jennifer replied frankly: "It worked because I think everyone did it. I mean, I don't think [my appeal] technically worked. I think that some parent [or] a few parent donors threatened." In other words, the goal of their appeal was achieved—the punishment was lessened—but Jennifer does not believe that it was her act of writing an appeal that achieved that goal. She benefited from what other people's parents somehow made happen behind closed doors. In this way, racialized privilege from outside the bubble enabled increased agency for affluent students, an example of how the racialization of an organization might emerge from social networks that exist independently of organizational hierarchies. In this case, connections between students and donors—organizational actors of markedly different statuses—somehow swayed administrators.

Thanks to these outside interventions, the punishments from the deans were universally reduced. Megan's (white woman) retelling strategically blurred over the impact of those power players but highlighted the impact for the implicated students: "The administration handed out our punishment and then everyone appealed their punishment, and it was marked down a notch. So, I went from social probation to a reprimand which is basically like, 'Don't do it again!' technically. Then the people that [were reprimanded] went from reprimand to nothing." Punitive and educational measures lingered on the horizon for only a handful of students, and even those were significantly lessened from their original form.

Money Wins: Rescinding the Articles of Impeachment

In addition to significantly shrinking the scope and impact of formal disciplinary measures, administrators (at the bidding of lawyers and parents), also made the impeachment threat disappear. Between the leaked announcement of the proposed impeachment on Wednesday and the scheduled advent of the proceedings that Saturday, students and their families threatened legal action convincingly enough to shut down the entire enterprise. One of the partygoers described the rumors circulating campus, "A lot of parents had lawyers who were trying to get involved with the impeachment process too, and that's why the impeachment process was dropped apparently. Apparently, a lawyer came through. I don't know what [actually] happened. That person denies it." The secrecy and resulting absence of reliable information fed the sense that administrators answered to a higher power and not to students working through established channels. Despite the fanciful depiction of the college as a "bubble" removed from the outside world, wealthy parents and donors exercised leverage that protected the partiers—not from the spectacle of impeachment or media coverage, but from any lasting material consequences.

Owing to white ignorance, many of those students did not understand how and why pressure from their families and professional contacts amounted to an exercise of racialized privilege. According to one of the partygoers:

> My dad's an attorney and he wrote a letter to the college after our punishment and after the articles of impeachment were filed. He wrote a letter to the deans and [the president] and basically outlined why a lot of what was going on was not fair because we had been punished under a system that didn't exist prior to what had happened. He was basically saying, "Punish them for the hard alcohol, that's fine. But how is it fair to exercise punitive measures because of the sombreros?" He never got a response back. But right after that, the articles of impeachment were rescinded. . . . The president of the BSG at the time, he was like, "We're pulling the articles of impeachment," but didn't give a reason as to why. But then that whole thing—my dad just wrote a letter—got twisted into [partiers] hiring a lawyer and exercises all of white privilege and affluence by hiring a lawyer when my dad was just a concerned parent who happened to be a lawyer and wrote a letter.

This partier exhibited no comprehension of the privilege inherent in her statement, or the kind of power she exerted by having a lawyer in her family. After all, she was likely among the least wealthy of the partygoers. Interestingly, however, she could not imagine and did not know that other students' families had actually hired outside counsel.

For those on the other side—the coalition who authored the articles of impeachment—the experience was eye-opening, intimidating, and oppressive. One student recalled their meeting with the dean that week:

> Pretty much the conversation went . . . "You know in the US anyone can be sued for defamation at any point, right?" I'm like, "Yes, but what does that have to do with me?" He's like, "Well, just so you know there might be the potential that some people that you might be impeaching are trying to take legal action potentially against the college and that might implicate you. . . . So, I have been through a lot of different . . . lawsuits,"—just given his job—and he was like, "Trust me that is not something you want to have to deal with for the next five years of your life." So, he's like, "You can still go through this if you want but just know that the college isn't able to support you in any way."

The coalition of accusers met up afterward to confer, and begrudgingly decided to rescind the articles of impeachment: "We rescinded, and we made a statement very clearly [at the BSG meeting that] this is not what we wanted. . . . We still feel like this needed to happen, but we are happy at least people had a real conversation, [or] tried to have a conversation." The next week the *Orient* confirmed that the impeachment proceedings were postponed "after administrators warned [BSG leaders] that continuing to do so could place BSG members in a weakened position in case of a lawsuit."[9] Even as implicated students worked to hide their methods, student activists were transparent about their conversations with administrators and the threatened lawsuit.

Having their efforts squashed by wealthy outside actors gutted student activists, while exposing them to harsh treatment on campus. One of the accusers reflected, "I spent so much time and energy putting work into what I thought was important, but nothing happened out of that, from those impeachment proceedings." Luis (Latino man) agreed, "That time was a really rude awakening to the fact that I could do whatever I think I'm passionate about, but to an extent, the lack of privilege, the lack of money could only get you so far. And I think I really had to learn to acknowledge that and learn to acknowledge that I could put my heart into everything, but that's not going to change anyone." This was a lesson many low-income students and students of color came away with: that socioeconomic privilege and social capital would always trump the very real pain of marginalized students. In short, money wins.

Spending so much time and energy pushing for public accountability also came at a steep cost to student activists. One *Orient* columnist, who had already written about both parties, reflected on the burden the college had placed on students of color and called for change: "During times of crisis, friends of mine have spent more time in administrative meetings than in the classroom or library. Many involved have grown weary—in fact, 'I'm done' has become a common sentiment. Thus, both sides of the debate are beginning to abandon the possibility of discussion and understanding." She continued, "Bowdoin put effort into diversifying the student body. Now, the college—not its minority students—needs to grapple with that newfound diversity. The college—not its minority students—needs to address the inherent biases present in the student body. As of now, it is simply veiling them."[10] By failing to address the ignorance and bias of white and otherwise privileged students, the author argued, the college reinforced the "us versus them" mentality that exhausted and alienated marginalized students. But she stopped short of naming the ways that campus structures create and reinforce systems of power that privilege white students. In line with civilized diversity discourse, the author advocated for antibias training that might enable further

MONEY TALKS

discussion of the issues—keeping the focus on individuals rather than systems, structures, and resources.

The impeachment battle did, however, result in one small structural change. One week after students formally introduced the articles of impeachment, they were rescinded while "simultaneously creating the formal steps by which impeachment occurs."[11] That BSG meeting had a much lower attendance than the week before. Because BSG "bylaws offered almost no instructions as to how an impeachment would actually proceed in reality," the assembly began the less glamorous process of designing an impeachment process that could be used in future cases. Many white students, like Megan, had pushed back against the first round of impeachment proceedings on technical grounds: "I was upset about the impeachment articles [filed against the partygoers] because . . . there was no process for impeachment." She pointed out the "absurdity of forming rules and then punishing people for rules that were formed after the fact." Creating a process for impeachment would alleviate this concern in future cases. With the partiers placated by having their appeals granted and the responding students bullied into backing off, the turmoil finally began to subside.

Shifting Back to White Priorities: Sticking with Civilized Diversity Discourse

After significant breaches to the norms of civilized diversity discourse via the blog posts, on Yik Yak, and at the BSG meeting, key players worked to coax campus back to equilibrium. For example, the Student Center for Multicultural Life, sponsored a "My Culture Is Not a Costume" and "Their Culture Is Not Our Costume" photo shoot, to "show solidarity in the wake of recent acts of ethnic stereotyping and to help educate the campus community about the harmful effects of ethnic stereotyping."[12] The Director of the Student Center for Multicultural Life was quoted as saying, "We will try to educate, be proactive, instead of being reactive when things happen, such as the 'Gangster' party, such as 'Cracksgiving,' such as the 'Tequila' party." He continued, "I envision the photos to show Bowdoin students from different cultures and different backgrounds represented, and that representation is something that as a campus, as a community, we should celebrate."[13] Events like this exemplified the administration's tacit commitment to channeling the rage and hurt felt by some students of color into nondisruptive forms of activism and spotlighted the institution's underlying "diversity regime"[14] through its desire to display and tokenize non-white students in the name of diversity but not undertake structural changes.

134   CHAPTER SIX

That Friday, the president sent another campus-wide email, recognizing the escalation of the debate about the party and its aftermath in both local and national media outlets. He argued that "the issues we are dealing with are not really about hats or drinks," while portraying the college as "a place with a history and culture of tolerance, respect, and warmth."[15] He selectively cited broad historical changes that had made the college more welcoming, such as the admission of women in the 1970s and the disbanding of fraternities in the 1990s, implicitly arguing that positive structural change had already been accomplished and turning a blind eye to policies that perpetuated exclusion, segregation, and marginalization of students of color on campus. As scholar Melvin Whitehead and colleagues argued, "These omissions serve to exacerbate, rather than interrupt, the race-evasive, distorted sense of history that white students frequently consume in their precollege communities."[16] By selectively mentioning policies furthering inclusion but failing to mention how other policies furthered white agency and ignorance on campus, the president again tacitly indicated which kinds of racism would be condemned on campus and which kinds would be celebrated.

In addition, the president reiterated his call for civilized diversity discourse. He encouraged the campus community to engage "with the most uncomfortable and difficult ideas," including those that "may offend us, and where we may have a deep emotional reaction." This claim reminded readers that the chief harm of racism was hurt feelings. He urged that "every one of our students, must know themselves to be an equal member" of the campus community, because "anything less diminishes their ability to participate, to become educated, and it diminishes their ability to add to the learning and creation of knowledge for others."[17] In other words, he reverted to the diversity script, where all differences matter equally, and the real problem was not racism—either individual or institutional—but students' reticence to engage in uncomfortable conversations.

In his email, the president also reiterated the false notion that racism only impacts people of color by erasing the ways white people and institutions benefit from white supremacy. He expressed that actions in social settings "that caricature groups, that simplify a culture to some coarse or crude sense of its reality, or that use tokens of discrimination with deep and long-standing meaning, can have a profound effect on those in our community who identify as part of these groups, and can diminish their ability to engage academically,"[18] but remained silent on how such transgressions serve to benefit white students and the unmarked whiteness of the college itself. As scholars Wendy Leo Moore and Joyce Bell argued,[19] by calling out overt acts of racism administrators gave the signal that overt racism is the only kind of racism on campus—a sleight of hand that affirms the acceptability of white ignorance, color-evasive racism, and diversity ideology.[20]

The same day, the impeachment debate was front-page news in the *Orient* and the opinion pages were stacked with commentary—this time, from "both sides." Although the heated debate at the BSG meeting had centered on if, how, and when participants would be held accountable for their actions by the administration,[21] the editorial board also worked to shift the focus back to civilized discourse by advocating for educational rather than punitive measures. They qualified some disciplinary measures as "productive"— educational programs facilitated by a faculty member, active bystander training, and writing a letter or paper on these experiences—and others as "harsh" punishments, including being forced to move out of their dorm rooms (and into rooms in another dorm) and being banned from the two campus-wide parties.[22] The editorial board also took issue with the broader conversation about those actions: "It is concerning that the disagreement over punitive measures seems to be overshadowing the larger-scale problems and tensions on campus, both related and tangential to the 'Tequila' party and its predecessors. . . . This diversion is crowding out the opportunity to think critically about why some Latinx students (and other students of color) feel disrespected and hurt by this incident in the first place." They continued, reminding readers of the responsibilities that come with freedom of speech, and urging white students to "lean into" conversations about "systemic oppression and racism."[23] From the pages of the opinion section, it was clear that at least a few students were heeding this advice.

That week's issue showcased the range of opinions among Latinx students. One op-ed wrote about the history of PC culture and the false claims that minority students were to blame for the Tequila party kerfuffle. In response to claims on Yik Yak that minoritized students were overreacting, the author, who identified as Latino, wrote: "I will give you points for creativity because you are shifting the focus away from the perpetrators of the event. By saying we are the issue, you are putting the blame on us minorities. There is just one problem with this sort of thinking: we are not the ones who perpetrated this incident. We are the recipients of acts of this nature, which, I would add, are unprovoked by us minority students."[24] Another, also written by a student who identified as Latino, pushed back: "The party demonstrated ignorance because the Mexican culture is so much richer than that. But just because the culture was not fully represented does not mean it was an act of misappropriation, nor does it mean the students at the party should be punished."[25] Often assumed by white students to be monolithic, the breadth of diversity within the Latinx community on campus came into full display in the wake

136   CHAPTER SIX

of the party, with divisions often falling along socioeconomic lines. In part because of these divisions, the Latin American Student Association (LASO) was unwilling to engage with the partygoers in educational conversations in the same ways that the African American Society (AfAm) had in the wake of the Gangster party.

The range of opinions among white students was also on full display in the *Orient*. One white student encouraged education over punishment, urging restorative justice, better access to overenrolled sociology courses, and more faculty of color.[26] Another questioned the class privilege of the partiers, saying: "It's Pavlovian, really, when you've been told 'yes' all your life. Yes to elite Manhattan preschool; yes to firing the babysitter you hate; yes to a weekend in the Hamptons; yes to that spring break trip in Cabo; yes, yes, yes. Perhaps you've grown accustomed to hearing that word in response to your requests. You've grown accustomed—through no fault of your own—to expecting your demands to be met with a resounding, authority-uttered, definitive 'yes.'" The author encouraged white students to try to empathize, "even if they do not know what it's like to be told no."[27] Even while calling out their (often racialized) class privilege quite starkly, both authors argued that if people knew better, they would do better—if they could take a class or grow some empathy, somehow the world would be a better place. In short, they too pushed for a return to civilized diversity discourse.

The most talked about column came from the cis, white, male athlete who admitted to tipping off *Barstool Sports* and initiating the cascade of conservative media attention on campus. Like many of the partygoers in my interviews, he tried to leverage his white ignorance to gain leniency and sympathy. He wrote, "I understand I was born into privilege. However, I didn't choose to be born into a white family or go to a white high school, that's just how my life is. Just because I'm seemingly more fortunate than other people doesn't mean I should be brushed aside as another kid who just doesn't get it. I want to get it. I wish I understood—it would probably make this whole situation a lot easier. But the fact of the matter is that nothing in my life has even remotely prepared me for dealing with this kind of problem."[28] To his credit, this author identified many of the state-sanctioned systems complicit in white ignorance—namely segregated neighborhoods, schools, and families. Despite claiming to want to understand better, however, he admitted to not attending any of the events or conversations on campus since the party for fear of being ostracized. This dissonance was yet another example proving that simply offering educational resources was not enough because students' racialized emotions—in this case, fear—motivated them to value their reputations and social networks more than disrupting their own ignorance.

By giving up his anonymity, however, and coming clean in the pages of the *Orient*, he too bought in to the call for a return to civilized diversity discourse.

Enabling White Ignorance:
Making Civilized Diversity Discourse Optional

In the days and weeks after the parties, students either "opted in" or "opted out" of conversations about race. By sustaining an organizational context wherein many students—and particularly white students—could easily "opt out" of race talk, the college enabled white ignorance and white racial comfort and reinscribed its campus as a white space. Opting out erased all possibility of misspeaking and risking one's reputation, while opting in required conscious and careful thought to avoid "hurting anyone's feelings." Students who opted into conversations about race noted that they were prudent to avoid offending anyone and being labeled as racist. To this end, potentially controversial conversations happened only among close friends. Overall, students' behaviors demonstrated that the preservation of collective eminence via the existing racial order proved more compelling than enacting the promise of the diversity script—reinforcing the notion that the act of bringing a diverse cohort of students together and hoping they will learn from their differences indeed constitutes "magical thinking."[29]

Those who "opted in" chose to discuss race, diversity, and cultural appropriation with their close friends, much as they usually would. Jade (Asian woman) stated, "A lot of my POC friends and I will talk about race and stuff maybe once a week, [and] when the whole [party] stuff was happening, every day." Amy (white woman) recalled engaging in conversations about race: "A lot of times it's been with my friends who are from different ethnic backgrounds, just because I'm usually kind of interested in their experience and so I like to hear about that from them. But I do talk about it with my other friends who are also normal white people—who are pretty similar to me." In this comment Amy echoed the sentiments modeled by administrators via email—that there are two groups: "normal white people," and people of color who are impacted by racist words and acts. As Megan described, "There was so much volatility. . . . I just turned to my friends, and I know a lot of other people turned to their friends. But then students of color sort of found solidarity with one another and white students found solidarity with one another and that hardened the divide that already existed." Because structural factors molded homogeneous friend groups (as seen in chapter 2), this kind of race talk happened behind closed doors—what sociologists Picca and Feagin refer to as "backstage"[30]—where students felt comfortable speaking more freely.

White students varied in what kinds of conversations they had with their friends. A few who "opted in" had realizations about how race, and specifically whiteness, mattered in society. Madison (white woman) remembered, "For like three weeks straight . . . I'd go to dinner and talk about the cultural appropriation issue. And it was like, I stood pretty firmly in my position, but felt that I gathered more information about why—not why I was right, but why I was justified in thinking what I was thinking." Paige (white woman) recounted: "I remember talking again with this closest group of people, one of whom is a sociology minor. And she's someone who's thought very intentionally about race and difference of many kinds and so I remember talking to her a lot during the Tequila party and the Gangster party and stuff like that about our thoughts about . . . the culture of whiteness, why white students would do these things, and what our place was as fellow white students. . . . We're well intentioned, but that isn't enough." Cindy (white woman) recalled, "One thing I did often think about was how easy it would have been for me to be at that party as a white person and not really think about [it]. I remember thinking, 'What if I had had just a slightly different group of friends?' . . . I could have so easily been complicit in what was happening and in a lot of ways I don't deny that I'm still complicit in those things." Many of these students noted that the conversations they were having about the Tequila party were the first conversations they had on campus where people really disagreed, and students ended up learning a lot from hearing divergent perspectives within their friend groups. Previously, students' incentives to preserve their reputations outweighed any possible benefits from rigorous debate but, in this moment, increasing numbers of white students felt they had something to gain from weighing in—at least among their close friends.

Other white students "opted in" to conversations deliberating whether the Tequila party was somehow different from the prior parties. Ben (white man) believed the Tequila party was not as problematic as the other parties, "I guess the first two parties I understood why they were bad. But the third one I was fed up. I was like, 'All right, this is ridiculous now. This is kind of getting out of control.'" Riley (white woman) agreed but was sensitive to becoming more aware, "Only at Bowdoin something like having a Tequila party could become a natural disaster. Where, you know, every other big state school has Cinco de Mayo parties and kids wear sombreros. . . . Coming into Bowdoin and seeing that blow up was like, 'Wow! Why is this a thing?!' But I think people learn their lesson and it's important to be more mindful of who is being offended." But Amy disagreed, positing this was no different and that the prior parties should have given students ample notice: "The people who planned that [party], they were there the year before with Cracksgiving. So,

MONEY TALKS   139

you were there. Why wouldn't you learn your lesson? There's no longer an excuse of . . . innocence or like you couldn't say, 'Oh, I didn't know.'" Students whose friends were involved on one side or the other tended to have stronger convictions, but again these conversations largely happened within established friend groups.

Students of color felt more pressured to "opt in," due to the ways the diversity script presented them as resources for their white peers to consume. This sudden pressure to educate their white peers felt affirming to some but alienating to others. For example, Danielle (white, Hispanic, and African American woman) felt good about the ways she could help educate her white friends:

> One of my roommates, after the Tequila party and cultural appropriation incidents, started asking me a bunch of questions because I wasn't white. [I remember] having this discussion with her and having to explain there is such thing as a Black Hispanic person and things like that. I never thought that I would have to explain that. I didn't really have a problem with it. I realized that a lot of people have no idea, and this is a very genuine person who cares and it's just something that she's never been exposed to, and she just didn't know. So, realizing that, if she's like that, then there are other people like that. . . . Having that discussion, I think was good for me in affirming who I am and how I feel about myself and then just helping her to learn.

In these moments, Danielle felt seen in a new way within her existing friend group. For others, however, being asked to educate their white peers felt complicated and confusing. After all, many students of color did not know any more than their white peers when it came to academic debates about cultural appropriation or structural racism. For example, Cassie (Asian American woman) confessed:

> I felt very almost like "outed" as being a person of color and having to have a stance on how I felt and be able to talk about it intelligently. And by that time, I definitely was more aware of things like that, but I wasn't ready to talk about it. And I think it was really difficult for me to be so visibly a person of color and not being so outspoken, because I felt like if I wasn't saying anything then I was just—what is that quote? If you don't actively do something, you're just siding with the [enemy]—I felt kind of like that. I felt like I had to speak up in order to show that I was on [students' of color] side.

The prevailing diversity script positioned Cassie and Danielle—visibly identifiable students of color—as resources available for the edification of their white peers. While Danielle embraced the role, Cassie felt ill-equipped. For her part, Cassie wanted to do right and show support for her fellow students of color. But in this campus context, the socially ordained way of showing support entailed engaging in civilized diversity discourse—to "talk about it intelligently"—and she did not yet feel prepared for that task.

In other cases, students of color who sided with the partiers felt as though their peers were expecting them to side with activists simply because of their identity. Carlos (white and Latino man), for example, had no issue with the Tequila party. Instead, he resented being lumped together with other students of color, saying: "That's totally great you have your Black Girl Brunch, and you have your Latino Boy Brunch and whatever, but we talk about diversity at Bowdoin, how diversity is really important to understanding different perspectives and different ideas and how people feel. But sometimes I feel like you're not really accomplishing that by creating these other low diversity groups, where it's like everyone has to feel the same way." Even though he did not take issue with the costume parties, dominant assumptions painting all students of color as a monolith meant he too was pressured to "opt in" and speak on behalf of his entire ethnic group.

In this way, students of color who were not involved in the party were called upon by their peers to respond in ways that white students were not. Unlike their white peers who could "opt out" of conversations about race, students of color tended to feel as though they were expected to have a strong yet eloquent reaction. As was the case with prior parties, admissions decisions limiting the number of students of color on campus paved the way for their tokenization. Structures segregating students' social interactions also mattered, as what was expected of students of color varied dramatically based on the racial composition of their peer group. Regardless of their feelings about the parties, however, many students of color felt commodified and on display.

Meanwhile, despite attracting considerable media attention, many students were not impacted by the controversial parties at all. In our interviews, two years after the Tequila party, some respondents failed to recall the events entirely, while others simply "opted out" of conversations because they were too busy or felt their race exempted them. Steve (white man) reported, he "didn't have time [*laughs*] to really get washed down in it. I wanted to focus on football and academics and job searching." Many white students who opted out of conversations about race in the wake of the parties felt discussions were not relevant to them because they were white, a clear example of the minimization tenet of colorblind racism,[31] but also of how whiteness as a credential enhances the agency of white students by allowing them to opt out. Anthony (white and Latino man) explained, "I don't see anything as a big issue because nothing is a big issue to me because I'm a white male. I don't need to care about anything." By surrounding themselves with like-minded students and

MONEY TALKS   141

validating social segregation through naturalization script, these students could ignore racialized controversies altogether. By sustaining a racialized organizational context wherein many students—and particularly white students and athletes—could easily "opt out" of race talk, the college facilitated greater agency for those students.

Money Wins, Coda

As the college closed for its two-week spring break, it appeared to most students that the controversy might finally dissipate. But for the students most implicated and their families, a lightened version of their consequences still lingered on the horizon. And for some, even that was too much. Those with the most influence continued to pressure top administrators to make it all go away. One of the partygoers recalled, "I remember being in the lobby of this hotel [on spring vacation] and my dad is on the phone with [the president] and I'm sitting there and they're fighting with each other. . . . It was so dramatic!" Even though many partygoers reported their parents' calls to the president went unanswered initially, at least one family had the leverage to eventually get a call back. Based on those conversations, what little remained of the partiers' punishments started to disappear. Vanessa recalled, "Our punishment kept getting pushed further and further. We got back from spring break, and they were like 'Oh you're coming back from spring break, so we don't want to make you [move rooms].' I was like, 'Okay, that's weird.' . . . Then it kept getting pushed off and pushed off. So, we were like, 'Are we moving? What's happening?'" The students tried to return to life as it had been before the party, but the drawn-out campaign to challenge all formal consequences continued.

The accused students remained in limbo until another closed-door meeting yet again turned the tide in their favor. One of the hosts recounted, "I got called into [the dean's] office and he was like, 'I just want you to know if we had seen this piece of evidence at the beginning, things would've been so different. Blah blah blah.' Then he pulls out this email that I sent to the head of LASO the day after [the party] happened." The host detailed the backstory of the email:

> That Sunday . . . Aubree's roommate showed me all the texts [from a LASO leader], I was like, "Should I email him?" And she was like, "Yeah, I don't see why not." Then I emailed him and apologized. I was like, "I'm sorry if this is how it came off, wasn't my intention at all, and I know with everything that happened this year and the Gangster party it added fuel to the fire and I'm

sorry." So, [the dean] produces this email printed out and he was like, "Why didn't you say anything about this? This shows your remorse and great character. We would have treated you so differently." I was like, "Are you kidding me?!"

The host credited that meeting as the cause of consequences continuing to evaporate, "It helped me out because we didn't have to move out of our room and our punishments were way lessened. I was like, 'You're delusional! You are just trying to dig yourself out of this crazy hole that you got yourself in.' It was so crazy. Then that was it! [The dean] was like, 'If by the end of senior year, you've proven that you've been a good member of the Bowdoin community, I'll rip up all of the documents ever. We can pretend like it never happened.'" With that, administrators returned to the standard that a sincere apology could, in itself, act as the appropriate consequence. Under pressure from major donors and in line with the diversity ideology, administrators prioritized intent over impact, thus allowing racialized power structures to remain in place.

Many students experienced similar feelings of uncertainty as the semester wound down and the previously decreed consequences somehow vanished. Not knowing about the closed-door meetings, Megan wondered if the extended appeals process had interfered with administrators' plans for educational programming. "Part of our punishment was to engage in discussions with members of LASO, but because like forty members that they had punished appealed and got their punishment moved down, the conversations that the school meant to organize never happened. I think it was maybe that, but more than anything, I think they just ran out of time at the end of the semester. So, there were supposed to be conversations orchestrated between Tequila party attendees and LASO members—because the sailing team did some with AfAm after the Gangster party—and that just never happened." Jennifer had no clear explanation either, "Our social probation letter said that we were required to attend . . . a class session on Latinx cultures, but they never held that session." After that, according to Jennifer, "People just tried to forget about it." Forgetting, like ignorance, is a choice not an accident. In this case, administrators "forgetting" to go forward with the gesture of providing educational programming carried clearly racialized implications for the campus. This is another example of Ray's tenet of racialized organizations wherein formal rules are decoupled from organizational practices in a racialized manner.[32]

The only educational session that was held was the active bystander training, led unsurprisingly by trained student volunteers, most of whom were students of color. Even the students who led the training were skeptical of its efficacy. One of the student facilitators recalled, "They asked me to [lead a training] and I said yes, but they didn't tell me that it would be with the group of students that did the Tequila party, so that was weird." The student explained their skepticism: "Active bystander training is more about sexual violence. . . . That can be applied to other things, but you can't stop something that you don't know is happening. Like if you can't identify racism, then how are you going to be active? You're just an unconscious bystander. So how are we going to bring consciousness to people? At the time I was just trying to help out in whatever way, because I was an advocate of education, like workshops to tackle these things. But we just didn't have a very good toolset." Some students, even those who had spent so much time responding to the Gangster party, were so invested in using education as a remedy they continued to volunteer their labor. But as this student facilitator acknowledged, the tools the college offered were not the right tools for the job. White ignorance was not being challenged, or even recognized.

What Students Learned

In one of the only lingering formal consequences for the partiers, at the end of the school year, they were asked to write a letter to the dean reporting what they had learned. As many of them noted, the premise was flawed from the outset. After all, administrators never actually required this cadre of partiers to participate in any educational programming. Jennifer complained, "I didn't learn anything because I was never taught during any of this!" As a result, the students did not cop to the same heartfelt revelations that Ben and Trevor felt after their session with Native American students in the wake of Cracksgiving or that Scott and Nora experienced from participating in dialogues with AfAm after the Gangster party. Those students accepted their consequences and played along with civilized diversity discourse, allowing the campus to quickly return to equilibrium while a small legion of student activists continued to agitate for structural change. But these partygoers weaponized their racial status and fought back. They did not learn the lesson about individualized acts of racism that the administration had worked so hard to promote—that when privileged people overstep, they can quietly maintain their institutional power by acting contrite, making efforts to learn, and evangelizing civilized diversity discourse. Instead, these students learned that wealth wins; but because each came from a different degree of wealth, their lessons varied according to what they knew of the behind-the-scenes negotiations conducted by parents, donors, and lawyers, and therefore varied by class status.

144   CHAPTER SIX

Megan felt bad and sought to undo some of her ignorance. She followed a similar trajectory to Trevor (from Cracksgiving) and Scott (from the Gangster party), also white, graduates of public schools, and recruited athletes. While Megan agreed the institution failed to educate the offending partygoers, she earnestly sought to understand her wrongdoings. Megan leaned on her friends for support, but like most athletes, she had a homogeneous peer group. Her redemption finally came from a former teammate, whose friend circle shifted when she left the team. No longer beholden to the intensive scheduling demands of athletics, this student adopted different and more diverse extracurriculars, learned about social inequities, and made new friends. Thanks to this friendship, Megan gained a new perspective:

> I had never thought about race before this whole experience. I had never thought about my position at Bowdoin as being one of privilege either because I come from a tight-knit community of white people—but middle class, my family is middle class. I hadn't thought of myself as privileged at this college in any way before, honestly, the conversation that I had with my friend that was a [sociology] major. Seeing the hurt that everything that we had done [had] caused other people was also a really interesting check in with my own social position. I had never really been forced to engage in any really difficult conversations before. . . . There was a large group of people that hated me on campus. There wasn't really anything I could do to change that other than just try and be nice to them when I saw them, but even that—I don't know if that fixes things.

Because she did not want to risk more potentially negative attention on campus, Megan gained most of her insights from trusted white peers, rather than formal programs or classes: "I hadn't really been exposed to any sort of discussion or thought on sociology prior to all of this and that honestly was one of the best educations I've received in sociology. But I remember talking to someone about it and them explaining why so many people were hurt about it. . . . I had one of my friends who is a [sociology] major and was on my team explain it to me—explain the notion of white privilege, explain that there are connotations to appropriating another culture and why it could've been hurtful, and it was the most perspective-shifting moment. . . . I'm lucky that I knew her and was able to talk to her." This was "backstage" race conversation at its best—peers of the same race translating their classroom learning to perpetuate better understandings of the social world. But it only worked because Megan had close friends and teammates who she listened to and trusted, and those white students had already chosen to educate themselves on systematic oppression, structural violence, and institutionalized racism—they "opted in" and took the work seriously. Although this work had little structural impact, this is one example of how white students can relieve students of color of having to assume sole responsibility for pushing back against white ignorance.

Other students who shared a similar upper-middle-class background with Megan, however, came out of the ordeal more impacted. Many students of this ilk on both sides of the conflict considered transferring to another college and at least a few did. For these students, the oppressive silencing and social exclusion exacted by "friends" with access to the kind of power that accompanies extreme wealth became too much to bear. While they were not included in my interview sample, stories from the students who permanently left campus because of these events could certainly deepen our understandings of the collateral damage resulting from a handful of uber-wealthy students choosing to defend their own interests at all costs.

Jennifer, who considered herself a "normal person" because she attended an affluent private school but was gifted a used car by her parents instead of a new, luxury vehicle, remained indignant and shifted blame back to the college. Resentful that punitive consequences had ever been threatened, Jennifer recalled the letter she wrote for the deans at the end of that semester, "I basically said I didn't learn anything because [administrators] interfered. . . . We were supposed to say what we learned about cultural appropriation. . . . So, I basically just said I learned that you can't appropriate other cultures or something. It was such a bullshit letter." Jennifer played along with what she knew was expected of her and continued to be appalled at the ways her peers wielded their wealth, without ever giving up her belief that the entire investigation was beneath her dignity.

Vanessa, the most affluent of the students profiled, also learned from the experience—but only a fraction of her learning centered on racism. She did, after all, have some inkling the party's theme was inappropriate before the invitation ever went out—that "preexisting butthurt insurance"[33] in saying it was "not *not* a fiesta." Vanessa learned firsthand the lesson that allows elite children to reproduce their parents' status; she learned why elite networks must remain exclusive. When asked what she learned, Vanessa joked, "I've learned don't invite girls you don't like to your party. I'm kidding!" Granovetter[34] famously wrote about the "strength of weak ties," meaning that for most people infrequent, arms-length relationships—known as weak ties—are more beneficial for employment opportunities, promotions, and wages than strong ties—like family or close friends. This theory explains why most undergraduates on small, elite campuses work so hard to maintain a respectable reputation: the "collective eminence"[35] of the alumni network that acts as a hub for these invaluable weak ties. But, as Khan[36] has argued, elites do not need weak ties to improve their position—they are already at the top. Instead, they cultivate dense, robust networks to prevent their wealth and status from getting watered down. From her experience with the Tequila party, Vanessa learned exactly why.

Vanessa also learned about the consequences of getting caught. As argued by a peer in the *Orient* opinion piece quoted earlier about students who were used to hearing "yes" all the time, Vanessa learned what it was like to hear "no." She admitted, "I've learned about so much—action and reaction, when it comes down to it your actions have consequences and I think in my life I have been a rule tester. This was the first time that I ever got caught. . . . It was a hard alcohol event and that's why I got in trouble. I mean, [we] did—[we] threw a Tequila party and there is no hard alcohol allowed on this campus." Even though she marshaled her privilege to escape most formal consequences, the public fallout was jarring to a person who had always been the beneficiary of backroom dealings. Vanessa reflected, "I never had to form an opinion about anything in my life up until then. Then [the party] happened and I had to form a belief. It was hard and confusing." Vanessa had, up until that point, been protected by her family's wealth and connections. Instead of learning how white people defend their privilege through the diversity script, she learned how superrich people defend their privilege by staying above the law.

In the end, Vanessa expressed remorse. As a white-presenting person, she had never had to deal with racism before. She stated:

> I feel bad that I hurt people . . . obviously I made a mistake. I wouldn't do it again. I mean I know now that it's wrong. . . . Because this whole thing is a huge reminder for the people that were negatively affected of it about all of the discrimination and acts of biases and racism that exists in society and is so real and so impactful upon people. I think that I've learned obviously how real that is because of how much it can be triggered by these little episodes and that is obviously something that I wasn't aware of. I had never experienced that kind of reaction to those kinds of things in my life. I think it really put into perspective how much that actually matters to people.

Like Megan, Vanessa took something valuable from her conversations with her peers. In the end, she became more sensitive to interpersonal differences and how much racism matters to other people.

Conclusion

For a few months, the Tequila party and its aftermath wreaked havoc on campus. In part because it came on the heels of the Gangster party and in part

MONEY TALKS   147

because the implicated students refused culpability, lobbied against formal consequences, and escalated the scope of visibility and involvement well beyond the campus bubble, many more students were impacted by the fallout than had been impacted by the Gangster party or Cracksgiving. While many of the students involved were athletes and the athlete community rallied in their defense, because they were not all part of the same team, their response to the formal disciplinary proceedings was not orchestrated with the coercive pressure or bureaucratic assistance of their coaches. As they leaned into their socioeconomic and racial status, drawing on family members, lawyers, and media contacts who were not part of the campus community, they unmasked the myth of the campus bubble.

The events that followed spotlighted just how much major donors matter. Due to the decentralization, free-market competition, and intimate ties to private equity and hedge funds in elite higher education,[37] money talks. Likely due to their social status, the partiers felt no obligation to submit to the demands of their peers or the administration; instead, they rallied their allies and stood their ground. They took direct action by involving their parents, contacting lawyers, and alerting the media. As Binder and Wood argued, civilized discourse has become the norm on small campuses due to students' profound investment in their reputation among peers.[38] For students for whom their reputation on campus is their most valuable asset, engaging in respectful dialogue might be a savvy course of action. But for uber-wealthy and well-connected students, those embedded in dense and resource-rich social networks already, off-campus networks matter more. Given the choice between admitting wrongdoing to ameliorate community ties and defending oneself at the expense of campus harmony, high-status students chose themselves over their fellow students.

After the Tequila party, costume parties of this ilk abruptly stopped. Because students on both sides doubled down, the controversy exploded and left a much bigger blast zone than the prior parties. Students, even those mostly removed, now knew the consequences for overstepping if word were to get out and, with the rise of social media, word was almost certain to get out. At the end of that tumultuous semester, the final issue of the *Orient* featured a full centerfold feature on race on campus. There were columns and opinion pieces reflecting on the drama of the party, the impeachment, and the media coverage—most continuing the trend of pressing for greater dialogue across differences. In this spirit, one writer even celebrated the increased vitality of the *Orient* itself, "Since my first year, the *Orient* opinion section has gone from the boring domain of a few white guys (sorry—it's true) to a vibrant space where all kinds of Bowdoin students discuss ideas. I'm proud to have been a part of that, and I know it will continue."[39] While many students came to appreciate the educative power of difficult conversations, this narrative also served to promote the diversity script, norms of civilized diversity discourse, and the ways whiteness was centered by organizational policies and practices.

7

The Aftermath

How does a college recover from the kinds of public and anonymous vitriol spewed in the wake of the Tequila party? After all, the class of 2018 still had two more years left on campus together before graduation. Following Cracksgiving and the Gangster party, racialized organizational structures reproduced white supremacy. Administrators orchestrated educational programming for the partiers (only) that passed as accountability. This charade required students of color to give their time and labor freely, pawns of a system implicitly and explicitly reinforcing the myth that racism's chief harm is hurt feelings. Students on all sides played their parts obediently because most could not afford to alienate themselves from the potential for lifetime dividends embedded in campus networks. The institution remained unchanged, and the parties continued. Yet in the wake of the Tequila party, due to anguish, exhaustion, and entitlement, the drama did not proceed according to script. Individual actors inhabited their roles differently—calling in the conservative media, fabricating articles of impeachment, summoning donors and lawyers, responding with satire instead of servitude. Instead of playing their parts in the established cycle of contrition and inertia, students on both sides summoned weapons of war. By the end of that semester, they had reached a ceasefire, but not a lasting peace.

Over their next two years on campus, the class of 2018 would have to sort out how to deal with this uneasy coexistence. Administrators, for the most part, were quick to move on—after all, parties like this had happened many times before without prompting soul searching or seismic shifts. But for these students, things were different. They were in middle school when Barack Obama was elected president, in high school when Black Lives Matter (BLM) was founded, and walked onto campus for the first time the day after Michael

150   CHAPTER SEVEN

Brown's funeral in Ferguson, Missouri. The series of parties that shaped the first half of their college experience had imparted contradictory lessons—on the one hand that racism is an individual problem we can educate away, on the other hand that when wealth wins, process, context, and justice no longer matter. For young people embedded in a small, elite, residential community, watching the national racial reckoning on their iPads, finding a resolution felt both important and impossible.

How the next two years played out stemmed from myriad factors. National events spurred structural consciousness. Student activism continued. Generational and isomorphic pressures caused the bureaucracy of the college to evolve. But because core organizational structures remained intact and funding streams remained the same, what students learned in their final two years on campus primarily echoed prior lessons about the pros and cons of civilized diversity discourse, in a context where wealth and whiteness always win.

Inching toward Structural Change

When students left campus for the summer of 2016, the controversy surrounding the Tequila party quieted, but the national context surrounding issues of racism and equity continued to churn. That summer, two more high profile police killings of Black men captured the media spotlight. In early July, Alton Sterling was shot and killed after an encounter with two Baton Rouge, Louisiana, police officers, and Philando Castile was shot and killed by a police officer during a traffic stop in Falcon Heights, Minnesota. The BLM movement grew in size and sophistication. In addition, each political party chose its candidate for the 2016 presidential election; the November ballot would feature Donald Trump (Republican) and Hillary Clinton (Democrat). Pressure from all sides to elevate issues of race as they related to each party's visions of justice caused tension and momentum to build.

By the time students returned to campus that fall, some changes were beginning to take shape. The class of 2016 graduated, meaning that several outspoken student activists were not returning to campus, and many students in the class of 2018 were spending all or part of their junior years abroad. In addition, the class of 2020 matriculated. As administrators had promised after the "Meeting in the Union" in 2015, the college sponsored a new required program in first-year orientation about race. But questions arose about how and what to tell incoming students about the now infamous parties of the past year. In the end, administrators and formal programs stayed mum and any transmission of information was left to students. Articles in the *Orient*

THE AFTERMATH   151

captured incoming students' curiosity and confusion, as the unsettled aftermath of the parties continued to be a topic of intense conversation on campus.

When the outside consultants who had visited campus in February 2016
(just days before the Tequila party) issued their report to the president that
summer, it detailed the sense of "fatigue," "trepidation," and "confusion"
shared by many members of the student body, faculty, and staff, particularly
in wake of the parties. In an article in the *Orient*[1] that fall, the new Multicultural Coalition representative to Bowdoin Student Government (BSG)
summarized one key takeaway, "[The report] does not just take the side of
the student of color. It also talks about how there's this divided perception
that white students . . . [feel as if] there's not enough space to talk about these
things and they feel unwelcome, while non-white students feel like there are
so many opportunities, but these white students don't come out." The report
recommended five structural changes: create an office for diversity and inclusion that reports to the president, update the existing Exploring Social Difference curricular requirement to focus on contemporary inequities, increase
support and professional development, implement inclusive excellence in
teaching and advising, and inspire campus-wide engagement in conversations about race. Instead of acting on the recommendations, however, the
president created an internal committee and gave them a year to review the
report and devise their own recommendations.

Throughout that academic year, structural shifts began to trickle down
from the administration. Admissions eliminated the application fee for first-
generation college students and those seeking financial aid. The Dean of
Students' office expanded access to its intensive first-year advising program.
The Office of Residential Life implemented new restrictions on access to off-
campus housing. New gender-neutral bathrooms were created in the student
union and other buildings.

Meanwhile, administrators also continued to promote a performative diversity script. For example, despite student opposition, the college merged
the Women's Resource Center and Resource Center for Gender and Sexual
Diversity. This tracks with other efforts on campus to homogenize nondominant groups—such as the "Center for Multicultural Life"—lumping all
types of diversity together. In another example, the college unveiled a plaque
to commemorate Dr. Martin Luther King Jr.'s visit to campus—a visit that
had taken place more than fifty years earlier and had never been formally
commemorated.

Students continued to work for structural change, albeit with limited authority. BSG grew the Intergroup Dialogue (IGD) program to include more
topics and more students. The Latin American Student Organization (LASO)

and the African American Society (AfAm) cosponsored parties with college houses, hoping to modify the music and diversify those social spaces. After Trump's election, students launched a petition to become a sanctuary campus. The Asian Student Association and the South Asian Student Association collaborated on a photo exhibit in the student union drawing attention to microaggressions, titled "Shit White People Say to POC #ThisIs2016"; the exhibit went viral on social media. Student athletes of color started a new coalition to give support and voice to athletes of color on campus for the first time. And the tradition of lively, respectable dialogue about race, class, and diversity continued in the opinion pages of the *Orient*.

Even so, campus had not transformed into a woke paradise overnight. In what was heralded as a transphobic bias incident, someone pooped in a tampon box (provided through the "Free Flow initiative") in a men's bathroom. Because the act was anonymous, however, there was no public tribunal as in the wake of the prior year's parties. Student activists returned to the script of nondisruptive collective action and cogently worded opinion pieces. While racially charged costume parties seemed to have stopped, other acts making marginalized students feel unwelcome and degraded continued.

By the time the class of 2018 arrived back on campus for their senior year, Trump was in the second half of his first year in office and racialized tensions had continued to grow nationwide. The "Unite the Right" rally that had drawn hundreds of white nationalists to Charlottesville, Virginia to protest plans to remove a Confederate statue in August 2017 had been met with counterprotesters and became one of the largest, most violent gatherings in the US in decades. Sensitive to national trends, Bowdoin announced its decision to move a plaque commemorating graduates who fought for the Confederacy from the lobby of its main auditorium to the archives area of the library. Notably, the plaque had been there since 1965, a time when other schools were implementing affirmative action, but Bowdoin was not yet on board, and one year after Dr. Martin Luther King Jr.'s visit to campus. Unlike in Charlottesville, Bowdoin's decision to move its plaque commemorating Confederate soldiers was not met with significant fanfare or resistance.

The college also inaugurated two significant structural changes that autumn. The committee that had reviewed the external consultants' report from 2016 recommended creating the role of Vice President for Inclusion and Diversity, and the college soon began the hiring process. In addition, the college secured a $5 million donation to develop a new program to support low-income students, first-generation students, and students historically excluded from elite college campuses. These two changes seemed to bring hope that campus might evolve into a more equitable and inclusive space.

THE AFTERMATH   153

Yet, at the same time, the president doubled down on "intellectual fear-lessness,"—this time to a national audience. During the first week of classes, the president published an op-ed in *TIME* magazine, continuing to push the narrative that difficult conversations were the key to unlocking hope for the future. He wrote, "At Bowdoin, we work hard to create an environment where students can be intellectually fearless, where they can consider ideas and mate-rial that challenge their points of view, may run counter to deeply held beliefs, unsettles them or may make them uncomfortable." He continued, "We want our students to understand and celebrate their wonderfully diverse identities, experiences and backgrounds, while also enjoying and appreciating the deep bonds of being a part of our college community. Being part of a strong and di-verse community requires an ability to talk honestly with one another about the real issues. That's why we push our students to develop skills and an abil-ity to engage in thoughtful and respectful ways with those who have varying perspectives, and with whom they may disagree—sometimes profoundly."[2] Readers were urged to celebrate diversity and engage with others, a strategy that had indeed been transformational for a small number of predominantly white students in the wake of each party.

While the president also made similar remarks on campus, the audience for this piece was obviously different. The brand reach of *TIME* magazine in the US tends to be middle-aged readers with a higher-than-average annual household income.[3] This piece was therefore likely intended to reassert the college's marketability to an audience of prospective parents and donors after the prior year's fiery press. That the article included no reference to or plans for structural change that might address institutionalized racism or white ig-norance shows the kinds of messaging the college believed would reassure its donors. Most donors, after all, do not want to disrupt the racialized systems that have enabled their accumulation of wealth. In the context of the sum-mer of 2017, however, the president gambled that his vision of pretending we could all talk about hard things from an even playing field might be a version of racial progress that even conservative donors would support.

Although (or perhaps because) the college continued to inch toward structural change while continuing to promote civilized diversity discourse, a bias incident again shook campus during the first week of classes. Accord-ing to the *Orient*, whiteboards in an academic building "had been defaced with numerous graphic and inappropriate images, including two drawings of male genitalia, a swastika, the letters 'FUKKK,' the names of two individuals, and homophobic language."[4] In a victory for the white-centering logic of the diversity ideology, students responded by returning to the ordained script. Security investigated the incident. BSG organized posters and a banner for

154   CHAPTER SEVEN

the student union to reaffirm Bowdoin's values. While some students lined up to sign the "We Do Not Tolerate Hate" banner, one *Orient* writer urged students to go beyond such "trendy," "lazy" activism.[5] With college leadership pointing students toward "intellectual fearlessness," civilized diversity discourse seemed to have returned to its former glory. Yet for some students, the events of their sophomore year were still unfinished.

Civilized Diversity Discourse, Revisited

Even with the time that had passed, the changes that had taken root on campus, and the other bias incidents, neither the college nor the students involved had made any concrete steps toward a direct resolution of the Tequila party. While many students and administrators were relieved to think the controversy might finally be water under the bridge, a small cadre of students of color sought to rethink their legacy on campus as they prepared for graduation. Lacking the family wealth that would exempt them from adhering to respectability politics on campus, they still hoped that they might be able to orchestrate systemic change by playing along with the norms of civilized diversity discourse.

By the fall of their senior year, the upperclassmen on the sailing team had resolved to be more proactive about the legacy of their Gangster party. Ella (Asian American woman), who was a member of the sailing team but had not attended the party, recalled, "My junior year, the team didn't do anything to address the Gangster party for the underclassmen, so a lot of the underclassmen didn't know very much and that was a concern to me particularly. And I think in reflecting on all the race stuff and as one of the only people of color on the team I was like, 'We need to talk about these things.' This is really important to me. And realizing the institutional memory and that we would be leaving soon and then there would be only one class that remembered it." The impetus for Ella's undertaking is yet another example of students of color feeling pressured to engage in diversity work on campus. She felt strongly the work was important, could see no one else taking it on, and knew the college hoped to soon engage in the kind of institutional "forgetting" that bolsters white ignorance.

Based on his experiences dressing up for the Gangster party and taking to heart the educational programming offered to the team afterward, Scott (white man) partnered with Ella in this mission. According to Scott, "The first week [of the season] we told our coach, 'Listen, we need to cut practice short and have an hour or two to talk about this.' We sat down in a circle, and I explained to everybody what had happened. And we explained what we were doing and then we had an IGD and then we met with [a sociology professor] and . . . there were four or five weeks in a row where every week we had an hour or two to talk about this. And really to show first-years how serious this is to the team." Even though the college had washed their hands of the Gangster party, these students used their seniority to pass on their learning to another cohort of predominantly white students. In contrast to how upperclassmen on the lacrosse team had twisted controversial costumes into a rite of passage for new players, the ethos of the sailing team began to change because this pair of leaders did the work to reeducate their peers and model a new way forward.

Based on the team's fruitful conversations, the seniors were inspired to host a more public event. Seniors on the sailing team began reaching out to friends across campus, floating the idea of a "Gangster party two years later thing." First, they reached out to AfAm; thanks to their IGD process after the party, the seniors of the two groups were now friendly. Because their earlier conversations with the sailing team had been productive and this event seemed like it would give voice to AfAm's ongoing anti-racism work, AfAm leaders were on board. From there, the seniors in AfAm reached out to their friends in BSG. The seniors in BSG were on board but suggested broadening the idea to also include students who had been involved in the Tequila party. They reached out to friends in LASO, who were also excited about the idea. But LASO as a group voted not to participate—not wanting to revisit the controversy. Even so, a few seniors were on board. Through networks of student leaders of color and their close allies, the idea grew to having a few representatives from both "sides" of each party put on a public panel discussion.

The only missing link was to find willing volunteers from among the Tequila party attendees. Because of the way those implicated in the Gangster party apologized and participated in educational programming, the team and AfAm were both amenable to continuing a conversation they had begun two years earlier. But the Tequila party had no comparable resolution. Students had retreated into their separate social circles, seething and hurt. Because their party ended in more of a cease-fire than peace talks, neither side was sure of what might come from revisiting their conflict. Many of the partiers who had been publicly identified did not want to be in the spotlight again. Megan (white woman) turned down the invitation saying, "They asked me to [participate] and I said no. . . . I have been approached by the college a few times to tell my story of the Tequila story. And I felt a little like—I don't mean to use the term 'tokenize' trivially, but there were forty people that attended the party and . . . my name got attached to it." She continued, "I didn't feel comfortable then getting on a stage and talking about things." Most partygoers agreed with Megan, taking advantage of whiteness as a credential that allowed them to simply "opt out."

But finally, one white student who had attended the party stepped up and agreed to participate in the panel. Unlike her friends who opted out to stay within the racial comfort of their tight-knit and homogeneous friend group, this partygoer believed the opportunity for public contrition might finally ingratiate her to a broader network of peers, allowing her to garner the kind of respect that would bring her back into the fold; "It sounded like an amazing opportunity for reconciliation from the Bowdoin community," she recalled. She continued, "I thought that I'd provide a good perspective because I attended the party, wore a sombrero, got the social probation, but I'm also a [social science] major so I kind of understand how the issues work and understand the language of it." Because the partygoers had never been required to participate in any educational programming, most still lacked the language to engage in civilized diversity discourse according to the pervasive campus norms—sounding "smart" was still widely valued. This student, however, credited her coursework with giving her the vocabulary to competently participate in such conversations.

When the event finally came together, the panel included a diverse group. According to one organizer there were, "Two people from the sailing team, two from AfAm, one from LASO, then one person who was at the Tequila party, and then . . . two other white students, one was loosely affiliated with the Tequila party." Because they could not convince any other representatives from LASO or the Tequila party to join, the group had settled for two white athletes who seemed to represent some common ground. Given the time that had passed and the looming end of their tenure on campus, the event was an attempt to heal, offer closure, and set an example for their peers.

Most importantly, the panelists hoped their event would prevent the recurrence of similar parties. In the spirit of civilized diversity discourse and intellectual fearlessness, they envisioned a panel discussion, to model dialogue across differences. Those among them who had benefited from educational programming essentially sought to expand that model; after all that had happened, they still believed that if their peers knew better, they would do better. One panelist explained, "Those issues all happened, but people all went off into their separate corners with their heads down and we never got back together to talk about them." According to another, "We wanted it to be an opportunity to recount what happened, in order to continue the historical knowledge here at Bowdoin, but at the same time show that we're able to sit down and have productive conversations and dialogue. . . . So, we're willing to sit down and have this conversation even if it's late, and hopefully you'll be

THE AFTERMATH   157

willing to have this conversation in the future, too." A third panelist agreed
that one key goal was, "How do we prevent this? Because it sounds like a lot
of the campus—like half the campus—wasn't here at the time of those parties.
And soon it'll be none of the campus. We were trying to set up an institutional
memory for these parties because they did play such a big role in so many
people's college experience." A fourth panelist also affirmed, "We can finally
pass on the knowledge that we have learned from this entire experience from
our first year really, until now. And to show them that these things shouldn't
happen. That we as a community should recognize that this is an institutional
problem that we should fight to not allow, and that we should hold the community responsible together and this should not be just the students of color
handling the situation on their own." The participants, like the president, saw
great hope in the idea of earnestly diving into difficult conversations. But,
beyond that, they believed that talking about the parties openly might create
more collective accountability. Their version of civilized discourse gave equal
voice to all sides, but together their voices took a definitive stand against cultural appropriation, acts of bias, and the ways these costume parties had further marginalized students of color on campus. Even after all they had been
through, the panelists were still hopeful.

    In the months leading up to the panel, that eclectic cadre of panelists re-
alized the elusive promise of conversations across difference. Together they
built trust and engaged honestly. One panelist, a student of color, recalled,
"Once we got all the people we wanted to get on board, we . . . had a really
productive, really powerful, emotional meeting. Just having all those people
in the same room was incredible. I cannot think of another time in my time
at Bowdoin where people representing such different perspectives and ideas
came together out of their own volition, not because of a class or something,
just to talk to each other!" Another student of color agreed, "The first time
we met it was actually really great. I felt like we all opened up and like I had
talked to people that I had never even met before." A third student of color
added, "We had our first couple of brunches where we had our conversations,
and they were really, really important to me. Because I felt like I carried a lot
of negative feelings towards my class still from sophomore year. And I felt
like this was finally a time to reconcile all of that. I didn't know that one of
the people in the room was the person who wore the cornrows. I was in awe
really, of the wide variety of experiences, and I was thinking the whole time,
'I am so excited I am doing this because we can finally pass on the knowledge
that we have learned from this entire experience.'" After nearly four years on
campus, students of color on the panel finally felt validated and listened to.
Some were able to forgive and form new friendships within the group. For

the individuals who chose to be involved, these meetings were healing and transformational.

The white panelists were also excited, but for different reasons. By apologizing and joining their peers of color in the work of educating white students, they felt like they were earning forgiveness and friendship. One white panelist recalled, "I felt like people who had once hated me for being a part of a certain group or attending that party respected me and I felt like I gained a lot of friendships in those seven people." They wanted to escape their notoriety on campus and worked to be seen as "good white people," the kind that were allied with people of color instead of the kind that wore controversial costumes unknowingly.[6] At the micro level, this kind of work is important, too. At least for a moment, these white students began to understand what allyship could look like. Out of shared commitment and respect, the group met every Saturday that winter to plan what they would say and prepare for the panel.

Money Wins: Opting Out, Again

While one Tequila partygoer felt comfortable talking about her role in the party, Megan and others—even two years later—still felt uneasy broaching the topic in public. Leaning into the ways whiteness acted as a credential within the college, allowing her to preserve her own racial comfort, Megan concluded that she should not have to engage with her past mistakes. Because she felt like she could not speak freely on campus, or be above reproach, she would not speak at all—and she would not allow anyone else to speak for her. She falsely projected her discomfort onto all her fellow partiers, saying: "No one wanted to get up from the Tequila party side and speak about things. . . . That just speaks to how much discomfort there is, even as a white person. I feel uncomfortable talking about [the party] sometimes because I feel like I can't say certain things." In short, because of the ways the college, as an organization, was racialized, white students could employ racialized emotions—in this case, fear of exposure—to exert power over campus events.

The same structural forces that made the panel improbable to begin with worked behind the scenes to shut it down. After a short time, other Tequila party attendees pressured their friend to quit. One partier explained, "A good friend of mine agreed to do [the panel] without talking to any of us first. I was bothered by it because I didn't want anyone else sharing our story without talking to us about it. I don't know, [the party] is a weirdly traumatic event to look back on sometimes." She continued, "I asked [my friend] not to do [the panel]. I went back and forth because obviously she had her freedom to

THE AFTERMATH   159

go up and speak on her experiences, but it was something that we were all
so heavily implicated by." Other friends also pressured the panelist to bow
out. White students who were accustomed to the privilege of opting out and
maintaining racial comfort, insisted on preserving that privilege—even to the
point of threatening their "close friends." They exercised individual agency in
ways that directly contradicted the president's calls for "intellectual fearlessness," yet another example of racialized decoupling within the college as an
organization.

Working from a now-familiar playbook, the partiers also called in support from off campus. Parents called administrators to threaten to either pull
their donations or bring in their lawyers. As had happened before, the Dean
of Students subsequently reached out to BSG leaders to warn them the panel
could have dire consequences. The combination of one panelist pulling out
and threats via the dean caused the group spearheading the panel to decide to
cancel. Organizers worried that the panel would end up being more divisive
than reconciliatory, which was not their goal.

The remaining panelists were hurt and angry. For the students of color
involved, the withdrawal and threats from the dean were a stinging reminder
of the ways white wealth and racial privilege had gotten the partiers off the
hook once before. One panelist pushed hard to get the Tequila party at-
tendee to reconsider saying, "[My friends] didn't want to participate either,
but they're going to be supportive of me because this is my voice. We're not
trying to down-talk everybody who was at the event, that is not our goal. I
offered up . . . I'm willing to have a sit-down conversation with every single
one of [your friends] about how this event is going to go." Another panelist
also pushed back, "I felt bad [for her] at first. And then I talked to [another
panelist] who was just mad. He was just like, 'There's literally no reason why
she can't do it! This is an important thing; she knows it's an important thing.
It's killing the whole event!'" The panelists thought they were following the
script. They believed that dialogue could change things on campus. But their
college and their white peers once again reminded them, in the free-market
landscape of elite higher education, money wins.

Meanwhile, the panelist in question hoped to appease both sides. She did
not want to lose her core friend group over the panel, but she also did not
want to lose the respect she had gained from her fellow panelists as a white
person willing to engage in dialogue about her transgressions. That panelist
shared how a few of her friends pressured her:

> They were extremely angry. . . . They thought that it was disrespectful that
> I didn't ask them if I could be on this panel. I really tried to get across that I

160   CHAPTER SEVEN

thought they'd be happy and thankful that I had volunteered to do it, since it's
not something someone technically wants to talk about. But I thought it'd be
interesting to talk about and I felt like I could stand up for people. And they
were like, "What gives you that right?!" . . . They told me that they were deeply
uncomfortable, and they would never think of me in the same light as a friend
if I did it.

While that panelist ultimately pulled out, she also stated, "I definitely reevalu-
ated my friendships," adding, "I'm really upset that . . . people who I thought
were . . . my best friends could be so ignorant and could take something
so personally and not see that the problem is bigger than them. It's actually
an institutional problem." For a white student who felt comfortable with the
rules of opting in, the panelist resented her peers' racialized ignorance. But
ultimately, she too chose to opt out to appease those friends.

Yet she simultaneously sought to maintain the respect of her fellow panelists. To achieve this goal, she met with each of the other panelists individually,
"I talked to each person on the panel, and I was like, 'Look, these people—and
I said their names—told me they're not going to be my friend. It's my senior
year. I'm so sorry but I have to honor that.' That really sucked because I was
really excited for those conversations, and I feel like I earned a lot of respect."
In the end, the dividends that participating in civilized diversity discourse
on a small campus promised actualized for her without even going through
with the panel. As one fellow panelist recognized, "Big kudos to them because
they met with each other panel people individually and was like, 'This is why
I'm dropping but I want to respect what we had.' And so huge props to that.
That was a really hard conversation to have." That panelist felt like she had
gained respect, and she had. While she earned social capital for her willingness to try—Mayorga's diversity as intent[7]—she remained stubbornly blind to
the ways her ability to opt out gave power to her friends' racialized emotions
and bolstered normative whiteness on campus.

Civilized Diversity Discourse, Revisited Again

Despite their devastation from the setback, the remaining panelists returned
to the norm of civilized diversity discourse in the days and weeks that followed. One of them recalled, "I was just so frustrated that weekend because I
had put so much time and energy into wanting to have a conversation. I was
happy something was finally going to happen. So that's when I wrote my *Orient* article. I pretty much outlined all my frustrations. I was just so annoyed.
And I sent it to [another panelist], and I was like, 'I want to do this, but I don't

THE AFTERMATH 161

want any of you guys to be affiliated with this because this is just my own beliefs, but there is no way for me not to drag everybody else in this.' And then all of them were like, 'No, this is actually a really good idea.'" The opinion piece was published in the *Orient* and received positively by fellow panelists. If the conversation could not continue in person, at least it could continue through the student newspaper.

The author felt positive about reclaiming his voice and his power through writing for a public audience. The article spoke about his family and how the Tequila party invalidated his Mexican identity. He wrote about listening to students of color testify in the BSG meeting about their pain and alienation. He wrote, "As one of the coauthors and introducers of the articles of impeachment, I was in the middle of everything: long conversations, tears, arguments, and tensions so evident across campus, you couldn't ignore them—unless you had the privilege to."[8] He continued, "My intention was to keep our student government members accountable for committing the very acts they voted to condemn. Across campus, however, by many white students, I was seen as a mad Latino rather than a BSG leader trying to uphold our community standards." He concluded, "'Tequila' party attendees, you have the luxury to be able to ride out the semester and avoid discourse. If only avoiding marginalization as a person of color was that easy. If only racism and discrimination, for students of color, ended on [graduation day]. Wouldn't that be nice." He turned the spotlight to the ways white students would be able to leave campus controversies behind when they graduated that spring, but students of color would continue to experience individual and institutional racism throughout their lives. Because the *Orient* was written and edited entirely by students, without administrative oversight, the op-ed went to print before the partiers could rally their defenses.

With that opening salvo, other panelists began to write and submit their work. The next week one student wrote about how the panel came to be, and the time the panelists had put into preparing. He wrote, "Our brunches were characterized by vulnerable discussion and genuine compassion, facilitated by two students who were uninvolved with either event. For sure, animosities were resurrected, and pain resurfaced. But more than anything, we found common ground and understanding. In former classmates who I labeled 'racists,' I found friendship. In the eyes of people who had hurt me, I saw anguish and resentment born from sleepless nights of grappling with the pain they had caused others. We were a year and a half late, but we were healing."[9] He continued, telling the story of how the panel came apart, "That made it all the more devastating when some members of our class felt they had to stop us.

They never even gave it a chance. They just broke us." He concluded by saying, "I've given up on this group of students who are so determined to erase themselves from the narrative. We were never interested in shaming them, but the unintended consequence of their action is that everyone will now know that in 2016 and still today, they are the reason why we are not having a roundtable discussion in pursuit of a better tomorrow." While he wrote with the tone of defeat, he definitively pointed out which students were obstructing civilized discourse on campus: those who, by the ways the campus (and US society) was structured, had racialized incentives to opt out.

That same week, one of the leaders of the sailing team wrote with a call to action for her classmates. "Passive complicity in racism is still racism. In fact, passive racism is dangerous because we believe we're doing nothing wrong. It gives the illusion of nonexistence. This passive acceptance and perpetuation of behaviors over time is what defines the culture of a community. It becomes the unnoticed normalization of institutionalized marginalization we thought we knew how to recognize."[10] With those words, the author described how normative whiteness feeds systems of white supremacy, enabling the unmarked whiteness of core organizational structures within the college. She concluded, "I do not claim to be an expert on talking about race, nor do I claim to have formulated answers to all the questions that both you and I have. All I know is that the only way we learn from one another and learn how to have these conversations is by having them—perhaps over brunch." She, too, pointed to structural problems, yet still pushed for dialogue.

In the coming weeks, two more opinion articles authored by would-be panelists were printed. One discussed her experience of the Gangster party and of feeling disrespected and upset during that semester. She talked about coming together in conversation this year with people who had really hurt her two years earlier, saying: "We came together because we believed it was still possible to change how Bowdoin's community understands race and acknowledges incidents of bias."[11] She recognized that Bowdoin had changed over the last two years, but lamented that the panel had been "deliberately stopped by members of the senior class." She shared her hope that future students would take up the mantle and do better. Another wrote about his experience wearing cornrows to the Gangster party, writing: "I laughed when friends showed me the fake chains in their Amazon shopping carts. I patiently sat as a housemate braided my hair, nodding along as my roommate told me stories of braiding his sister's hair the same way when they were growing up. It didn't register with me that as we spoke, I was undergoing a transformation that trivialized his experience and that of so many other Black students."[12] He made a plea to his fellow white students, "Too often, the people responsible

THE AFTERMATH   163

for incidents of racial bias plead ignorance. I was certainly one of them. I never held outwardly racist views, so it felt like the only way to rationalize my participation in a racist event. But in retrospect, I had infinite opportunities for enlightenment. Fueling my ignorance was apathy—a general indifference to an issue that didn't directly affect me. Throughout my life, I had been able to go about my day without confronting racial issues. This was a privilege, and an inherently white one." He wrote in plain language about Mills' conception of white ignorance, that it is not a blameless predicament, but an intentional choice—a choice enabled by the college and by broader societal structures.[13]

During the same period, student researchers who helped collect data for this book published a series of articles in the *Orient* featuring preliminary analysis of our data. Their articles began to lay bare some of the structures that sustained white supremacy on campus. The first article focused on how housing policies and extracurricular structures promoted de facto social segregation, explaining how many students believed social segregation is just natural and others see it as a legacy of the college's history as a historically and predominantly white institution (PWI).[14] The second article addressed the question of why students have so little understanding of race and racism, detailing how the general curricular requirements and the coursework required for most majors fail to address these issues adequately, if at all, and proposing guidelines for a new requirement to help bridge the knowledge gap.[15] The third article addressed the three racially charged parties detailed in this book, citing students' confusion and resentment, as well as structural barriers to productive discussions or resolutions.[16] The final article revealed how students defined diversity and where they saw its role on campus, showing how students—like administrators—largely applauded diversity but failed to acknowledge structural inequities.[17] Based on their writings, the authors were invited to give workshops to faculty and staff on campus that spring.

As their senior spring semester began to wind down, these op-eds and articles spurred more conversations among students. For instance, the *Orient* columnist who had initially explained the Gangster party and then turned to satire in the wake of the Tequila party reprised her column to write about a conversation and reconciliation with one of the students who attended the Tequila party at a local bar on Senior Night.[18] Megan, too, finally began to work to restore dialogue. Instead of continuing to opt out, she began to opt in. Megan recalled, "After the *Orient* articles were published, I had conversations with all of the people that wrote them individually because I feel like the most meaningful headway is made when you just sit with another person and talk things out." She also agreed to a recorded conversation with one of

164 CHAPTER SEVEN

the students who had written the articles of impeachment that was part of a publicly available podcast for another student's class project. After the conversation Megan confessed, "It makes me realize there [are] probably more similarities than differences between all of us, but the differences were what were highlighted our sophomore year. . . . It was a nice form of closure because [they] thought I hated [them], and I thought [they] hated me. . . . I just feel like everything got misrepresented on both sides." Megan came to the realization that dialogue could break down barriers later than some of her white peers, yet perhaps sooner than many others. This resolution—of some students finding peace through difficult conversations—represents perhaps the best of what civilized diversity discourse has to offer. Indeed, changing individual's hearts and minds might be one small step toward racial justice— particularly if it is the paid work of college faculty and staff. But when it falls to students of color to defend their dignity and humanity to ignorant peers, there is also a steep cost.

"Not My Problem": Individualism and the Rejection of Responsibility

As we have seen repeatedly throughout this book, even well intended panels, articles, research projects, and podcasts only reach audiences that choose to engage. They do not single-handedly change attitudes, behaviors, or systems. Systemic change would require powerful people to redistribute resources and give up privileges, not just offer workshops or tinker with advising programs. In this case, a small group of students dedicating a tremendous amount of time and energy to dismantling white ignorance had some poetic ripple effects but did not inspire a significant shift to the racialization of the college as an organization. Offering a case in point, the senior class council decided to host a brunch that spring stemming from this series of articles and invited everyone in the class to come reflect on the events of their sophomore year. According to the would-be panelists, nearly all of whom attended, the conversation was rich, but the crowd was small and mostly "the people you'd expect to be there." Given one last chance to show up, most seniors still chose to opt out. Sustaining a campus environment where most students, and especially white students, can simply opt out of conversations about racism, ignorance, and white privilege is one of the many ways PWIs sustain white supremacy and one of the reasons why racialized costume parties recur.

In short, for most students, other people's controversies were simply not their concerns. On a small residential campus, they saw no reason to engage in a conversation that held no clear benefit to themselves but came with huge reputational risks should it go poorly. Vanessa (white and Hispanic), for example, was livid when she read the articles by the would-be panelists in the *Orient*. Although she helped plan the party, Vanessa claims she was never invited to be part of the panel and felt "very rattled" that others were publicly digging up the past, without talking to her first. Yet she did not heed the article's call to reengage, remembering: "When that article was published in the *Orient* on the two-year anniversary of the party, it was a call out for people [who have] the privilege to leave [the party] in the past and not bring it up again—because 'you don't have to be affected by these issues once you graduate, but we always will.' I was like, 'Excuse you . . . that's not my problem!' I'm sorry. I literally cannot do anything to fix your problem. That is society's shit!" Although Vanessa correctly identified systemic racism as "society's shit," she refused any personal responsibility for addressing those issues or her own actions. Her response swung in the opposite direction from scripts painting racism as an individual problem; Vanessa argued that because racism is a systemic issue, she—as an individual—should be freed from accountability. While Vanessa's remarks veered from the most common student scripts, she similarly shirked responsibility for contrition or reparations.

Simultaneously, however, Vanessa insisted she should have been consulted about the panel, saying, "You're displacing anger right now onto me and that's wrong because . . . you've never contacted me [about joining the panel]." Accustomed to having access to power, Vanessa and her friends wanted to control the narrative. Although the hosts of the party were never publicly identified in the *Orient* or any other media sources, Vanessa insisted she was "not hard to find." But in fact, very few of my respondents knew who had planned the Tequila party—both the random sample comprising 10% of the senior class and the targeted sample of students directly involved with the parties—and if they knew, they were very reticent to say. Just as in the immediate wake of the party, in the aftermath senior year, Vanessa and her friends leaned into their privilege to stay out of the public eye as much as possible. They wanted to control the narrative without having to take the heat of public exposure.

By the time the class of 2018 graduated at the end of May, some members of the class felt as though they had achieved a modicum of closure while others continued to opt out. While many felt hopeful for the college's future, others remained angry about how the last four years had unraveled. One would-be panelist stated, "I wanted the underclassmen to learn from us. And I wanted all underclassmen, not just white underclassmen, to learn. It was just really disappointing. I am glad we found ways to make it happen in some shape or form. But [the panel] still could have been the best event ever to happen at Bowdoin and it was just canceled." Two years after the notorious string of costume parties, the college was inching toward structural change, doubling down on civilized diversity discourse, and preserving the racial comfort of white students. Even the most dedicated student activists still bought into the racialized norms of campus culture, desperately wishing for dialogue rather than disruption.

"Not a Bubble" Revisited:
Isomorphic Change in the Wake of National Upheaval

The two years following the class of 2018's graduation were filled with global upheaval and strife. The college would continue to make progress on issues of race and diversity, but it would take the largest protests in US history—those following the murder of George Floyd by Minneapolis police officers on May 26, 2020—to push the narrative beyond civilized diversity discourse and toward meaningful structural change. As evidenced in the snapshots of its history presented in this book, Bowdoin has not made a habit of responding to pressures from student activists quickly. Structural shifts have come only after the institution knows that change will be supported by those who fill its coffers—major donors and tuition-paying families. Following Floyd's murder and the ensuing protests, the ways wealthy white people talk about race had to shift to mask newly exposed power structures.

In an email to the campus community more than two weeks after Floyd's murder, the president initiated a marked change to campus conversations about race.[19] He admitted that he and the college had come up short: "I have come up well short as an ally, and I need to learn how to be better and how to make a more meaningful difference in the fight against racism and to the aspiration of being anti-racist." He continued, "As for our college, we talk proudly about preparing our students to tackle the most difficult challenges and to lead in solving the world's biggest problems. This is real. We are genuinely successful at this. But, when it comes to racism, we have not lived up to our promise." Having passed up many opportunities to admit to this in prior years, the president's timing provides an example of how higher education, as an institution, is linked with other social institutions. As racialized organizations theory posits, events outside the campus bubble acted as a powerful lever to spur internal organizational shifts.[20]

Finally, instead of urging for "intellectual fearlessness" as he had so many times before, the president committed himself and the college to action: "Deliberate, focused, and persistent commitment and action are required if we expect these outcomes to be different." His plan was lengthy and specific, including requiring and supporting every division of the college "for the education of its members on institutional racism and anti-racism" and "building allyship"; asking the faculty to provide "robust educational opportunities for students to engage across the curriculum with the phenomenon of institutional racism, its persistence, and the inequalities, injustices, and harm that result"; creating "the mechanisms to have greater success in recruiting more Black faculty and staff, and in providing them with the opportunity to thrive and succeed"; creating "the mechanisms to have greater success in recruiting more Black students, and students from other communities of color, and give them the support necessary for success"; and "improving the engagement and understanding" among students, the campus community, and the alumni body with regard to issues of structural racism. The manifesto included a commitment to funding and assessing such work. With this commitment to undertaking and allocating resources toward anti-racism work on campus, the president began the slow process of shifting the racial climate. As Ray argues, racialized organizations legitimate the unequal distribution of resources, shifting how resources are distributed is key to shifting how the organization itself is racialized.[21]

The president concluded his email by underscoring the main finding of this book: "We have been in this place many times before—where we see and participate in a collective cry of outrage over the horrific history and evidence of racial violence in this country, but little actually changes." This time, however, he vowed would be different: "My commitment is to carry out this work and I am accountable for the results." Indeed, in the months and years that followed, many structural changes materialized. Mandatory antibias training, new hiring initiatives, updated curricular requirements, changes to the demographics of admitted students, and other equity measures for students, such as free iPads and laptops for all. Whether any of these changes will shift the normative culture of whiteness on campus remains to be seen, especially given what has not changed—the primacy of financial solvency for every college and the racialization of wealth and power in this country.[22]

8

Conclusion

I began this book by telling the story of the cold February evening when a crowd of undergraduates gathered in a dorm room to drink tequila at a party that was "not *not* a fiesta." Using the series of costume parties that took place on that campus between 2014 and 2016 as a window into racialized organizational processes, this book has shown how students have navigated intersecting pressures from macro-, meso-, and micro-level forces differently over time. Macro-level forces include capitalism, the market orientation of higher education, affirmative action, the anti-PC movement, and the Black Lives Matter (BLM) movement. At the organizational level, structures and systems like admissions, Division III (DIII) varsity athletics, housing, scripts, and civilized diversity discourse matter. At the micro level, social actors inhabit these structures and scripts based on their social position and personal networks. Answering the question of why racialized costume parties persist requires recognizing and interrogating the interplay between structure and agency in the context of these overlapping forces.

Making light of racialized stereotypes as a means of cementing the structural power of whiteness is a long-standing American tradition.[1] Dating back to even before the advent of blackface and minstrel shows and continuing today, dressing up in costumes from other people's cultural traditions has been one way of perpetuating harmful stereotypes that contribute to the ongoing marginalization and oppression of nondominant groups.[2] But as our national conversations about race have begun to shift in recent years, criticisms of this practice have begun to garner more attention.[3] Campuses where similar parties have been happening for generations now suddenly find themselves thrust into the front lines of a culture war.

CONCLUSION 169

In this chapter, I summarize key findings and delve into the implications of this work for scholars and practitioners. This case study explores the ways one elite college promoted the diversity ideology and color-evasive racism through structures and scripts, and how students "inhabited" white normativity by opting out of conversations about race and/or engaging in civilized diversity discourse. In this way, the college produces collective eminence that relies on and reinforces white racial comfort, and ultimately strengthens its own institutional status and solvency. While elite colleges largely serve to facilitate credentialism and social reproduction, this study shows that part of what students are socialized into on campus are contemporary norms for how white elites talk (or avoid talking) about race. Most graduates leave ill-equipped to acknowledge or address racial inequities, and thus continue to sustain and reinvent systematic and institutional structures that maintain and reproduce white supremacy.

Why Racially Themed Costume Parties Persist

Why, then, did racially themed parties persist on small elite campuses? This question has been answered across each of the substantive chapters in this book. First, the parties persisted because they emerged as a product of the normative culture of white supremacy on campus. As discussed in chapter 2, the unmarked whiteness of core organizational structures—in this case admissions, DIII athletics, and housing policies—bolstered white ignorance even while small pockets of committed students learned to recognize and push back against interpersonal and institutionalized racism. Without changes to core organizational structures, the scripts and behaviors of most students remained unchallenged—they continued to espouse the diversity script, believe segregation results from human instinct, and hole up in homogeneous friend groups. In addition, as chapters 3 and 4 highlighted, the parties persisted because the college ignored these racialized structures and instead portrayed racist acts as the failings of individual students. In doing so, administrators promoted civilized diversity discourse and limited educational measures as the solution. These measures were largely executed by students of color, uncompensated for their time and labor, which served to exacerbate inequities on campus. Finally, as chapters 5 and 6 showed, campus is not a bubble. Administrators were beholden to tuition-paying parents and major donors to maintain the status and solvency of the institution. Therefore, when controversies became heated, money won. As we saw in chapter 7, despite their best efforts, students advocating for change made only small and gradual gains until the changing national context finally dictated that the college would need to find new ways of dealing with racialized inequities on campus. Together these findings depict the college as a racialized organization that systematically incentivized white ignorance and sustained white supremacy.

A RACIALIZED INSTITUTION

As this book has shown, elite liberal arts colleges are structurally, culturally, and historically racialized, and Bowdoin has its own racialized structures, culture, and history. As per inhabited institutional theory,[4] structural features of the college—including its history and endowment, admissions practices, and commitment to maintaining a robust DIII athletic program—shaped the context that students "inhabited" when they matriculated. According to sociologist Victor Ray, racialized organizations limit agency of subordinate racial groups and magnify agency among dominant racial groups, legitimate unequal distribution of resources, treat whiteness as a credential, and decouple formal rules from organizational practices in a racialized manner.[5] We see examples of each of these processes in examining the college as a racialized organization.

Admissions. Germinating from the civil rights movement and continuing today, elite and historically white colleges have invested in cultivating "diverse" student bodies as a marker of status.[6] Although the college upheld a commitment to need-blind admissions and curated a racially diverse student body, these priorities were balanced such that the college could remain competitive among peer institutions regarding its "diversity statistics," while white and upper-class students remained the majority on campus.[7] Given that Bowdoin's acceptance rate hovered between 10% and 15% each year of this study, it is safe to assume that its admissions practices were deliberate.

In his 1978 "diversity rationale," Supreme Court Justice Powell argued that the educational benefits of learning alongside people different from oneself justify using race as one factor in selective college admissions. Scholars, however, have contended that expecting students to benefit simply from proximity constitutes "magical thinking."[8] Even as selective colleges have matriculated more students of color and educators unpack the latent potential of intentionally diverse residential communities, studies have shown that elite campuses remain white spaces—where white norms, values, and cultural representations shape the student experience.[9] In agreement with prior research, this study shows that admitting a cohort that is disproportionately white, wealthy, and drawn from private high schools created an indelible blueprint

CONCLUSION

for the norms of social interaction on campus, engendering greater feelings of belonging for students who fit that mold.

Athletics and Housing. That students agreed that the social scene was divided into "athletes, nonathletes, [and] kids in the Outing Club," was also a direct product of the college's history, structures, and funding streams. Because extracurricular activities were the most common foundation for students' closest friendships, structures governing extracurricular participation played a central role in social networking. But, like admissions, they too were rigged to disproportionately advantage white and wealthy students.

For example, the college retained admissions priorities that gave athletic "boosts" to 15% of each incoming class, disproportionately white, wealthy students from highly resourced suburban neighborhoods.[10] And, unlike other extracurricular activities, the college supported varsity athletic teams with large budgets, dedicated facilities, massive collections of gear, and professional staff members. The ways that athletes, in aggregate, differed from nonathletes created social rifts on campus. Athletic teams—due to their intensive practice and competition schedules—tended to not only work out together, but eat together, live together, and party together. Because of how much structured time athletes spent together, teams ended up feeling like impenetrable cliques, both for those on teams and those who were not. In other words, the disproportionate allocation of resources to activities that served primarily white and wealthy students scaffolded de facto segregation. While NARPs ("nonathletic regular people") found friendship through other activities, including racial and ethnic affinity groups, their relative lack of facilities, staff, and funding spotlights how the college, as a racialized organization, legitimated the unequal distribution of resources and magnified agency among dominant racial groups.

During the period of this study, apart from its first-year housing policy, the college did little to disrupt the racial and socioeconomic divisions created and normalized through the extracurricular hierarchy which awarded higher status to cost-intensive pursuits. The disproportionate number of white, wealthy athletes living off campus exacerbated de facto social segregation created by athletic teams and the Outing Club. Off-campus houses tended to become affiliated with an athletic team, inhabited by students who could afford the expense, and "handed down" to members of the team each year.

While some studies have focused on the ways diversity-related programming impacts racial equity on campuses, my data suggest that more mundane structures must also been seen as central to diversity-related initiatives. The unmarked whiteness of core organizational structures—in this case selective admissions, DIII athletics, and housing policies—shaped dominant norms by granting increased power and agency to wealthy and white students, and particularly recruited athletes. Together these systems bolstered white supremacy and white ignorance on campus.

Scripts. The data presented in this book demonstrate how these structures promoted scripts for talking about race that simultaneously emphasized civilized discourse, diversity ideology, and the naturalization of segregation on campus. The diversity script performed as civilized diversity discourse dominated campus norms, as similarly noted in studies of other elite campuses.[11] Another script, the naturalization script—building on Bonilla-Silva's conceptualization of colorblindness[12]—aligned with students' tendency to explain the formation of homogeneous friend groups as "comfortable" and "natural," rather than as the product of social structures on and off campus. To maintain civilized discourse in this context where students asserted the value of broad acceptance, defended the virtue of good intentions, and participated in the commodification of students of color, students often engaged in conversations within homogeneous groups or "opted out" of conversations about race altogether. Students claimed to want to avoid "hurting anyone's feelings," but at the same time enacted multiple tenets of colorblind racism—minimization ("opting out"), abstract liberalism (meritocratic rhetoric), and naturalization of segregation.[13] In doing so, students used these scripts to preserve their respectability and racial comfort, and thus potential access to their resource-rich peer cohort and college alumni networks.[14]

Considering the pervasive naturalization of social segregation on campus, the diversity script emerged as a product of the elite status of the institution and the contemporary expectation for elites to project cultural omnivorousness.[15] Yet, for the most part, students' behaviors did not align with this script. The diversity script promoted colorblind inclusivity and integration of all identities, without acknowledging structural inequities and institutionalized racism. Many white students only talked about race when it was safe and favorable to them (i.e., in the classroom or IGD [Intergroup Dialogue]) and, as a result, some students of color felt like they existed on campus only to benefit the omnivorous consumption of their white peers.[16] Students of low socioeconomic status and students of color were told repeatedly that they were included equally at Bowdoin but were less likely to actually feel like they belonged than their white and affluent peers.

As evidenced by their prevalence in prior studies, these scripts are not unique to one college. The fact that similar scripts pervade many elite campuses, and wider swaths of contemporary US society,[17] suggests social actors on elite campuses are not acting in a vacuum. Rather—as neo-institutional theory would suggest—elite campuses are responding to macro-level pres-

CONCLUSION   173

sures to reproduce contemporary, white, elite norms for talking about race
and diversity via organizational processes.[18] Rivera's work has shown how
elite undergraduates use extracurricular activities generally, and sports in
particular, to match with elite employers[19]—an example of how the practices
and scripts prioritized at Bowdoin are not necessarily a product of this college
in particular, but rather contemporary norms for the white elite more broadly.
In reality, the college would not likely see itself as benefiting from teaching
undergraduates new or divergent ways of talking about race. Instead, the college benefits from maintaining systems, practices, and scripts that socialize
students into the contemporary norms of the elite employers and upper-class
patrons who bolster the college's solvency and reputation.

TREATING RACISM AS AN INDIVIDUAL PROBLEM

Racially themed costume parties also persisted in part because the college
treated racism as an individual action, rather than as a structural problem.
The deans alternately punished or sought to educate individual offenders or,
in the case of the Gangster party, the easily identifiable team that hosted the
party. They did not seek to educate the rest of the student body and, at best,
dragged their feet on addressing the structures that enabled white ignorance.
In doing so, they treated the parties as a product of the ignorance of a small
group of partiers rather than the product of a broader culture of white supremacy. Doing so, in the words of scholar Sara Ahmed, "underestimates the
scope and scale of racism, thus leaving us without an account of how racism
gets reproduced."[20] Confronting unmarked whiteness would force students
to recognize that institutionalized racism operated within the admissions
and athletic recruiting systems; dismantling the myth of meritocracy would
threaten one foundation of white supremacy.

When administrators responded to transgressions by educating only the offending students, they reinforced false notions that racism is only the product
of individual actions. By calling out students wearing costumes that perpetuated derogatory stereotypes, administrators clearly signaled that *this* kind of
racism was problematic; such messaging simultaneously implied that all other
kinds of racism were, therefore, acceptable. Then, rather than assuming the
onus, administrators furthered racialized inequities by leaning on the unpaid
labor of students of color to educate their white peers. This kind of work to de-
marcate and limit the definition of racism to only overt acts kept attention away
from structural racism and the unmarked whiteness of the college.

In these ways, treating racism as an individual problem unambiguously
bolstered white ignorance. Arguing that ignorance, like knowledge, is a social

product grounded in both explicit and tacit practices, sociologist Jennifer Mueller's work shows how racial ignorance works as a core process that helps "maintain white supremacy by allowing white people to experience their inequitable and unjust power, status, and wealth as legitimate."[21] Dominant groups hold a rational investment in not understanding racism and racial domination; the "possessive investment in whiteness" creates real material and psychic benefits.[22] All major US institutions have been formed as white institutions, and structured to normalize white interests as common interests. As a result, as philosopher Charles Mills argued, white people act ignorantly because they can trust that societal institutions will approve of their racialized not-knowing.[23] Because white administrators empathized with partygoers' lack of *intent* to harm, the *impact* of their actions was not fully addressed.[24] Even while the debate grew heated, the coercive power of campus culture became clear: The two options—educate or punish—were both grounded in the portrayal of racism as an individual act.

RELYING ON CIVILIZED DIVERSITY DISCOURSE

Prior studies have argued that because small, elite campuses engender a strong sense of community and lack of anonymity, activism most often takes the form of deliberation and dialogue, what Binder and Wood dubbed "civilized discourse."[25] Applying this notion to conversations about race, this study develops the concept of "civilized diversity discourse."[26] By placing all students' experiences on a level playing field and centering individuals' feelings, rather than structural inequities and oppression, civilized diversity discourse maintains racialized organizational processes that benefit white people and institutions. While the diversity and naturalization scripts characterized what students said when asked how diversity matters for campus life, civilized diversity discourse describes the rules of engagement for talking about race and other kinds of diversity on campus.

On the surface, civilized diversity discourse has pros and cons. The stated purpose is to educate students; as one of the deans posited, if racism is a product of ignorance, education is the solution. In fact, my interviews suggest that some white students did become more racially aware from participating in civilized diversity discourse. Thoughtful communication about difficult topics is a valuable life skill. When it works well, some students gain from this upside. However, this benefit impacted only a small number of students and came at a steep cost to many students of color.[27] A tireless cadre of students of color gave testimony at Bowdoin Student Government (BSG) meetings, participated in IGD sessions, met with administrators, and organized

CONCLUSION   175

programming to educate their peers. In large part, administrators relinquished their educational roles and relied on students of color to do the work of educating white students. When students of color are, at best, uncompensated, and, more often, penalized for their labor, "conversations across differences" serve to exacerbate inequities. These educational ventures extract time, labor, and creative capital, while serving as painful reminders of the symbolic and emotional violence inflicted upon students of color by their institution and their peers.

In addition, relying exclusively on this discourse masked the need for structural change. Administrators often elided the power-infused issue of racism by calling it "difference" or "multiculturalism" and encouraged students to "communicate across differences" rather than recognizing and trying to redress long-standing systematic power imbalances that make race unlike less power-infused differences. Most civilized diversity discourse reinforced the notion that the main problem with cultural appropriation and racism was that they hurt people's feelings. While this is certainly one impact, focusing on hurt feelings reinforces white ignorance by erasing the structural impacts of white supremacy. Racism is about more than hurt feelings, and conversations about differences that ignore the role of power and oppression rarely serve to disrupt systems of exploitation.

A larger body of research documents how white Americans strive to avoid being perceived as racist, primarily for moral reasons.[28] We see these efforts, for example, in the statements made by BSG. In the case of elite liberal arts colleges, however, because students stand to earn individual dividends—on campus and postgraduation—from preserving their reputations, the incentives are not only moral, but also social and economic. All students—but especially those who were not already embedded in resource-rich networks—strived to maintain respectability when discussing "sensitive topics" like race to avoid being excluded from resource-rich alumni networks.

This study shows how, at small elite schools, collective eminence is maintained through preserving racial comfort by "opting out" or employing civilized diversity discourse when "opting in" to conversations about race. By sustaining an organizational context wherein many students—and particularly white students—could easily "opt out" of race talk, the college enabled white ignorance and reinscribed its campus as a white space. Opting out erases all possibility of misspeaking and risking one's reputation, while opting in requires conscious and careful thought to avoid "hurting anyone's feelings." Students who opted into conversations about race noted that they were prudent to avoid offending anyone and being labeled as racist. Yet the persistence of racist words, acts, and structures on campus (as evidenced repeatedly in interviews with students of color) underscores that most students valued maintaining their reputation more than the opportunity to "learn from diversity." In the end, students' behaviors demonstrated that the preservation of collective eminence via the existing racial order proved more compelling than enacting the promise of the diversity script.

CAMPUS IS NOT A BUBBLE

Students often talked about campus as a "bubble," removed from the outside world. In some ways this was true; students would eat, sleep, work, study, and play, all without leaving the grounds. This all-inclusive residential model encouraged students to invest in the kinds of relationships and traditions that would cultivate a robust alumni network and promote broad ignorance to the ways the college was embedded within and dependent upon other social institutions. But even though liberal arts colleges were founded in idyllic rural hamlets to ward off the corrupting influences of urbanization, no campus is a world unto itself.

Students arrived with preconceived notions of race, status, and merit.[29] White students brought with them various racialized privileges and practices characteristic of US society. They also maintained access to whatever resources and liabilities might be embedded in their existing social networks. To those outside "the bubble," the controversies surrounding the parties seemed trivial and passing. When the going got tough on campus, however, privileged students drew economic, social, and cultural capital from their networks,[30] reaching out to friends and relatives, who exerted their power in ways that upheld white dominance.

In addition, media platforms played a role in how the aftermath of each party played out. In the case of the Gangster party, Black students confronted the sailing team in person in the dining hall, but word of their encounter spread through campus via apps like Instagram and Yik Yak. In the case of the Tequila party, no outsiders were privy to the party itself or the costumes, and word spread exclusively via photos posted online. In an earlier generation, this kind of party would have remained in the "backstage"[31] discourse of white and white-presenting students—as the Cracksgiving party had for many years. But by 2016, social media was instrumental to campus life. Many students could not conceive of attending an epic party without posting evidence on their socials. The anonymity of Yik Yak provided a platform for the kinds of hateful vitriol that violated campus norms of civilized diversity discourse; there students could express overt racism without risking access to social capital on and off campus.

CONCLUSION   177

Furthermore, taking a page from the broader anti-PC campaign rampant at the time, white students unironically used outsized media platforms to claim they were being silenced. Intentionally bringing in outside media sources not only violated the norms of civilized diversity discourse, but also allowed the partiers to evade accountability—all while escalating the scope and scale of the controversy. Activating the conservative national media successfully spread word of the controversy beyond campus to an audience that held particular sway with college administrators. In this way, racialization within the college as an organization was reinforced not only by macro-level social forces and internal shifts (as theorized by sociologist Victor Ray[32]) but also via social networks linking organizational actors—in this case between students and donors.

MONEY TALKS

Because the American system of higher education is largely privately funded—through donations that serve as tax write-offs for the wealthy—and the broader political and economic machine feeds on racialized exploitation, a college's legitimacy and survival depends chiefly on the largess of donors who have benefited from racialized capitalism.[33] Small colleges therefore have powerful disincentives to engage in interventions that might alienate major donors. Their survival depends on the broader US system of racial and economic injustice that privileges wealthy white people—not only their money, but also their approval (because graduates' success depends, in part, on wealthy white employers).[34] Thus, when the right donor parents and alumni fought back against punishments, the administration sided with them and against student activists. After all, costumes that play on derogatory stereotypes may be harmful, but they do not violate any laws. Because elite colleges are dependent on wealthy donors, white wealth has the power to tip the scales of justice in its favor. Just as the unmarked whiteness of core organizational structures conveyed advantages to white students, so too did the market dependency of higher education more broadly.

In the case of Cracksgiving and the Gangster party, the structures surrounding DIII athletics created white spaces that nurtured white ignorance. Those structures sustained generations of exclusion, but they also nurtured team cohesion. And when it came time for administrators to respond to those parties, they took advantage of preexisting hierarchies within each team. Cracksgiving and the Gangster party were handled within the campus bubble largely because administrators treated racism as an individual act and the students involved, squeezed by the cultish enticements of their DIII teams, abided by established norms for white ignorance and civilized diversity discourse. The structures of DIII athletics gave the college leverage to produce an outcome that would satisfy the needs of all consequential parties—just enough reprimand to appear concerned, not enough disruption to inflame most donors and tuition-paying families.

But in the case of the Tequila party, the implicated students were not incentivized by athletic consequences, and therefore acted as free agents striving to maintain their race and class privilege. Doing so, they drew from a familiar playbook that included activating their own racialized emotions as well as friends, relatives, and the anti-PC foot soldiers of the national media. Students pointedly learned the power of extreme wealth to work covertly and supersede stated rules. Perhaps unsurprisingly, administrators soon buckled under the pressure from parents and donors. Despite the fanciful depiction of the college as a "bubble" removed from the outside world, wealthy parents and donors exercised leverage that protected the partiers—not from the spectacle of impeachment or media coverage, but from any lasting material consequences. In this way, influences from outside the bubble prompted decoupling of rules and practices in a racialized manner, while also enabling increased agency for privileged students.

Even the most affluent students, however, did not want to let it be known that they were calling in outside reinforcements. As Khan argued in his ethnography of an elite boarding school, while the children of wealthy families once openly leveraged their upper-class connections and entitlements, contemporary elite norms dictate that even the wealthiest of students should strive to appear as though they earned their privilege in a class-neutral meritocratic system.[35] The ways the highly selective admissions process continues to privilege wealthy applicants while masking the ways that privilege matters plays heavily into this charade.[36] Elite colleges thus provide the credentials that facilitate social reproduction while helping maintain the myth of meritocracy. Because wealth still conveys coveted power but flaunting one's wealth in mixed company violates the elite code of conduct, students seeking to escape reprimand tried not to call attention to their methods. Owing to white ignorance, many of those students claimed not to understand how and why pressure from their families and professional contacts amounted to an exercise of racialized power.

By failing to address the ignorance and bias of white and otherwise privileged students, the college reinforced the "us versus them" mentality that exhausted and alienated marginalized students. Student activists were tired and angry from volunteering their labor and seeing little payout. Having their efforts squashed by wealthy outside actors gutted student activists, while

CONCLUSION 179

exposing them to harsh treatment on campus. Students of color felt more pressured to "opt in" to conversations about race due to the ways the diversity script presented them as resources for their white peers to consume. This sudden pressure to educate their white peers felt affirming to some but alienating to others. In the wake of disruptions to civilized diversity discourse, the administration worked to reinforce its tacit commitment to channeling the rage and hurt felt by students of color into nondisruptive forms of activism and conversation. These actions spotlighted the institution's underlying "plantation politics"[37] through its desire to display and tokenize non-white students in the name of diversity, but not undertake structural changes.

The college had meaningful incentives to perpetuate this cycle. Because it is essentially at the mercy of consumer demands, it must maintain its legitimacy within its cohort of peer schools. In recent decades, this has meant adding racial diversity to its student body. However, it must simultaneously maintain its legitimacy in the eyes of wealthy donors. In Bowdoin's case, those donors are often white men, and historically conservative. Even while the college has admitted more students of color, it has maintained the systems and policies that please its benefactors—the admission of a disproportionately large number students from private schools and the upper sliver of the wealth spectrum, the robust DIII athletics program, options for housing that facilitate the agency of athletes and the segregation of peer groups, and diversity programming that does not disrupt the status quo. The college is invested in sustaining the racial ignorance of its students because it produces new cohorts of alumni that will succeed in the same elite circles as current benefactors and continue—through philanthropic homophily—to support the college.[38]

What Students Learned

So, what do undergraduates on a small, white, elite campus learn from racially charged costume parties? They learned what they were taught. A small number of perpetrators and motivated bystanders soaked up educational interventions and changed their ways. This learning came at a direct cost to the students of color drafted to educate their peers. Students of color coerced into educating their peers learned that the college would protect its own interests over theirs, regardless of how selflessly they gave of their time, labor, and intellect. Meanwhile, campus structures and practices encouraged most other students to maintain the status quo.

Because of the ways the implicated students reacted differently to being called out for their actions, we can see how social actors maintain some agency in how they inhabit racialized organizational scripts, norms, and policies. The students involved in the Tequila party, in part because they were not structurally situated within the same varsity team, made different choices than the sailing and lacrosse teams. They did not cop to the same heartfelt revelations that Ben and Trevor felt after their session with Native American students in the wake of Cracksgiving or that Scott and Nora experienced from participating in dialogues with AfAm after the Gangster party. Those students accepted their consequences and played along with civilized diversity discourse, allowing the campus to quickly return to equilibrium while a small legion of student activists continued to agitate for structural change. But these partygoers weaponized their privilege and fought back. They did not learn the lesson about individualized acts of racism that the administration had worked so hard to promote—that when privileged people overstep, they can quietly maintain their institutional power by acting contrite, making efforts to learn, and evangelizing civilized diversity discourse. Instead, these students (and their families) imposed on everyone the lesson that wealth always wins.

What students learned from this series of parties varied somewhat based on their race and class backgrounds. Granovetter[39] wrote about the "strength of weak ties," meaning that for most people infrequent, arms-length relationships—known as weak ties—are more beneficial for employment opportunities, promotions, and wages than strong ties—like family or close friends. This theory explains why most undergraduates on small, elite campuses work so hard to maintain a respectable reputation; the "collective eminence"[40] of the alumni network that acts as a hub for these invaluable weak ties. But elites do not need weak ties to improve their positions—they are already at the top.[41] Instead, they cultivate dense, robust networks to prevent their wealth and status from getting watered down.[42] From her experience with the Tequila party, for example, Vanessa learned exactly why. Vanessa had, up until that point, been protected by her family's wealth and connections. Instead of learning how white people defend their privilege through the diversity script, she learned how rich people defend their privilege via insular ties.

Meanwhile, most students were indoctrinated by how the college responded to each party. They learned to recite the "white-centering" script of the diversity ideology—that all kinds of diversity matter (even those that have never been tied to systemic oppression or privilege), that diversity is vital (but only to the extent that it benefits white and wealthy students), and that the benign intent of the partiers matters more than the harmful impact of their actions. Because campus structures provided the scaffolding for the naturalization of de facto social segregation, however, students also recited

CONCLUSION   181

colorblind scripts and remained ensconced in homogeneous peer groups. Students were incentivized to engage in "civilized diversity discourse," when talking about race or diversity, and went to great lengths to avoid hurting anyone's feelings. Most students, including students of color, complied with this hegemonic norm because, in this small, elite setting, students believed that their reputation on campus would matter for their postgraduation prospects. Thus, students learned to talk about race to the extent that they could without disrupting white racial comfort, or they learned to not talk about it at all in mixed company.

Racialized Organizations, Inhabited Institutions, and Higher Education

Sociologist Randall Collins argued that the struggle between groups within a society is fought both over organizations and through organizations.[43] Such is the case in the battle for racial justice in the US, being fought over and through many types of organizations, but particularly colleges and universities. This study adopts an inhabited institutional theory lens to spotlight how social actors bridge local meanings and institutional structures, underlining the meso-level role that organizations play.[44] In the experiential core of campus life, administrators and students must interpret—and perhaps adapt or resist—what we are expected to say and do each day. Indeed, in this book we have seen that students, administrators, and parents made different choices in the case of each party, exercising agency amid structural constraints to varying outcomes.

Racialized organizations theory reminds us that the ways institutions become inhabited are never race neutral and this case study provides evidence of that claim. While prior studies have shown that institutional size and status shape campus interactions, colleges are also racialized organizations. Research on large universities has begun to investigate how institutional structures support a divergence of discourse and behaviors. In a case study of a public flagship university, sociologist James Thomas described how a "diversity regime"—a set of meanings and practices that institutionalize a benign commitment to diversity but prohibit meaningful change to the ways power, resources, and opportunities are distributed—obscures, entrenches, and intensifies existing racial inequalities on campus.[45] Through the lens of neoliberal conceptualizations of diversity, individuals and organizations are no longer pretending to exist in a post-racial society (i.e., color-evasiveness), rather race is strategically highlighted and consumed in ways that benefit white people and white institutions.[46] At Thomas's "Diversity University," however, the work was intentionally diffuse. During the period of this study, at Bowdoin, in fact, the opposite was true. Diversity work was concentrated in the division of Student Life—under resourced, yet still marketed and commodified for the benefit of white people and institutions.

The experiential core of these small elite campuses shapes the scripts and behaviors of the next generations of America's power brokers.[47] Incoming students tend to choose elite liberal arts colleges, not for the vocational value of the degree, but for the freedom it gives them to pursue a wide variety of vocations and the social networks that accompany the credential. Unlike at larger schools, where students can be more anonymous, or less elite schools, where students receive career-specific training, students (and parents) choose small liberal arts colleges not for the concrete skills but specifically so that they will be *known* on campus. Students are invested in the welfare of the institution and of their peers because those social networks matter for upward social mobility postgraduation. But the pressures to be known somewhat exacerbate the pressures to conform. Even though the media has characterized higher education as a liberal bastion and Gen Z as a woke generation, small, elite colleges continue to incentivize adherence to elite, white norms because of the coercive power of these social networks.[48]

This study spotlights what students at elite schools are really learning about race in the contemporary era. Contrary to the media narrative, students are not learning to tear down the establishment, but rather to work within it. They are not learning about anti-racism, but instead about the diversity ideology and color-evasiveness. They are not learning about reallocating resources or disrupting racial hierarchies. Instead, they are learning how to rise within the systems that already exist. As a result, they often unknowingly walk the line between performative outrage that reifies the individual nature of racist acts, and quietly sustaining racialized organizational structures and policies that cater to white racial comfort.

Building on racialized organizations theory, this book explores how the unmarked whiteness of core organizational structures aids in the production of white ignorance, even—or perhaps especially—in moments of racialized contestation. We have seen many examples of each of the four tenets of racialized organizations theory in action. The college shaped students' agency, both in how white normativity differentially impacted sense of belonging on campus, and in how resources were disproportionately allocated, as in the case of extracurricular activities that served predominantly white and wealthy students (i.e., athletics and the Outing Club). In moments of racialized controversy, whiteness acted as a credential and formal rules were decoupled from practices in ways that advantaged white students and their

CONCLUSION

families, for example the case of the Tequila partygoers' disappearing consequences. As Ray argued, these racialized processes were maintained and contested by internal and external forces, such as changes to hiring practices and diversity training in response to the national BLM movement. But this case study also showcases other ways that racialized organizational processes become contested and reinforced. For example, links between social institutions can play a role—as was the case when the national media weighed in on the aftermath of the Tequila party—as can parallel social networks—such as the links between students and donors. For colleges, then, changes to the racialization of organizational norms and processes must be considered in the context of their webs of interdependencies.

By design, this case study is limited in its generalizability, and future research should investigate how institutional histories, structures, and geographies differently shape undergraduates' race-related scripts and behaviors. This study is also limited by the cross-sectional design of the interviews and surveys, and future research should longitudinally examine how undergraduates' racial scripts and behaviors change during college to parse out whether institutional contexts are amplifying existing scripts or reshaping them. Because graduates of elite colleges and universities wield disproportionate economic and cultural influence in US society,[49] better understanding how these institutions shape students' conceptions of race and racism over time will provide a critical window into pathways for social change.

Why Do Costume Parties Matter?

Events of the last decade have pushed issues of institutionalized racism into the foreground of nearly every arena of life in the US, from the police to the playground to the Oscars. Because of our centuries-long history of racialized oppression, we can find evidence of racial inequity everywhere we look—housing, the labor market, the justice system, and the list goes on. If we are to take steps toward crafting a more just and equitable society, we must have leaders who understand racism as both an individual and structural phenomenon and work to undo racialized social systems. Elite college students flaunting their white ignorance by dressing up in costumes that demean marginalized people and reinforce derogatory stereotypes is harmful. If the point of these parties is, as students largely claim, to dress up and get drunk, there should be plenty of other ways to achieve those goals without perpetuating symbolic and emotional violence.

But this book is not only about the harm caused by insensitive costumes and alcohol; in the retelling of the kerfuffle surrounding these parties we gain new insights into how white people and organizations maintain racialized power structures even in the face of public contestation. At this moment in American history, when cries to recognize and remediate racial injustices were louder than they had been in nearly half a century, addressing the relatively trivial question of costume parties is not the answer to centuries of oppression, exploitation, and exclusion. What we learn from this case study at the intersections of national political forces, organizational structures and scripts, and individual agency, however, is the myriad ways that white ignorance and white dominance get perpetuated within social institutions. Changing those institutions—both how they allocate agency and resources and how they train future leaders to think, talk, and act—arguably is part of the solution.

To those invested in maintaining white supremacy through institutions like elite colleges that serve a critical role in the cycle of social reproduction, taking a stand over tiny sombreros strategically diverts attention away from structural change. Tiny hats keep people on all sides of the argument fired up over something relatively small and symbolic, while Black men are dying in the streets and incarcerated at alarming rates. Tiny hats let administrators put on the performance of caring about students of color and about serious conversations, without doing anything to disrupt institutionalized oppression. If they label this an act of bias and educate the bad apples, they spare themselves the deep interrogation of the myriad ways elite institutions exploit and exclude. Just as people love to root for their favorite college sports teams, the media has rallied the public to reinforce white dominance and white ignorance as they decry these ridiculous woke campuses and mock already marginalized students. If we agree that tiny hats are the only problem, we do not have to talk about the ways that core organizational structures also matter. Participating in this charade allows the systems that perpetuate and incentivize white racial comfort and racial ignorance to continue. As racial scripts and norms change,[50] it is through these micro- and meso-level actions that whiteness stays on top.

What Is to Be Done?

The puzzle of how to advance racial justice in a system built largely on stolen lands and flourishing thanks to systems of slavery, exploitation, and oppression is complex. Because elite colleges depend on major donors, the puzzle will only be solved when wealthy white people agree to fund institutions that work to disrupt systems that have, until now, facilitated and legitimized intergenerational transmissions of wealth.[51] If we design elite colleges to disrupt

CONCLUSION

cycles of social reproduction and systemic racism, major donors would be funding systems that would advance a more equitable society, at the expense of their own interests.

At the most extreme, one solution is to simply get rid of elite colleges. Give the land back to Indigenous nations and abandon the uppermost tiers of the American higher education hierarchy. There are many less prestigious schools that are being more successful at leveling the playing field. Let us, as a society, invest in those models instead.

More realistically, if we are to tinker within the existing system, the data in this book remind us that changes in higher education are ultimately linked to the changing tides of our society. Public opinion and political will matter, and as a result isomorphism also matters. In other words, institutions must keep up with peer schools and together they must keep up with changing times. But within the context of each institution, localized leadership also matters.[52] Just look at the list of changes Bowdoin's president rolled out in the weeks following the murder of George Floyd in 2020. In the present era, we see that some elite institutions have diversified their student bodies, faculty, and allocation of resources earlier and more quickly than others. Boards, presidents, deans, and other administrators have a significant role to play in recognizing and decentering whiteness on the campuses of historically and predominantly white institution (PWIs).

Within each college, these leaders must take seriously the tenets of racialized organizations theory as they consider organizational change. Racialized organizations theory posits that organizations limit agency of subordinate racial groups and magnify agency among dominant racial groups, legitimate unequal distribution of resources, treat whiteness as a credential, and decouple formal rules from organizational practices in a racialized manner.[53] Unequal resource allocation, for example, is one place to begin. In the case of Bowdoin, the allocations of budget, staff, space, and other resources to varsity athletics likely dwarf the spending on staff, space, and resources allotted to affinity groups and other supports for students of color, low-income students, and first-generation students. How would the campus experience change if there were as many staff positions dedicated to supporting students from historically excluded groups as there were coaches and athletic trainers? Further, what would it look like to eliminate not only the legacy "boost" in admissions (as some peer schools have started to do) but also the athletic factor "slots"? Admissions, for example, could become more closely representative of the college-aged population, or work toward reparations for centuries of racialized exclusion. We could extend this line of argument to campus housing policies as well, to consider how whiteness acts as a credential in certain spaces, which students have more agency, and how resources are differentially allocated.[54]

These changes must take place within the constraints of the marketplace of US higher education that is disproportionately dependent on financiers.[55] Because of the ways white wealthy people work to maintain their advantages and wield their donations as leverage, many of the changes that would bring more equity on campus have the potential to jeopardize fundraising efforts and thereby lessen institutional prestige. Getting rid of athletic slots in admissions may impact teams' win records, and some research suggests that teams are important for fundraising.[56] Getting rid of legacy admissions preferences may also hurt fundraising.[57] To decenter whiteness, colleges must either change their sources of revenue, relinquish some of their prestige, or convince donors to buy into a way of thinking about equity on campus that disrupts the centuries-old practice of privileging white students—in access, in agency and in resources. The underlying capitalistic market logic makes this difficult.

Perhaps colleges could begin by convincing donors that reallocating resources on campus works in their favor. Much research has shown that more diverse teams make better decisions, and diversity is good for business.[58] Since today's students are largely tomorrow's donors, changing the way we educate students today could have a domino effect that the donors of tomorrow will be more likely to support initiatives that achieve greater equity. But changing the way elite colleges educate students about race cannot just arrive in the form of "conversations across difference," it must also be modeled in the everyday work of core organizational structures. Otherwise racially themed costume parties and other symptoms of white supremacy will continue to recur.

Acknowledgments

I am grateful to the students who agreed to be interviewed for this project, generously sharing their time, experiences, and candor. I am also grateful to all the students who have written articles and opinion pieces for the *Orient*, creating a record of your time on campus. Together, your words have inspired generative controversies, giving us the opportunity to grapple with meaningful questions about the kind of future we might build together.

I am also deeply grateful to the undergraduate researchers who helped get this adventure off the ground in fall 2017: Sydney Avitia-Jacques, Hannah Berman, Julia Conley, Sophie Cowen, Diana Furukawa, Hannah Graham, Zachary Hebert, Holly Hornbeck, Stephanie Intal, Joyce Kim, Parker Lemal-Brown, Bettina Mariano, Sophie Sadovnikoff, Kendall Schutzer, Juliana Villa, and Kayli Weiss. The energy, curiosity, and talent you poured into your work revising the interview protocol, contacting respondents, conducting and transcribing interviews, and engaging in the first stages of data analysis breathed life into this project and laid the groundwork for authentic connections between scholarly questions and the joy, grief, chaos, and confusion of the student experience. Your thinking is embedded in every aspect of this project, and I could not have done this without each of you. I also want to thank Pamela Zabala for early inspiration; working with Pamela on her undergraduate thesis introduced me to many unanswered questions about the parties and to the *Orient* archives.

A special shout out to Sophie Cowen and Sydney Avitia-Jacques for leading the team of student researchers who coalesced early findings into articles for the *Orient*, including coauthors Hannah Berman, Zach Hebert, Joyce Kim, and Kayli Weiss. Your voices brought sociological research to the campus community, and I am so proud of your conviction, creativity, and collaboration.

I am also indebted to my undergraduate research team from the summer of 2018: Beatrice Cabrera, Hannah Graham, and Natalie Rudin. In cleaning and coding the data, you completed some of the most tedious labor on this project, yet you showed impeccable commitment, intellectual engagement, and good humor. It was truly a pleasure to get to work so closely with each of you. In addition, I want to thank Hannah Graham and Natalie Rudin for being ambitious and diligent coauthors as we developed the analytical argument that provided the framework for chapter 2. I am also grateful for research assistance from Praise Hall and Marcus Williams.

This research came to fruition thanks to invaluable support provided by many colleagues at Bowdoin. Thanks to Marieke van der Steenhoven for introducing me to the possibilities within the Bowdoin College archives and to the rest of the team in the archives and the library for tirelessly tracking down sources. Thanks to Tina Finneran and the Institutional Research, Analytics, and Consulting team for research support and sampling assistance. And thanks to many named and unnamed others behind the scenes, including (but not limited to) Cara Martin-Tetreault, Lynne Toussaint, Bowdoin IT, the amazing campus grounds, facilities, and dining crews, and the exceptional staff at the Bowdoin College Children's Center. Finally, I am so grateful to Lori Brackett for, among many other things, your unending kindness.

To my intellectual community, I am grateful for incisive feedback throughout the many stages of the research process. Thanks to the anonymous reviewers working with the University of Chicago Press whose suggestions have greatly improved this manuscript, and to the many other colleagues and reviewers who have offered generative feedback on journal articles, conference proposals, and presentations related to this book. I am deeply indebted to Shaun Golding, who read and commented on countless early chapter drafts; to Michael Rosenfeld, Craig McEwen, and Caroline Martinez for their enduring mentorship and for providing feedback on versions of this manuscript; to my colleagues in the Bowdoin College sociology department; and to Carrie Scanga for help and support along the way. In addition, this book would not be what it is without outstanding developmental editing from Kelly Besecke at Bookmark Editing. Finally, I am so grateful to Elizabeth Branch Dyson and the team at the University of Chicago Press for saying yes and for expertly guiding this book to print.

The research reported in this book was made possible in part by grants from the Spencer Foundation (201900209) and the Bowdoin College Faculty Development Fund. I am grateful to both funders for believing in the value of bringing these stories to light. That said, the views expressed in this book

ACKNOWLEDGMENTS

are those of the author and do not necessarily reflect the views of the Spencer Foundation or Bowdoin College.

Most of this book was written during the COVID-19 pandemic, while schools and offices were closed, and the life of the college was happening on Zoom. If you've ever tried to write a book while assisting with a remote kindergarten class, you have my most sincere empathy. I am eternally grateful to my coconspirators in virtual schooling and real-life parenting, Barbara Elias and Jens Klenner, and to the teachers who worked so hard to engage our children during those extraordinary years.

Finally, I will always be grateful to my extended family for being my foundation and for always cheering me on. Thank you especially to my parents for all that they made possible. Thank you to my wife, Allyson, for your unending love and support. And to Miles and Lydia, I am grateful for you every day; you give me reasons to believe tomorrow might be better.

Appendix A

Respondents' Gender, Race, and Ethnic Identities

TABLE A.1. Interview respondents' gender, race, and ethnic identities

Respondent	Gender	Race/ethnicity, survey[a]	Race/ethnicity, interview[b]
Adrian	Man	ME, W	"White. I'm 15 percent Lebanese or something like that."
Alexis	Woman	W	"White"
Amy	Woman	W	"Caucasian"
Andrea	Woman	H, W	"I definitely identify as white, but [one side of my family] is Hispanic, so then I'm half-Hispanic."
Annie	Woman	W	"Caucasian and Jewish"
Anthony	Man	H, W	"A little bit German, and a little bit Argentinian, and a little bit American"
Ben	Man	W	"White, Caucasian"
Brooke	Woman	W	"White"
Caleb	Man	A, PI, W	"White and Filipino"
Cali	Woman	H	"Woman of color . . . Colombian"
Carlos	Man	H, W	"I'm white. Ethnically, I'm Latino."
Cassie	Woman	A	"Asian American, Korean American"
Chase	Man	W	"White"
Cindy	Woman	W	"White, European, and Jewish"
Cody	Man	W	"White, half Catholic, half Episcopalian"
Courtney	Woman	W	"White as fuck"
Crystal	Woman	H, W	"I can use the benefits of being Hispanic and not have any of the prejudices against me because I'm white. . . . I feel like I'm a fake Hispanic person even though I was born and raised in a Latin country."
Danielle	Woman	B, H, W	"What race am I if I look white but I'm all these other things? I mostly identify with being Hispanic and having some African American in me."
Edgar	Man	H, W	"White and Hispanic"
Elijah	Woman	H, A	
Ella	Woman	A	"Asian American"
Erika	Woman	B	"Black, Haitian American"

(*continued*)

TABLE A.1. (continued)

Respondent	Gender	Race/ethnicity, survey[a]	Race/ethnicity, interview[b]
Evan	Man	W	"White"
Gabe	Man	H	"Hispanic/Latino"
Garrett	Man	W	"White"
Genesis	Woman	B	"African American"
Isabella	Woman	W	"I'm white with a lot of [recently immigrated] European ancestors."
Jacob	Man	H, W	"[One] side of the family is Mexican and [the other] side is European, so I think I definitely identify obviously as white but also I'm pretty careful to not play up being Hispanic."
Jade	Woman	A	"Chinese"
Jaden	Man	B	"Black, but I'm Jamaican."
Jasmine	Woman	B	"African American"
Jeff	Man	W	"White"
Jennifer	Woman	W	"Pretty white"
Jesse	Other gender	H, W	"I'm Cuban, I'm Latino. . . . But . . . I don't look Latino. . . . I'm half white."
José	Man	H	"Latino and Hispanic. I'm of Mexican descent. I'm a Mexican American."
Lauren	Woman	B	"Black"
Lily	Woman	A	"Chinese definitely, ethnically. Race—I'm expanding the definition of American I guess in a sense for myself."
Logan	Man	W	"Irish and German"
Luis	Man	H	"Latino"
Madison	Woman	W	"White Caucasian"
Margaret	Woman	A	"Asian, South Asian"
Maria	Woman	H, W	"I'm a quarter [Central American], but I identify as white, Caucasian."
Mark	Man	A	"Japanese, Asian"
Megan	Woman	W	"White"
Nori	Woman	A	"Asian"
Ophelia	Woman	W	
Otis	Man	W	"White"
Owen	Man	A	"I'm a lot of things. . . . My white friends think I'm Asian and my Asian friends think I'm white."
Paige	Woman	W	"White, Jewish"
Peter	Man	W	"White, Jewish, American"
Rachel	Woman	A	"Appear Asian and feel very white"
Rebecca	Woman	W	"White"
Remington	Man	W	"Just white"
Riley	Woman	W	"About as white as you can get"
Ruth	Woman	W	"I'm white, but I'm Jewish and my grandparents were immigrants from eastern Europe."
Scott	Man	W	"Pretty white"
Steve	Man	W	"White"
Tanner	Man	W	"White"
Taylor	Woman	W	"White, Jewish"

RESPONDENTS' GENDER, RACE, AND ETHNIC IDENTITIES 193

TABLE A.1. (*continued*)

Respondent	Gender	Race/ethnicity, survey[a]	Race/ethnicity, interview[b]
Trevor	Man	W	"White, Jewish"
Tristan	Man	W	"White. I identify with being Sicilian."
Tyler	Man	W	"Racially, I'm white. Ethnically, my father is Jewish."
Vanessa	Woman	H, W	"I'm white? I'm American!"
Victor	Man	H	"Mexican American"
Xavier	Man	B	"African American"

[a] Race/ethnicity marked on post-interview demographic survey (A = Asian or Asian American; B = Black or African American; H = Hispanic, Latino, or Spanish origin; ME = Middle Eastern or North African; PI = Pacific Islander; W = White).

[b] Race/ethnicity as described during in-depth interview.

Appendix B

Interview Protocol

Precollege

- Tell me about where you grew up. What was your city/town/neighborhood like?
- Who was in your home growing up? What did the adults in your home do for work?
- What was your high school like?
- How did you decide to go to college?
- What was the college application process like for you? How did you end up coming to Bowdoin?

For Each Year on Campus

- Thinking back to when you arrived on campus your [first, sophomore, junior, senior] year, tell me about that transition.
- How would you describe your academic preparedness your [first, sophomore, junior, senior] year?
- With regard to academics, to what extent did you feel like you belonged or didn't belong at Bowdoin? Why?
- Were you involved in any school or community activities outside of classes? [If so,] Tell me about those. How did you get involved in each activity? What, if anything, did you take away from participating in each activity?
- Did you work during your [first, sophomore, junior, senior] year? Can you tell me about that?
- Tell me about your social life. How was it the same or different from the year before? What was your relationship like with your floor? What were your close friends like? How did you meet them? What kinds of things did you do together?

- To what extent did you feel like you belonged or didn't belong at Bowdoin, socially? Why?
- Were there any events or controversies that came up on campus that year that stand out to you? If so, could you tell me about those? How did those impact you personally?
- Did you feel like you changed during your [first, sophomore, junior, senior] year here? If so, how?
- Did you go home during your [first, sophomore, junior, senior] year? [If so,] What was it like when you visited home?
- Tell me about any challenges you experienced during your [first, sophomore, junior, senior] year. How did you handle each challenge?
- How did you decide where to live and who to room with for your next year?
- What did you do in the summer between your [first, sophomore, junior] and [sophomore, junior, senior] years?

SOPHOMORE YEAR ADDITIONAL QUESTIONS

- Tell me about how you went about choosing your major.
- How did you go about deciding whether or not to study abroad?

SENIOR YEAR ADDITIONAL QUESTIONS

- What are your plans for the future in terms of school and career? What events, people or experiences have had an impact on your plans?
- Have your educational and career goals changed since you left high school? If so, how?

For Each Identity

- How would you describe your [social class, race, gender, sexual orientation]?
- Has how you identify or present yourself changed during your time at Bowdoin? If so, how?
- Since arriving at Bowdoin, how much do you feel like you have thought about your [social class, race, gender, sexual orientation]? What prompts you to think about it?
- Would you say your [social class, race, gender, sexual orientation] has opened up social opportunities for you on campus? Can you tell me about a time or a specific memory?
- Has your [social class, race, gender, sexual orientation] ever caused you to be left out or discriminated against? Can you tell me about a time?

- Has your [social class, race, gender, sexual orientation] ever been a factor in your interactions with your peers on campus? In choosing friends, sexual, or romantic partners?
- Has your [social class, race, gender, sexual orientation] ever been a factor in your interactions with faculty, staff or administrators on campus?
- In general, would you say that students of different [social class, race, gender, sexual orientation] identities mix at Bowdoin? What about you? Are any of your close friends from a different [social class, race, gender, sexual orientation] than you? How do you know?

Diversity

- In your own words, what does diversity mean?
- Based on your experiences thus far, what do you think about diversity at Bowdoin?
- How does diversity affect life on Bowdoin's campus, if at all? How has diversity enhanced life at Bowdoin, if at all? What problems has diversity created at Bowdoin, if any?
- Have you had meaningful, honest conversations with other students about diversity? If so, how often would you say this happens? Could you tell me about one of those conversations? Overall, what do you take away from these conversations?
- Has your academic experience been affected by diversity? In what ways?
- Has your social experience been affected by diversity on campus? In what ways?
- Have your future plans been affected by diversity here? In what ways?
- How have events at Bowdoin over the last four years shaped your views on diversity? What about controversies that have come up? Tell me about those and how they have shaped your thinking.

Campus Life Reflections

- I've asked a few times during this interview whether, at certain points in time, you felt like you belonged at Bowdoin socially and academically. Overall, what do you think it takes to belong here?
- At this point in time, to what extent do you feel like you belong here?
- What do you think it takes to be successful at Bowdoin?
- Do you feel like you have been successful at Bowdoin? Why or why not?
- Overall, how do you feel like you've changed during your time at Bowdoin?
- What could Bowdoin do, if anything, to make this a better place for you?
- What could Bowdoin do, if anything, to make this a better place for students in general?

Notes

Chapter One

1. Koos Couve, "Students Offered Counselling over Small Sombrero Hats at Tequila-Themed Birthday Party," *Independent*, March 6, 2016, accessed January 23, 2020, https://www.independent.co.uk/news/world/americas/students-offered-counselling-over-small-sombrero-hats-at-tequilathemed-birthday-party-a6915521.html.

2. See also Gina García et al., "When Parties Become Racialized: Deconstructing Racially Themed Parties," *Journal of Student Affairs Research and Practice* 48, no. 1 (2011): 5–21.

3. Courtney Kueppers, "Beyond Sombreros, Tequila, and 'Gangster' Parties," *Chronicle of Higher Education*, March 18, 2016, accessed October 30, 2019, https://www-chronicle-com.ezproxy.bowdoin.edu/article/Beyond-Sombreros-Tequila-and/235750.

4. "Beyond a 'Compton Cookout,'" *Los Angeles Times*, March 1, 2010, accessed January 23, 2020, https://www.latimes.com/archives/la-xpm-2010-mar-01-la-ed-ucsd2-2010mar02-story.html.

5. Edward Sifuentes, "Sorority Pics Spark Call for Sensitivity," *San Diego Union Tribune*, May 8, 2013, accessed January 28, 2020, https://www.sandiegouniontribune.com/news/education/sdut-csusm-chola-sorority-greeks-2013may08-htmlstory.html.

6. Joseph Asch, "Breaking: Of Crips and Bloods and Memories of Ghetto Parties," *Dartblog*, August 14, 2013, accessed January 22, 2020, http://www.dartblog.com/data/2013/08/010998.php.

7. Fernanda Santos, "Arizona Fraternity Party Stirs Concerns of Racism," *New York Times*, January 22, 2014, accessed January 21, 2020, https://www.nytimes.com/2014/01/23/us/arizona-fraternity-party-stirs-concerns-of-racism.html.

8. Tanzina Vega, "Colorblind Notion Aside, Colleges Grapple with Racial Tension," *New York Times*, February 24, 2014, accessed January 21, 2020, https://www.nytimes.com/2014/02/25/us/colorblind-notion-aside-colleges-grapple-with-racial-tension.html.

9. "Racial Tension and Protests on Campuses Across the Country," *New York Times*, November 10, 2015, accessed January 21, 2020, https://www.nytimes.com/2015/11/11/us/racial-tension-and-protests-on-campuses-across-the-country.html.

10. Liam Stack, "Yale's Halloween Advice Stokes a Racially Charged Debate," *New York Times*, November 8, 2015, accessed January 21, 2020, https://www.nytimes.com/2015/11/09/nyregion/yale-culturally-insensitive-halloween-costumes-free-speech.html.

11. Jamie Altman, "Claremont McKenna Dean of Students Resigns Following Student Protests," *USA Today*, November 13, 2015, accessed January 22, 2020, https://www.usatoday.com /story/college/2015/11/13/claremont-mckenna-dean-of-students-resigns-following-student-pro tests/37408843/.

12. Stack, "Yale's Halloween Advice."

13. Vivian Wang, "Once at Center of Yale Protests, Professor Wins the School's Highest Honor," *New York Times*, August 14, 2018, accessed January 22, 2020, https://www.nytimes.com /2018/08/14/nyregion/yale-professor-protests-christakis-honored-sterling.html.

14. Conor Friedersdorf, "The Perils of Writing a Provocative Email at Yale," *The Atlantic*, May 26, 2016, accessed January 21, 2020, https://www.theatlantic.com/politics/archive/2016/05/the -peril-of-writing-a-provocative-email-at-yale/484418/.

15. Adam Harris, "America Can't Seem to Kick Its Racist Costume Habit," *The Atlantic*, October 31, 2018, accessed February 13, 2020, https://www.theatlantic.com/education/archive /2018/10/americans-keep-wearing-racist-halloween-costumes/574516/.

16. Larry Buchanan, Quoctrung Bui, and Jugal Patel, "Black Lives Matter May Be the Largest Movement in U.S. History," *New York Times*, July 3, 2020, accessed September 18, 2023, https:// www.nytimes.com/interactive/2020/07/03/us/george-floyd-protests-crowd-size.html.

17. Rob Eschmann, *When the Hood Comes Off: Racism and Resistance in the Digital Age* (Berkeley: University of California Press, 2023), 214–15.

18. Zeus Leonardo, "The Trump Presidency, Post-Color Blindness, and the Reconstruction of Public Race Speech," in *Trumpism and Its Discontents*, ed. Osagie Obasogie (Berkeley, CA: Berkeley Public Policy Press, 2020), 18–37.

19. Zak Foste and Tenisha Tevis, "On the Enormity of Whiteness in Higher Education," in *Critical Whiteness Praxis in Higher Education*, ed. Zak Foste and Tenisha Tevis (Sterling, VA: Stylus, 2022), 1–18.

20. Sara Ahmed, *On Being Included: Racism and Diversity in Institutional Life* (Durham, NC: Duke University Press, 2012); James Thomas, *Diversity Regimes: Why Talk Is Not Enough to Fix Racial Inequality at Universities* (New Brunswick, NJ: Rutgers University Press, 2020).

21. Amy Binder, "Afterword: New Institutional, Inhabited Institutional, and a Cultural-Organizational Approach to Studying Elites and Higher Education," in *Universities and the Production of Elites*, ed. Roland Bloch et al. (New York: Palgrave Macmillan, 2018), 373–85.

22. Victor Ray, "A Theory of Racialized Organizations," *American Sociological Review* 84, no. 1 (2019): 26–53.

23. David Labaree, *A Perfect Mess: The Unlikely Ascendancy of American Higher Education* (Chicago: University of Chicago Press, 2017).

24. Michael Hout, "Social and Economic Returns to College Education in the United States," *Annual Review of Sociology* 38 (2012): 379–400; Steven Brint et al., "Where Ivy Matters: The Educational Background of U.S. Cultural Elites," *Sociology of Education* 93, no. 2 (2020): 153–72.

25. Lauren Rivera, *Pedigree: How Elite Students Get Elite Jobs* (Princeton, NJ: Princeton University Press, 2015).

26. Marvin Harris, *Our Kind: Who We Are, Where We Came from and Where We Are Going* (New York: Harper Perennial, 1990).

27. Theodore Allen, *The Invention of the White Race: The Origin of Racial Oppression* (New York: Verso, 2021).

28. Lerone Bennett, Jr., *The Shaping of Black America: The Struggles and Triumphs of African Americans, 1619–1990s* (New York: Penguin Books, 1993).

NOTES TO PAGES 5–6

29. Throughout the book, white supremacy refers to the system of racial domination that benefits white people and harms people of color, using violence and discrimination to normalize unequal power relations. (Moira Ozias and Penny Pasque, "Toward Definitions of Whiteness and Critical Whiteness Studies," in *Critical Whiteness Praxis in Higher Education*, 21–47).

30. Nolan Cabrera, *White Guys on Campus: Racism, White Immunity, and the Myth of "Post-Racial" Higher Education* (New Brunswick, NJ: Rutgers University Press, 2019).

31. Michelle Alexander, *The New Jim Crow: Mass Incarceration in the Age of Colorblindness* (New York: New Press, 2010).

32. Noel Ignatiev, *How the Irish Became White* (New York: Routledge, 1995).

33. Evelyn Glenn, *Unequal Freedom: How Race and Gender Shaped American Citizenship and Labor* (Cambridge, MA: Harvard University Press, 2002); Mae Ngai, *Impossible Subjects: Illegal Aliens and the Making of Modern America* (Princeton, NJ: Princeton University Press, 2004).

34. Ian Haney Lopez, *White by Law: The Legal Construction of Race* (New York: New York University Press, 2006).

35. Alexander, *The New Jim Crow*.

36. Eduardo Bonilla-Silva, "Rethinking Racism: Toward a Structural Interpretation," *American Sociological Review* 62, no. 3 (1997): 465–80.

37. Thomas Shapiro, *The Hidden Cost of Being African American* (New York: Oxford University Press, 2004).

38. Charles Mills, *The Racial Contract* (Ithaca, NY: Cornell University Press, 1997).

39. Cheryl Harris, "Whiteness as Property," *Harvard Law Review* 106, no. 8 (1993): 1707–91.

40. Zeus Leonardo, *Race, Whiteness, and Education* (New York: Routledge, 2009).

41. Michael Omi and Howard Winant, *Racial Formation in the United States: From the 1960s to the 1990s* (New York: Routledge, 1994).

42. Nolan Cabrera, "Where is the Racial Theory in Critical Race Theory? A Constructive Criticism of the Crits," *Review of Higher Education* 42, no. 2 (2018): 209–33; Lauren Irwin, "White Normativity," in *Critical Whiteness Praxis in Higher Education*, 48–69; Lawrence Bobo, Camille Charles, Maria Krysan, and Alicia Simmons, "The Real Record on Racial Attitudes," in *Social Trends in American Life: Findings from the General Social Survey Since 1972*, ed. Peter Marsden (Princeton, NJ: Princeton University Press, 2012), 38–83.

43. Matthew F. Jacobson, *Roots, Too: White Ethnic Revival in Post-Civil Rights America* (Cambridge, MA: Harvard University Press, 2008).

44. Mary Waters, *Ethnic Options: Choosing Identities in America* (Berkeley: University of California Press, 1990).

45. Mills, *The Racial Contract*.

46. Mills, *The Racial Contract*, 19. As cited in Amanda Lewis, Tyrone Forman, Margaret Hagerman, "Charles Mills Ain't Dead! Keeping the Spirit of Mills' Work Alive by Understanding and Challenging the Unrepentant Whiteness of the Academy," *Race, Ethnicity, and Education* 26, no. 4 (2023): 555 (italics in the original).

47. Charles Mills, "White Ignorance," in *Race and Epistemologies of Ignorance*, ed. Shannon Sullivan and Nancy Tuana (Albany: State University of New York Press, 2007), 28. As cited by Cheryl Matias and Colleen Boucher, "From Critical Whiteness Studies to a Critical Study of Whiteness: Restoring Criticality in Critical Whiteness Studies," *Whiteness and Education* 8, no. 1 (2023): 64–81.

48. Matias and Boucher, "From Critical Whiteness Studies."

49. Linda Alcoff, "Epistemologies of Ignorance: Three Types," in *Race and Epistemologies of Ignorance*, 39–58.

50. Mills, *The Racial Contract*, 11. As cited in Lewis, Forman, and Hagerman, "Charles Mills Ain't Dead!"

51. Jennifer Mueller, "Racial Ideology or Racial Ignorance? An Alternative Theory of Racial Cognition," *Sociological Theory* 38, no. 2 (2020).

52. Harvey Cormier, "Ever Not Quite: Unfinished Theories, Unfinished Societies, and Pragmatism," in *Race and Epistemologies of Ignorance*, 59–76.

53. Wil Haygood, "Why Won't Blackface Go Away? It's Part of America's Troubled Cultural Legacy," *New York Times*, February 10, 2019, accessed February 7, 2020, https://www.nytimes .com/2019/02/07/arts/blackface-american-pop-culture.html.

54. "Blackface: The Birth of an American Stereotype," National Museum of African American History and Culture, September 13, 2018, accessed February 7, 2020, https://nmaahc.si.edu /blog-post/blackface-birth-american-stereotype.

55. Brent Staples, "How Blackface Feeds White Supremacy," *New York Times*, March 31, 2019, accessed February 7, 2020, https://www.nytimes.com/2019/03/31/opinion/blackface-white-su premacy.html.

56. Richard Fausset and Campbell Robertson, "Beyond College Campuses and Public Scandals, a Racist Tradition Lingers," *New York Times*, February 8, 2019, accessed February 7, 2020, https://www.nytimes.com/2019/02/08/us/northam-blackface-virginia.html; Matthew W. Hughey, "A Paradox of Participation: Nonwhites in White Sororities and Fraternities," *Social Problems* 57, no. 4 (2010): 653–79.

57. Raul Perez, *The Souls of White Jokes: How Racist Humor Fuels White Supremacy* (Stanford, CA: Stanford University Press, 2022).

58. John Koblin and Michael Grynbaum, "Megyn Kelly's Crash at NBC in One Word (Hers): 'Wow,'" *New York Times*, October 26, 2018, accessed February 7, 2020, https://www.nytimes.com /2018/10/26/business/media/megyn-kelly-today-canceled-nbc.html.

59. John Koblin and Michael M. Grynbaum, "It's Final: Megyn Kelly and NBC Part Ways. And She Will Be Paid in Full," *New York Times*, January 12, 2019, https://www.nytimes .com/2019/01/11/business/media/megyn-kelly-nbc.html.

60. Brett Murphy, "Blackface, KKK Hoods and Mock Lynchings: Review of 900 Yearbooks Finds Blatant Racism," *USA Today*, February 20, 2019, accessed February 7, 2020, https://www .usatoday.com/in-depth/news/investigations/2019/02/20/blackface-racist-photos-yearbooks -colleges-kkk-lynching-mockery-fraternities-black-70-s-80-s/2858921002/.

61. Anna Purna Kambhampaty, Madeleine Carlisle, and Melissa Chan, "Justin Trudeau Wore Brownface at 2001 'Arabian Nights' Party While He Taught at a Private School," *TIME*, September 18, 2019, accessed February 7, 2020, https://time.com/5680759/justin-trudeau-brownface-photo/.

62. Ray, "A Theory of Racialized Organizations."

63. Ray, "A Theory of Racialized Organizations," 31.

64. Ray, "A Theory of Racialized Organizations," 31.

65. Adia Wingfield and Koji Chavez, "Getting In, Getting Hired, Getting Sideways Looks: Organizational Hierarchy and Perceptions of Racial Discrimination," *American Sociological Review* 85, no. 1 (2020): 31–57.

66. Ray, "A Theory of Racialized Organizations," 36.

67. Craig Steven Wilder, *Ebony and Ivy: Race, Slavery and the Troubled History of America's Universities* (New York: Bloomsbury, 2013), 1–2.

NOTES TO PAGES 9–13

68. A parallel system of higher education—schools now known as historically Black colleges and universities (HBCUs)—were erected to serve students of color. Women were also excluded from many institutions, prompting the emergence of women's colleges.

69. Labaree, *A Perfect Mess*.

70. Charlie Eaton, *Bankers in the Ivory Tower: The Troubling Rise of Financiers in U.S. Higher Education* (Chicago: University of Chicago Press, 2022).

71. Labaree, *A Perfect Mess*.

72. Labaree, *A Perfect Mess*, 67.

73. Brown (as cited by Labaree in *A Perfect Mess*).

74. Labaree, *A Perfect Mess*, 14.

75. Labaree, *A Perfect Mess*, 14.

76. Bianca Williams, Dian Squire, and Frank Tuitt, *Plantation Politics and Campus Rebellions: Power, Diversity, and the Emancipatory Struggle in Higher Education* (Albany: State University of New York Press, 2021).

77. Party City, accessed February 7, 2020, https://www.partycity.com/.

78. Adrienne Keene, "Representations Matter," *Journal Committed to Social Change on Race and Ethnicity* 1, no. 1 (2015): 102–11.

79. Ayana Byrd and Lori Tharpes, *Hair Story: Untangling the Roots of Black Hair in America* (New York: St. Martin's, 2014).

80. Ayana Byrd, "How Braids Tell America's Black Hair History," *Elle*, December 27, 2017, accessed February 28, 2020, https://www.elle.com/beauty/hair/a14380845/braids-tell-americas -black-hair-history/.

81. Kenya Evelyn, "Virginia Becomes First Southern US State to Ban Hair Discrimination," *Guardian*, March 11, 2020, https://www.theguardian.com/us-news/2020/mar/06/virginia-hair -discrimination-ban.

82. "The Crown Act," 2023, accessed October 3, 2023, https://www.thecrownact.com/about.

83. Parul Sehgal, "Is Cultural Appropriation Always Wrong?," *New York Times*, September 29, 2015, accessed January 28, 2020, https://www.nytimes.com/2015/10/04/magazine/is-cultural -appropriation-always-wrong.html.

84. Caitlin Gibson, "How 'Politically Correct' Went from Compliment to Insult," *Washington Post*, June 5, 2023, accessed February 10, 2020, https://www.washingtonpost.com/lifestyle/style /how-politically-correct-went-from-compliment-to-insult/2016/01/13/b1cf5918-b61a-11e5 -a76a-0b5145e8679a_story.html.

85. Moira Weigel, "Political Correctness: How the Right Invented a Phantom Enemy," *Guardian*, November 30, 2016, accessed February 10, 2020, https://www.theguardian.com/us-news/2016 /nov/30/political-correctness-how-the-right-invented-phantom-enemy-donald-trump.

86. Jane Mayer, *Dark Money: The Hidden History of the Billionaires Behind the Rise of the Radical Right* (New York: Random House, 2016); Alexander Hertel-Fernandez, Theda Skocpol, and Jason Sclar, "When Political Mega-Donors Join Forces: How the Koch Network and the Democracy Alliance Influence Organized U.S. Politics on the Right and Left," *Studies in American Political Development* 32, no. 2 (2018): 127–65.

87. For example, Allan Bloom's *The Closing of the American Mind: How Higher Education Has Failed Democracy and Impoverished the Souls of Today's Students* (New York: Simon & Schuster, 1987); Roger Kimball's *Tenured Radicals: How Politics Has Corrupted Our Higher Education* (New York: HarperCollins, 1991), and Dinesh D'Souza's *Illiberal Education: The Politics of Race and Sex on Campus* (New York: Simon & Schuster, 1991).

88. Maureen Dowd, "Bush Sees Threat to Flow of Ideas on U.S. Campuses," *New York Times*, May 5, 1991, accessed February 10, 2020, https://timesmachine.nytimes.com/timesmachine/1991/05/05/642191.html?pageNumber=1.

89. Dowd, "Bush Sees Threat to Flow of Ideas."

90. Heidi Kitrosser, "Free Speech, Higher Education, and the PC Narrative," *Minnesota Law Review* 101 (2017): 1987–2064.

91. Weigel, "Political Correctness."

92. Sydney Allen, "CDS and Students Discuss Cultural Appropriation," *Oberlin Review*, December 4, 2015, accessed March 9, 2020, https://oberlinreview.org/9303/news/cds-and-students-discuss-cultural-appropriation/.

93. Vimal Patel, "Colleges Are Losing Control of Their Story: The Banh-Mi Affair at Oberlin Shows How," *Chronicle of Higher Education*, October 31, 2019, accessed February 13, 2020, https://www.chronicle.com/article/Colleges-Are-Losing-Control-of/247465.

94. Gibson, "From Compliment to Insult."

95. Weigel, "Political Correctness."

96. Irin Camron, "Donald Trump's Worst Offense? Mocking Disabled Reporter, Poll Finds," *NBC News*, August 11, 2016, accessed March 10, 2020, https://www.nbcnews.com/politics/2016-election/trump-s-worst-offense-mocking-disabled-reporter-poll-finds-n627736.

97. Hannah Fingerhut, "In 'Political Correctness' Debate, Most Americans Think Too Many People Are Easily Offended," *Pew Research Center*, July 20, 2016, accessed February 10, 2020, https://www.pewresearch.org/fact-tank/2016/07/20/in-political-correctness-debate-most-americans-think-too-many-people-are-easily-offended/.

98. Yascha Mounk, "Americans Strongly Dislike PC Culture," *The Atlantic*, October 10, 2018, accessed February 13, 2020, https://www.theatlantic.com/ideas/archive/2018/10/large-majorities-dislike-political-correctness/572581/.

99. National Center for Educational Statistics (NCES), "Indicator 22: Hate Crime Incidents at Post-Secondary Institutions," *Indicators of School Crime and Safety*, 2019, accessed February 3, 2020, https://nces.ed.gov/programs/crimeindicators/ind_22.asp.

100. Wendy Leo Moore and Joyce Bell, "The Limits of Community: Deconstructing the White Framing of Racist Speech in Universities," *American Behavioral Scientist* 63, no. 13 (2019): 1760–75.

101. Bowdoin College, "The Social Code," *Bowdoin College Code of Community Standards*, 2023, accessed April 17, 2023, https://www.bowdoin.edu/dean-of-students/ccs/community-standards/the-codes.html.

102. Walter DeKeseredy, James Nolan, and Amanda Hall-Sanchez, "Hate Crimes and Bias Incidents in the Ivory Tower: Results from a Large-Scale Campus Survey," *American Behavioral Scientist* (2019), https://doi.org/10.1177%2F0002764219831733.

103. Jeffrey Snyder and Amna Khalid, "The Rise of 'Bias Response Teams' on Campus," *New Republic*, March 30, 2016, accessed February 4, 2020, https://newrepublic.com/article/132195/rise-bias-response-teams-campus; FIRE, "Bias Response Team Report 2017," *The Foundation for Individual Rights and Expression*, 2017, accessed February 4, 2020, https://www.thefire.org/research/publications/bias-response-team-report-2017/report-on-bias-reporting-systems-2017/#executiveSummary.

104. Anna Boch, "The Limits of Tolerance: Extreme Speakers on Campus," *Social Problems* 69 (2022): 143–63; Lawrence Bobo, "Group Conflict, Prejudice, and the Paradox of Contemporary Racial Attitudes," in *Eliminating Racism: Profiles in Controversy*, ed. Phyllis Katz and Dalmas Taylor (New York: Plenum, 1988), 85–144.

NOTES TO PAGES 16–18

105. Paul DiMaggio and Walter Powell, "The Iron Cage Revisited: Collective Rationality and Institutional Isomorphism in Organizational Fields," *American Sociological Review* 48, no. 2 (1983): 147–60.

106. Ray, "A Theory of Racialized Organizations," 28; Binder, "Afterword"; Tim Hallett, "The Myth Incarnate: Recoupling Processes, Turmoil, And Inhabited Institutions in An Urban Elementary School," *American Sociological Review* 75, no. 1 (2010): 52–74.

107. Hallett, "The Myth Incarnate"; Lisa Nunn, *Defining Student Success: The Role of School and Culture* (New Brunswick, NJ: Rutgers University Press, 2014).

108. Ray, "A Theory of Racialized Organizations," 36.

109. Wingfield and Chavez, "Getting In, Getting Hired"; Diane Gusa, "White Institutional Presence: The Impact of Whiteness on Campus Climate," *Harvard Educational Review* 80, no. 4 (2010): 464–89.

110. Amy Binder and Kate Wood, *Becoming Right: How Campuses Shape Young Conservatives* (Princeton, NJ: Princeton University Press, 2013).

111. Daisy Reyes, "Inhabiting Latino Politics: How Colleges Shape Students' Political Styles," *Sociology of Education* 88, no. 4 (2015): 302–19; Daisy Reyes, *Learning to Be Latino: How Colleges Shape Identity Politics* (New Brunswick, NJ: Rutgers University Press, 2018).

112. Binder and Wood, *Becoming Right*.

113. Reyes, "Inhabiting Latino Politics," 308.

114. Shamus Khan, *Privilege: The Making of an Adolescent Elite at St. Paul's School* (Princeton, NJ: Princeton University Press, 2011).

115. Shamus Khan, "The Sociology of Elites," *Annual Review of Sociology* 38 (2012): 361–77.

116. Ruben Gaztambide-Fernandez and Leila Angod, "Approximating Whiteness: Race, Class, and Empire in the Making of Modern Elite/White Subjects," *Educational Theory* 69, no. 6 (2019): 719–43.

117. Khan, *Privilege*; Khan, "The Sociology of Elites."

118. Zeus Leonardo and Alicia Broderick, "Smartness as Property: A Critical Exploration of Intersections Between Whiteness and Disability Studies," *Teachers College Record* 113, no. 10 (2011): 2206–32.

119. Robert Granfield and Thomas Koenig, "Learning Collective Eminence: Harvard Law School and the Social Production of Elite Lawyers," *Sociological Quarterly* 33, no. 4 (1992): 503–20.

120. Lauren Rivera, "Diversity within Reach: Recruitment versus Hiring in Elite Firms," *Annals of the American Academy of Political and Social Science* 639 (2012): 71–90; Lauren Rivera, "Hiring as Cultural Matching: The Case of Elite Professional Service Firms," *American Sociological Review* 77, no. 6 (2012): 999–1022; Rivera, *Pedigree*.

121. Mark Granovetter, "The Strength of Weak Ties," *American Journal of Sociology* 78, no. 6 (1973): 1360–80; Karthik Rajkumar et al., "A Causal Test of The Strength of Weak Ties," *Science* 377, no. 6612 (2022): 1304–10.

122. Khan, "The Sociology of Elites," 373.

123. Ozias and Pasque, "Toward Definitions of Whiteness and Critical Whiteness Studies."

124. Gusa, "White Institutional Presence"; Irwin, "White Normativity."

125. Nolan Cabrera, "White Immunity: Working Through Some of the Pedagogical Pitfalls of Privilege," *Journal Committed to Social Change on Race and Ethnicity* 3, no. 1 (2017): 77–90; Leonardo, *Race, Whiteness, and Education*.

126. Cheryl Matias, *Feeling White: Whiteness, Emotionality, and Education* (Rotterdam: Sense, 2016); Zeus Leonardo and Michalinos Zembylas, "Whiteness as Technology of Affect: Implications for Educational Praxis," *Equity and Excellence in Education* 46, no. 1 (2013): 150–65.

127. Williams, Squire, and Tuitt, *Plantation Politics*; Frank Tuitt, Dian Squire, and Bianca Williams, "Plantation Politics and Neoliberal Racism in Higher Education: A Framework for Reconstructing Anti-Racist Institutions," *Teachers College Record* 120, no. 14 (2018): 1–20.

128. Nolan Cabrera, "Cause with Effect: Critical Whiteness Studies and the Material Consequences of Whiteness on Communities of Color," *International Journal of Qualitative Studies in Education* 35, no. 7 (2022): 711–18.

129. Ray, "A Theory of Racialized Organizations," 47.

130. Mueller, "Racial Ideology or Racial Ignorance?"

131. Hout, "Social and Economic Returns"; Rivera, *Pedigree*.

132. Randall Collins, *The Credential Society: An Historical Sociology of Education and Stratification* (New York: Academic, 1979).

133. Mitchell Stevens, Elizabeth Armstrong, and Richard Arum, "Sieve, Incubator, Temple, Hub: Empirical and Theoretical Advances in the Sociology of Higher Education," *Annual Review of Sociology* 34 (2008): 127–51.

134. Binder and Wood, *Becoming Right*; Reyes, *Learning to Be Latino*.

135. Elizabeth Aries and Richard Berman, *Speaking of Race and Class: The Student Experience at an Elite College* (Philadelphia: Temple University Press, 2013); Elizabeth Lee, *Class and Campus Life: Managing and Experiencing Inequality at an Elite College* (Ithaca, NY: Cornell University Press, 2016); Ann L. Mullen, *Degrees of Inequality: Culture, Class, and Gender in American Higher Education* (Baltimore, MD: Johns Hopkins University Press, 2011); Jenny M. Stuber, *Inside the College Gates: How Class and Culture Matter in Higher Education* (Lanham, MD: Rowman & Littlefield, 2012).

136. Antar Tichavakunda, *Black Campus Life: The Worlds Black Students Make at a Historically White Institution* (Albany: State University of New York Press, 2021); Janice McCabe, *Connecting in College: How Friendship Networks Matter for Academic and Social Success* (Chicago: University of Chicago Press, 2016).

137. Aries and Berman, *Speaking of Race and Class*; Maya A. Beasley, *Opting Out: Losing the Potential of America's Young Black Elite* (Chicago: University of Chicago Press, 2012); Cabrera, *White Guys on Campus*; Natasha Warikoo, *The Diversity Bargain: And Other Dilemmas of Race, Admissions, and Meritocracy at Elite Universities* (Chicago: University of Chicago Press, 2016); Sarah Susannah Willie, *Acting Black: College, Identity, and the Performance of Race* (New York: Routledge, 2003).

138. Elizabeth A. Armstrong and Laura T. Hamilton, *Paying for the Party: How College Maintains Inequality* (Cambridge, MA: Harvard University Press, 2013); Beasley, *Opting Out*.

139. Charles Ragin and Howard Becker, *What Is a Case? Exploring the Foundations of Social Inquiry* (Cambridge: Cambridge University Press, 1992).

140. Wendy Moore and Joyce Bell, "The Right to Be Racist in College: Racist Speech, White Institutional Space, and the First Amendment," *Law & Policy* 39, no. 2 (2017): 99–120.

141. At the time, the area was part of the state of Massachusetts.

142. Louis Hatch, *The History of Bowdoin College* (Portland, ME: Loring, Short & Harmon, 1927), 21.

NOTES TO PAGES 21–29

143. Hatch, *History of Bowdoin College*, 19.

144. Charles Calhoun, *A Small College in Maine: Two Hundred Years of Bowdoin* (Brunswick, ME: Bowdoin, 1993), 167; Scott Jaschik, "Bowdoin Will End Award in Name of Jefferson Davis," *Inside Higher Ed*, October 26, 2015, accessed April 8, 2020, https://www.insidehighered.com/quicktakes/2015/10/26/bowdoin-will-end-award-name-jefferson-davis.

145. NCES, "Indicator 22."

146. EADA, "Equity in Athletics," 2019, https://ope.ed.gov/athletics/#/.

147. To allow for comparisons with similar studies, some interview questions were based on questions used by Aries and Berman (*Speaking of Race and Class*); Lee Cuba et al., *Practice for Life: Making Decisions in College* (Cambridge, MA: Harvard University Press, 2016); and Warikoo (*Diversity Bargain*). Full protocol provided in appendix B.

148. "About the Orient," *Bowdoin Orient*, n.d., accessed January 10, 2023, https://bowdoinorient.com/about/.

149. "Agenda and Minutes," Bowdoin Student Government, 2019, accessed February 6, 2023, http://students.bowdoin.edu/bsg/about-us/agenda-minutes/.

150. Karly Sarita Ford and Ashley Patterson, "'Cosmetic Diversity': University Websites and the Transformation of Race Categories," *Journal of Diversity in Higher Education* 12, no. 2 (2019): 99–114.

151. Mitchell Stevens and Josipa Roksa, "The Diversity Imperative in Elite Admissions," in *Diversity in American Higher Education: Toward a More Comprehensive Approach*, ed. Lisa M. Stulberg and Sharon Lawner Weinberg (New York: Routledge, 2011), 63–73; Lisa M. Stulberg and Anthony S. Chen, "The Origins of Race-Conscious Affirmative Action in Undergraduate Admissions: A Comparative Analysis of Institutional Change in Higher Education," *Sociology of Education* 87, no. 1 (2014): 36–52.

152. W. E. B. DuBois, "Does the Negro Need Separate Schools?," *Journal of Negro Education* 4, no. 3 (1935): 328–35; Mitchell Chang and Maria Ledesma, "The Diversity Rationale," in *Diversity in American Higher Education*, 74–85.

153. David Brunsma, Eric Brown, and Peggy Placier, "Teaching Race at Historically White Colleges and Universities: Identifying and Dismantling the Walls of Whiteness," *Critical Sociology* 39, no. 5 (2013): 717–38; Wendy Moore, *Reproducing Racism: White Space, Elite Law Schools, and Racial Inequality* (Lanham, MD: Rowman & Littlefield, 2008); Joe R. Feagin, Hernan Vera, and Nikitah Imani, *The Agony of Education: Black Students at a White University* (New York: Routledge, 1996).

154. Warikoo, *Diversity Bargain*.

155. Khan, "The Sociology of Elites."

156. Eaton, *Bankers in the Ivory Tower*.

Chapter Two

1. Shamus Khan, *Privilege: The Making of an Adolescent Elite at St. Paul's School* (Princeton, NJ: Princeton University Press, 2011); Shamus Khan, "The Sociology of Elites," *Annual Review of Sociology* 38 (2012): 361–77.

2. Zeus Leonardo and Alicia Broderick, "Smartness as Property: A Critical Exploration of Intersections Between Whiteness and Disability Studies," *Teachers College Record* 113, no. 10 (2011): 2206–32.

3. Jerome Karabel, "Status Group Struggle, Organizational Interests, and the Limits of Institutional Autonomy: The Transformation of Harvard, Yale, and Princeton, 1918–1940," *Theory and Society* 13, no. 1 (1984): 1–40; Jerome Karabel, *The Chosen: The Hidden History of Admission and Exclusion at Harvard, Yale, and Princeton* (New York: Houghton Mifflin, 2005).

4. Karabel, "Status Group Struggle," 29.

5. Karabel, "Status Group Struggle," 26.

6. Charles Calhoun, *A Small College in Maine: Two Hundred Years of Bowdoin* (Brunswick, ME: Bowdoin, 1993), 248.

7. Lisa M. Stulberg and Anthony S. Chen, "The Origins of Race-Conscious Affirmative Action in Undergraduate Admissions: A Comparative Analysis of Institutional Change in Higher Education," *Sociology of Education* 87, no. 1 (2014): 36–52.

8. Bowdoin College Archive, *College Catalog* (Brunswick, ME: Bowdoin, 1969), 49–50, accessed February 10, 2023, https://archive.org/details/catalogue19691970bowd/page/50/mode/2up?ui =embed&view=theater.

9. Mitchell Chang and Maria Ledesma, "The Diversity Rationale," in *Diversity in American Higher Education: Toward a More Comprehensive Approach*, ed. Lisa M. Stulberg and Sharon Lawner Weinberg (New York: Routledge, 2011), 74–85.

10. Mitchell Stevens and Josipa Roksa, "The Diversity Imperative in Elite Admissions," in *Diversity in American Higher Education*, 63–73.

11. Adam Liptak, "Supreme Court Upholds Affirmative Action Program at University of Texas," *New York Times*, June 23, 2016, accessed February 3, 2020, https://www.nytimes.com /2016/06/24/us/politics/supreme-court-affirmative-action-university-of-texas.html.

12. Adam Liptak, "Supreme Court Rejects Affirmative Action Programs at Harvard and UNC," *New York Times*, June 29, 2023, accessed October 5, 2023, https://www.nytimes.com/2023 /06/29/us/politics/supreme-court-admissions-affirmative-action-harvard-unc.html.

13. Mitchell Stevens, *Creating a Class: College Admissions and the Education of Elites* (Cambridge, MA: Harvard University Press, 2007), 247.

14. Annette Lareau, *Unequal Childhoods: Class, Race, and Family Life* (Berkeley: University of California Press, 2003).

15. Lareau, *Unequal Childhoods*; Stevens, *Creating a Class*.

16. Stevens, *Creating a Class*, 191.

17. National Center for Educational Statistics (NCES), "Indicator 22: Hate Crime Incidents at Post-Secondary Institutions," *Indicators of School Crime and Safety*, 2019, accessed February 3, 2020, https://nces.ed.gov/programs/crimeindicators/ind_22.asp.

18. "Some Colleges Have More Students from the Top 1 Percent Than the Bottom 60," *New York Times*, January 18, 2017, accessed February 8, 2023, https://www.nytimes.com/interactive /2017/01/18/upshot/some-colleges-have-more-students-from-the-top-1-percent-than-the -bottom-60.html.

19. NCES, "Indicator 22."

20. Sherry Deckman, *Black Space: Negotiating Race, Diversity, and Belonging in the Ivory Tower* (New Brunswick, NJ: Rutgers University Press, 2022).

21. Ruben Gaztambide-Fernandez and Leila Angod, "Approximating Whiteness: Race, Class, and Empire in the Making of Modern Elite/White Subjects," *Educational Theory* 69, no. 6 (2019): 719–43.

22. Gaztambide-Fernandez and Angod, "Approximating Whiteness."

23. Karabel, *The Chosen*.

NOTES TO PAGES 34–38

24. Robert Granfield and Thomas Koenig, "Learning Collective Eminence: Harvard Law School and the Social Production of Elite Lawyers," *Sociological Quarterly* 33, no. 4 (1992): 503–20; Khan, *Privilege*; Natasha Warikoo, *The Diversity Bargain: And Other Dilemmas of Race, Admissions, and Meritocracy at Elite Universities* (Chicago: University of Chicago Press, 2016).

25. Hy Khong and Alex Mayer, "Into the Woods," *Bowdoin Orient*, March 27, 2015,

26. Victor Ray, "A Theory of Racialized Organizations," *American Sociological Review* 84, no. 1 (2019): 26–53.

27. "Our Three Divisions," NCAA, 2020, accessed June 9, 2020, https://www.ncaa.org/sports /2016/1/7/about-resources-media-center-ncaa-101-our-three-divisions.aspx.

28. Kirsten Hextrum, *Special Admission: How College Sports Recruitment Favors White Suburban Athletes* (New Brunswick, NJ: Rutgers University Press, 2021), 18.

29. Stevens, *Creating a Class.*

30. "About the NESCAC," New England Small College Athletic Conference (NESCAC), 2020, accessed June 9, 2020, https://www.nescac.com/about/about.

31. EADA, "Equity in Athletics," 2019, https://ope.ed.gov/athletics/#/.

32. Bill Pennington, "One Division III Conference Finds That Playing the Slots System Pays Off," *New York Times*, December 25, 2005, accessed June 11, 2020, https://www.nytimes.com /2005/12/25/sports/ncaafootball/one-division-iii-conference-finds-that-playing-the.html.

33. Bowdoin College, *Self-Study 2006*, accessed February 8, 2023, https://library.bowdoin .edu/arch/archives/a001/a001s029u001v006.pdf.

34. Pennington, "One Division III Conference."

35. Sam Weyrauch, "Banded Together: Recruited Athletes with Sub-Average Academics Can Receive Preference in Admissions," *Bowdoin Orient*, March 28, 2014, http://bowdoinorient.com /bonus/article/9151.

36. Hextrum, *Special Admission.*

37. Hextrum, *Special Admission*, 121.

38. Stevens, *Creating a Class.*

39. Lareau, *Unequal Childhoods.*

40. Anna Fauver, "ACC Hopes to Address Race in Athletics," *Bowdoin Orient*, September 29, 2017, https://bowdoinorient.com/2017/09/29/acc-hopes-to-address-race-in-athletics/.

41. From survey data I collected (see chap. 1 for methodology): 72% of recruited athletes identified as white, compared to 61% of students who were not recruited athletes.

42. Forty-five percent of recruited athletes attended private high school, compared to 40% of students who were not recruited athletes.

43. Ninety-three percent of recruited athletes had parents who received a bachelor's degree or higher, compared to 82% of students who were not recruited athletes.

44. Forty-three percent of recruited athletes came from neighborhoods they characterized as "mostly white" and an additional 39% came from neighborhoods they characterized as "mostly white, but with some racial diversity," compared to 38% of students who were not recruited athletes came from neighborhoods they characterized as "mostly white" and an additional 29% came from neighborhoods they characterized as "mostly white, but with some racial diversity."

45. Eighty-six percent of recruited athletes came from homes where English was the only language spoken, compared to 73% of students who were not recruited athletes.

46. Twenty-two percent of recruited athletes had one or more parents who were born outside the US, compared to 38% of students who were not recruited athletes.

47. Forty-one percent of recruited athletes received need-based financial aid, compared to 57% of students who were not recruited athletes.

48. Three percent of recruited athletes received accommodations for a disability, compared to 7% of students who were not recruited athletes.

49. Weyrauch, "Banded Together."

50. Some participants viewed this as a racialized two-tier system with the trainings for students of color being lower quality than traditional trainings.

51. Will Jacob, "30 College Street Becomes Multicultural Center," *Bowdoin Orient*, September 7, 2007, http://bowdoinorient.com/bonus/article/2741.

52. Pamela Zabala, "'Cooperate with Others for Common Ends?': Students as Gatekeepers of Culture and Tradition on College Campuses," Bowdoin College, 2017, https://digitalcommons .bowdoin.edu/honorsprojects/67/.

53. Allison Wei and Rachael Allen, "More Limits for Off-Campus Housing Recommended," *Bowdoin Orient*, September 15, 2017, https://bowdoinorient.com/2017/09/15/more-limits -for-off-campus-housing-recommended/.

54. Zabala, "Cooperate with Others?"

55. Wei and Allen, "More Limits for Off-Campus Housing."

56. Allison Wei, "New Off-Campus Housing Policy Announced," *Bowdoin Orient*, November 10, 2017, https://bowdoinorient.com/2017/11/10/new-off-campus-housing-policy-announced/.

57. Elijah Anderson, "The White Space," *Sociology of Race and Ethnicity* 1, no. 1 (2015): 10–21.

58. Zabala, "Cooperate with Others?"

59. Paul DiMaggio and Walter Powell, "The Iron Cage Revisited: Collective Rationality and Institutional Isomorphism in Organizational Fields," *American Sociological Review* 48, no. 2 (1983): 147–60.

60. Ray, "A Theory of Racialized Organizations."

61. Amy Binder, "Afterword: New Institutional, Inhabited Institutional, and a Cultural-Organizational Approach to Studying Elites and Higher Education," in *Universities and the Production of Elites*, ed. Roland Bloch et al. (New York: Palgrave Macmillan, 2018), 373–85.

62. Natasha Warikoo, *The Diversity Bargain: And Other Dilemmas of Race, Admissions, and Meritocracy at Elite Universities* (Chicago: University of Chicago Press, 2016).

63. E.g., Carson Byrd, *Poison in the Ivy: Race Relations and the Reproduction of Inequality on Elite College Campuses* (New Brunswick, NJ: Rutgers University Press, 2017); Camille Z. Charles et al., *Taming the River: Negotiating the Academic, Financial, and Social Currents in Selective Colleges and Universities* (Princeton, NJ: Princeton University Press, 2009); Thomas J. Espenshade and Alexandria Walton Radford, *No Longer Separate, Not Yet Equal: Race and Class in Elite College Admission and Campus Life* (Princeton, NJ: Princeton University Press, 2009).

64. Eduardo Bonilla-Silva, *Racism without Racists: Colorblind Racism and the Persistence of Racial Inequality in America* (Lanham, MD: Rowman & Littlefield, 2018); Eduardo Bonilla-Silva and Tyrone Forman, "'I'm Not Racist But...': Mapping White College Students' Racial Ideology in the USA," *Discourse & Society* 11, no. 1 (2000): 50–85.

65. Subini Ancy Annamma, Darrell Jackson, and Deb Morrison, "Conceptualizing Color-Evasiveness: Using Dis/Ability Critical Race Theory to Expand a Colorblind Racial Ideology in Education and Society," *Race, Ethnicity, and Education* 20, no. 2 (2017): 147–62.

66. Alex Manning, Douglas Hartmann, and Joseph Gerteis, "Colorblindness in Black and White: An Analysis of Core Tenets, Configurations, and Complexities," *Sociology of Race and*

NOTES TO PAGES 50–56

Ethnicity 1, no. 4 (2015): 539. As cited in Sarah Mayorga-Gallo, "The White-Centering Logic of Diversity Ideology," *American Behavioral Scientist* 63, no. 13 (2019): 1789–809.

67. Warikoo, *Diversity Bargain*.

68. Natasha Warikoo and Janine de Novais, "Colorblindness and Diversity: Race Frames and Their Consequences for White Undergraduates at Elite US Universities," *Ethnic and Racial Studies* 38, no. 6 (2015): 860–76.

69. Mayorga-Gallo, "White-Centering Logic"; Candis Smith and Sarah Mayorga-Gallo, "The New Principle-Policy Gap: How Diversity Ideology Subverts Diversity Initiatives," *Sociological Perspectives* 60, no. 5 (2017): 889–911.

70. Mayorga-Gallo, "White-Centering Logic," 1792.

71. Shametrice Davis and Jessica Harris, "But We Didn't Mean It Like That: A Critical Race Analysis of Campus Responses to Racial Incidents," *Journal of Critical Scholarship on Higher Education and Student Affairs* 2, no. 1 (2016): 62–78; Wendy Moore and Joyce Bell, "The Right to Be Racist in College: Racist Speech, White Institutional Space, and the First Amendment," *Law & Policy* 39, no. 2 (2017): 99–120; Rema Reynolds and Darquillius Mayweather, "Recounting Racism, Resistance, and Repression: Examining the Experiences and #Hashtag Activism of College Students with Critical Race Theory and Counternarratives," *Journal of Negro Education* 86, no. 3 (2017): 283–304.

72. Moore and Bell, "The Right to Be Racist in College."

73. Amanda Lewis and John Diamond, *Despite the Best Intentions: How Racial Inequality Thrives in Good Schools* (New York: Oxford University Press, 2015).

74. Bonilla-Silva, *Racism without Racists*; Warikoo, *Diversity Bargain*.

75. Mayorga-Gallo, "White-Centering Logic."

76. Smith and Mayorga-Gallo, "The New Principle-Policy Gap"; Warikoo, *Diversity Bargain*.

77. DiMaggio and Powell, "The Iron Cage Revisited."

78. Ray, "A Theory of Racialized Organizations."

79. Mayorga-Gallo, "White-Centering Logic."

80. Mayorga-Gallo, "White-Centering Logic."

81. Mayorga-Gallo, "White-Centering Logic," 1795.

82. Jennifer Mueller, "Racial Ideology or Racial Ignorance? An Alternative Theory of Racial Cognition," *Sociological Theory* 38, no. 2 (2020).

83. Veronica Lerma, Laura Hamilton, and Kelly Nielsen, "Racialized Equity Labor, University Appropriation and Student Resistance," *Social Problems* 67, no. 2 (2020): 286–303; Sara Ahmed, *On Being Included: Racism and Diversity in Institutional Life* (Durham, NC: Duke University Press, 2012).

84. Lerma, Hamilton, and Nielsen, "Racialized Equity Labor."

85. Special thanks to Sophie Cowen from my research team for early development of the theory involved in this concept.

86. Bonilla-Silva, *Racism without Racists*.

87. E.g., Mueller, "Racial Ideology or Racial Ignorance?"

88. Ingrid A. Nelson, Hannah J. Graham, and Natalie L. Rudin, "Saving Face While (Not) Talking about Race: How Undergraduates Inhabit Racialized Structures at an Elite and Predominantly White College," *Social Problems* 70, no. 2 (2023): 456–73, https://doi.org/10.1093/socpro/spab045.

Chapter Three

1. Bowdoin College, Members of the Junior Class, *Bowdoin Bugle* (Brunswick, ME: Bowdoin, 1905), 152.

2. Marisa McGarry, "Teach-in on Native American Appropriation Brings Oft-Ignored Campus Issues to Light," *Bowdoin Orient*, May 2, 2014, http://bowdoinorient.com/bonus/article/9381.

3. Veronica Lerma, Laura Hamilton, and Kelly Nielsen, "Racialized Equity Labor, University Appropriation and Student Resistance," *Social Problems* 67, no. 2 (2020): 286–303; Fabio Rojas, *From Black Power to Black Studies: How a Radical Social Movement Became an Academic Discipline* (Baltimore, MD: Johns Hopkins University Press, 2007).

4. In 2010, reporting guidelines changed and a new "two or more races" category was introduced, skewing comparisons from before and after this year.

5. Lisa M. Stulberg and Anthony S. Chen, "The Origins of Race-Conscious Affirmative Action in Undergraduate Admissions: A Comparative Analysis of Institutional Change in Higher Education," *Sociology of Education* 87, no. 1 (2014): 36–52.

6. Melvin Whitehead et al., "Disrupting the Big Lie: Higher Education and Whitelash in a Post/Colorblind Era," *Education Sciences* 11, no. 9 (2021): 486–500; Zeus Leonardo, "The Trump Presidency, Post-Color Blindness, and the Reconstruction of Public Race Speech," in *Trumpism and Its Discontents*, ed. Osagie Obasogie (Berkeley, CA: Berkeley Public Policy Press, 2020), 18–37.

7. Nathalie Baptiste, "Origins of a Movement," *The Nation*, February 9, 2017, accessed January 29, 2020, https://www.thenation.com/article/archive/origins-of-a-movement/; Patrisse Khan-Cullors. "6 Years Later and Black Activists Are Still Fighting," Black Lives Matter, July 13, 2019, accessed February 26, 2020, https://blacklivesmatter.com/six-years-strong/.

8. Victor Ray, "A Theory of Racialized Organizations," *American Sociological Review* 84, no. 1 (2019): 26–53.

9. "Race Centerfold," *Bowdoin Orient*, May 6, 2016, https://www.scribd.com/doc/311707042.

10. McGarry, "Teach-in on Native American Appropriation."

11. Al Baker, J. David Goodman, and Benjamin Mueller, "Beyond the Chokehold: The Path to Eric Garner's Death," *New York Times*, June 13, 2015, accessed February 26, 2020, https://www.nytimes.com/2015/06/14/nyregion/eric-garner-police-chokehold-staten-island.html.

12. Michael Pearson, "A Timeline of the University of Missouri Protests," CNN, November 10, 2015, accessed January 22, 2020, https://www.cnn.com/2015/11/09/us/missouri-protest-timeline/index.html.

13. Doug Cook, "The Record-Setting Class of 2018," News Archive 2009–2018, May 8, 2014, accessed June 1, 2020, http://community.bowdoin.edu/news/2014/05/the-record-setting-class-of-2018/.

14. Carolyn Finney, *Black Faces, White Spaces: Reimagining the Relationship of African Americans to the Great Outdoors* (Chapel Hill: University of North Carolina Press Books, 2014).

15. Rebecca Goldfine, "A Bowdoin Tradition: A Presidential Welcome on the Museum Steps," *News Archive 2009–2018*, September 2, 2014, accessed June 1, 2020, http://community.bowdoin.edu/news/2014/09/a-bowdoin-tradition-president-admissions-director-welcome-the-class-of-2018-on-museum-steps/.

16. Elizabeth Lee, *Class and Campus Life: Managing and Experiencing Inequality at an Elite College* (Ithaca, NY: Cornell University Press, 2016); Mitchell Stevens, *Creating a Class: College Admissions and the Education of Elites* (Cambridge, MA: Harvard University Press, 2007).

17. Daniel Mejia-Cruz and Alexander Thomas, "Breaking the Bowdoin Cycle of Angst," *Bowdoin Orient*, September 12, 2014, http://bowdoinorient.com/bonus/article/9418.

18. Jennifer Mueller, "Racial Ideology or Racial Ignorance? An Alternative Theory of Racial Cognition," *Sociological Theory* 38, no. 2 (2020).

19. George Lipsitz, *The Possessive Investment in Whiteness: How White People Profit from Identity Politics* (Philadelphia: Temple University Press, 1998).

NOTES TO PAGES 65–76

20. Charles Mills, *The Racial Contract* (Ithaca, NY: Cornell University Press, 1997); Charles Mills, "White Ignorance," in *Race and Epistemologies of Ignorance*, ed. Shannon Sullivan and Nancy Tuana (Albany: State University of New York Press, 2007), 28.

21. Sarah Mayorga-Gallo, "The White-Centering Logic of Diversity Ideology," *American Behavioral Scientist* 63, no. 13 (2019): 1789–809.

22. Tim Foster, "Students Who Dressed as Native Americans to Face Disciplinary Action," *Bowdoin Orient*, December 9, 2014, http://bowdoinorient.com/bonus/article/9826.

23. Whitehead et al., "Disrupting the Big Lie."

24. Caroline Martinez, "Why Hasn't the College Taken Stronger Stances, Actions on Racial Issues?" *Bowdoin Orient*, December 5, 2014, http://bowdoinorient.com/bonus/article/9794.

25. Andrew Seager, "Project '65," *Bowdoin Orient*, February 28, 1964, accessed April 16, 2020, https://digitalcommons.bowdoin.edu/bowdoinorient-1960s/5/.

26. Bowdoin Orient, "Project 65 Awarded Financial Grant Rockefeller Foundation Gives $150,000," *Bowdoin Orient*, April 7, 1967, accessed April 23, 2020, https://digitalcommons.bowdoin.edu/bowdoinorient-1960s/8/.

27. Julian Andrews, "Administration Falls Silent on 'Cracksgiving' Appropriation Incident," *Bowdoin Orient*, January 23, 2015, http://bowdoinorient.com/bonus/article/9858.

28. Amy Binder and Kate Wood, *Becoming Right: How Campuses Shape Young Conservatives* (Princeton, NJ: Princeton University Press, 2013). Daisy Reyes, *Learning to Be Latino: How Colleges Shape Identity Politics* (New Brunswick, NJ: Rutgers University Press, 2018).

29. Ingrid A. Nelson, Hannah J. Graham, and Natalie L. Rudin, "Saving Face While (Not) Talking about Race: How Undergraduates Inhabit Racialized Structures at an Elite and Predominantly White College," *Social Problems* 70, no. 2 (2023): 456–73, https://doi.org/10.1093/socpro/spab045.

30. Veronica Lerma, Laura Hamilton, and Kelly Nielsen, "Racialized Equity Labor, University Appropriation and Student Resistance," *Social Problems* 67, no. 2 (2020): 286–303.

31. Zeus Leonardo and Ronald Porter, "Pedagogy of Fear: Toward a Fanonian Theory of 'Safety' in Race Dialogue," *Race, Ethnicity, and Education* 13, no. 2 (2010): 139–57.

32. Frantz Fanon, *Black Skin, White Masks*, trans. C. L. Markmann (New York: Grove, 1967).

33. Leonardo and Porter, "Pedagogy of Fear," 147.

34. Frank Dobbin and Alexandra Kalev, *Getting to Diversity: What Works and What Doesn't* (Cambridge, MA: Harvard University Press, 2022).

35. Leslie Picca and Joe Feagin, *Two-Faced Racism: Whites in the Backstage and Frontstage* (New York: Routledge, 2007); Mayorga-Gallo, "White-Centering Logic."

36. Anderson, "The White Space."

37. Pamela Zabala, "'Cooperate with Others for Common Ends?': Students as Gatekeepers of Culture and Tradition on College Campuses," Bowdoin College, 2017, https://digitalcommons.bowdoin.edu/honorsprojects/67/.

38. Michelle Kruk et al., "Open Letter: Bowdoin Students Aching for Change," *Bowdoin Orient*, February 12, 2015, http://bowdoinorient.com/bonus/article/9954.

Chapter Four

1. John Eligon and Richard Pérez-Peña, "University of Missouri Protests Spur a Day of Change," *New York Times*, November 12, 2015, https://www.nytimes.com/2015/11/10/us/university-of-missouri-system-president-resigns.html.

2. Eligon and Pérez-Peña, "University of Missouri Protests Spur a Day of Change."

214   NOTES TO PAGES 76-89

3. Eligon and Pérez-Peña, "University of Missouri Protests Spur a Day of Change."

4. Michael Ndemanu, "Antecedents of College Campus Protests Nationwide: Exploring Black Student Activists' Demands," *Journal of Negro Education* 86, no. 3 (2017): 238–51.

5. National Center for Education Statistics (NCES), "Full-time Faculty in Degree-granting Postsecondary Institutions, by Race/Ethnicity, Sex, and Academic Rank: Fall 2015, Fall 2017, and Fall 2018," 2019, accessed April 12, 2023, https://nces.ed.gov/programs/digest/d19/tables/dt19 _315.20.asp.

6. Espinosa et al., "Race and Ethnicity in Higher Education: A Status Report," American Council on Education, November 23, 2020, accessed April 12, 2023, https://www.equityinhigh ered.org/resources/report-downloads/.

7. Clayton Rose, "Opening of the College," *Bowdoin College News*, September 3, 2015, accessed January 10, 2023, https://www.bowdoin.edu/news/2015/09/opening-of-the-college-con vocation-2015-bowdoin-president-clayton-rose.html.

8. Zeus Leonardo, Race, Whiteness, and Education (New York: Routledge, 2009).

9. Amy Binder and Kate Wood, *Becoming Right: How Campuses Shape Young Conservatives* (Princeton, NJ: Princeton University Press, 2013); Daisy Reyes, "Inhabiting Latino Politics: How Colleges Shape Students' Political Styles," *Sociology of Education* 88, no. 4 (2015): 302–19.

10. Ingrid A. Nelson, Hannah J. Graham, and Natalie L. Rudin, "Saving Face While (Not) Talking about Race: How Undergraduates Inhabit Racialized Structures at an Elite and Predominantly White College," *Social Problems* 70, no. 2 (2023): 456–73, https://doi.org/10.1093/socpro/spab045.

11. Adira Polite, "Cultural Appropriation: Why They're Not 'Just Clothes.'" *Bowdoin Orient*, October 27, 2015, http://bowdoinorient.com/bonus/article/10602.

12. Adira Polite, "Cultural Appropriation."

13. Gina García et al., "When Parties Become Racialized: Deconstructing Racially Themed Parties," *Journal of Student Affairs Research and Practice* 48, no. 1 (2011): 5–21; Zeus Leonardo and Ronald Porter, "Pedagogy of Fear: Toward a Fanonian Theory of 'Safety' in Race Dialogue," *Race, Ethnicity, and Education* 13, no. 2 (2010): 139–57.

14. Jenna Scott, "Statement of Solidarity re: The Sailing Team Party," Bowdoin Student Government, October 28, 2015, accessed January 11, 2023, https://students.bowdoin.edu/bsg/archive -2023/statement-of-solidarity-re-the-sailing-team-party/.

15. Sydney Avitia-Jacques, "How Didn't We Realize This Was Wrong?," *Bowdoin Orient*, October 29, 2015, http://bowdoinorient.com/bonus/article/10606.

16. James Jelin, "Campus Must Agree on What Progress Means Following 'Gangster' Party," *Bowdoin Orient*, October 29, 2015, http://bowdoinorient.com/bonus/article/10605.

17. Bowdoin Orient Editorial Board, "Broken Dialogue," *Bowdoin Orient*, October 30, 2015, http://bowdoinorient.com/bonus/article/10630.

18. Beth Brogan, "Bowdoin's Sailing Team's 'Gangster Party' Criticized as Racist," *Bangor Daily News*, October 28, 2015, accessed September 17, 2019, https://www.bangordailynews.com /2015/10/28/news/bowdoin-sailing-teams-gangster-party-criticized-as-racist/.

19. Mary Juetten, "Failed Start Ups: Yik Yak," *Forbes*, November 13, 2018, accessed January 11, 2023, https://www.forbes.com/sites/maryjuetten/2018/11/13/failed-startups-yik-yak/#294261d95725; Keith Wagstaff, "What is Yik Yak and Why Do College Students Love It So Much?" *NBC News*, November 11, 2015, accessed January 11, 2023, https://www.nbcnews.com/tech/mobile /what-yik-yak-why-do-college-students-love-it-so-n461471.

20. Calder McHugh, "Without Anonymity, Interest in Yik Yak Wanes," *Bowdoin Orient*, September 30, 2016, http://bowdoinorient.com/bonus/article/11401.

NOTES TO PAGES 89–100

21. Victor Ray, "A Theory of Racialized Organizations," *American Sociological Review* 84, no. 1 (2019): 45–46.

22. Rob Eschmann, *When the Hood Comes Off: Racism and Resistance in the Digital Age* (Berkeley: University of California Press, 2023), 214–15.

23. Veronica Lerma, Laura Hamilton, and Kelly Nielsen, "Racialized Equity Labor, University Appropriation and Student Resistance," *Social Problems* 67, no. 2 (2020): 286–303.

24. James Thomas, "The Economization of Diversity," *Sociology of Race and Ethnicity* 5, no. 4 (2019): 483.

25. Leonardo and Porter, "Pedagogy of Fear."

26. Zak Foste and Tenisha Tevis, "On the Enormity of Whiteness in Higher Education," in *Critical Whiteness Praxis in Higher Education*, ed. Zak Foste and Tenisha Tevis (Sterling, VA: Stylus, 2022), 1–18.

27. Caroline Martinez, "Administration Must Take Real Action and Stop Making Students Do Its Job," *Bowdoin Orient*, November 6, 2015, http://bowdoinorient.com/bonus/article /10639.

28. Rachael Allen, "Community Pack Union to Address Why Race Should Matter to White Students," *Bowdoin Orient*, December 11, 2015, http://bowdoinorient.com/bonus/article/10809.

29. Allen, "Community Pack Union."

30. John Branch, "Rose Hires Researchers to Investigate Race at Bowdoin," *Bowdoin Orient*, December 11, 2015, http://bowdoinorient.com/bonus/article/10810.

31. Nicole Wetsman, "Protest Draws Attention to Issues of Race on Campus," *Bowdoin Orient*, November 6, 2015, http://bowdoinorient.com/bonus/article/10659.

32. Bowdoin Orient Editorial Board, "System Administration," *Bowdoin Orient*, November 6, 2015, http://bowdoinorient.com/bonus/article/10661.

33. Bowdoin Orient Editorial Board, "System Administration."

34. Caroline Martinez, "Administration Must Take Real Action."

35. Lucia Ryan, "Bias Incident Display in Union Raises Awareness of Racial Issues on Campus," *Bowdoin Orient*, December 4, 2015, http://bowdoinorient.com/bonus/article/10777.

36. Adira Polite, "'Bowdoin Bubble' Means We Should Hold Ourselves to a Higher Standard," *Bowdoin Orient*, November 12, 2015, http://bowdoinorient.com/bonus/article/10676.

37. García et al., "When Parties Become Racialized."

38. Bianca Williams, Dian Squire, and Frank Tuitt, *Plantation Politics and Campus Rebellions: Power, Diversity, and the Emancipatory Struggle in Higher Education* (Albany: State University of New York Press, 2021).

39. Jesse Carr et al., "Future Thinking and Freedom Making: Antidiversity as an Intervention to the Plantation Politics of Higher Education," in *Plantation Politics*, 141–70.

40. Ray, "A Theory of Racialized Organizations."

Chapter Five

1. Fabio Rojas, *From Black Power to Black Studies: How a Radical Social Movement Became an Academic Discipline* (Baltimore, MD: Johns Hopkins University Press, 2007).

2. Victor Ray, "A Theory of Racialized Organizations," *American Sociological Review* 84, no. 1 (2019): 26–53.

3. Harry Rube, "Washington '17 Begins Term as Multicultural Rep," *Bowdoin Orient*, February 12, 2016, http://bowdoinorient.com/bonus/article/10920.

4. J. Kim, "Discrimination Will Always Be There, But Race and Ethnicity Still Matter," *Bowdoin Orient*, January 29, 2016, http://bowdoinorient.com/bonus/article/10835; Nick Distefano, "Political and Scientific Correctness are Both Forces for Good," *Bowdoin Orient*, February 4, 2016, http://bowdoinorient.com/bonus/article/10858.

5. Julian Andrews and Steff Chavez, "Call and Response," *Bowdoin Orient*, February 12, 2016, http://bowdoinorient.com/bonus/article/10917.

6. Kirsten Hextrum, *Special Admission: How College Sports Recruitment Favors White Suburban Athletes* (New Brunswick, NJ: Rutgers University Press, 2021).

7. Calder McHugh, "Ladd Hosts Discussion on Race in the College House System," *Bowdoin Orient*, February 12, 2016, http://bowdoinorient.com/bonus/article/10919.

8. Leslie Picca and Joe Feagin, *Two-Faced Racism: Whites in the Backstage and Frontstage* (New York: Routledge, 2007).

9. Charles Mills, *The Racial Contract* (Ithaca, NY: Cornell University Press, 1997); Charles Mills, "White Ignorance," in *Race and Epistemologies of Ignorance*, ed. Shannon Sullivan and Nancy Tuana (Albany: State University of New York Press, 2007), 28.

10. Douglas Lee et al., "Relinquishing White Innocence: Slaying a Defender of White Supremacy," in *Critical Whiteness Praxis in Higher Education*, ed. Zak Foste and Tenisha Tevis (Sterling, VA: Stylus, 2022), 90–112; Cheryl Matias, *Feeling White: Whiteness, Emotionality, and Education* (Rotterdam: Sense, 2016).

11. Eduardo Bonilla-Silva, "Feeling Race: Theorizing the Racial Economy of Emotions," *American Sociological Review* 84, no. 1 (2019): 1–25.

12. Matias, Feeling White.

13. John Branch and Jono Gruber, "Stereotyping at 'Tequila' Party Causes Backlash," *Bowdoin Orient*, February 26, 2016, http://bowdoinorient.com/bonus/article/10990.

14. Matias, *Feeling White*; Picca and Feagin, *Two-Faced Racism*; Raul Perez, *The Souls of White Jokes: How Racist Humor Fuels White Supremacy* (Stanford, CA: Stanford University Press, 2022).

15. Branch and Gruber, "Stereotyping at 'Tequila' Party."

16. Jenna Scott, "Statement of Solidarity re: 'Tequila' Party," Bowdoin Student Government, February 24, 2016, accessed February 22, 2023, https://students.bowdoin.edu/bsg/archive-2023 /statement-of-solidarity-re-tequila-party/.

17. Branch and Gruber, "Stereotyping at 'Tequila' Party."

18. Adira Polite, "A Satirical Exploration of the Tequila Party," *Bowdoin Orient*, February 25, 2016, http://bowdoinorient.com/bonus/article/10959.

19. Giselle Hernandez, "Somos Tequileros: A Personal Reaction to the 'Tequila' Party," *Bowdoin Orient*, February 26, 2016, http://bowdoinorient.com/bonus/article/10976.

20. "Listen and Learn," *Bowdoin Orient*, February 26, 2016, http://bowdoinorient.com/bonus /article/10975.

21. Carlos Holguin, "Criticisms of Political Correctness Are No Excuse," *Bowdoin Orient*, March 4, 2016, http://bowdoinorient.com/bonus/article/11023.

22. El Presidente, "Reader Email—Pussification of Bowdoin: Campus in Chaos After Tequila Party," *Barstool Sports*, February 29, 2016, https://www.barstoolsports.com/boston/reader-email -pussification-of-bowdoin-campus-in-chaos-after-tequila-party/.

23. Uncle Turtleboy, "Tequila Themed Party Deemed Racist by Bowdoin Students Who Had Their Feelings Hurt," Turtleboy, February 29, 2016, https://turtleboysports.com/tequila -themed-party-deemed-racist-by-bowdoin-students-who-had-their-feelings-hurt/.

NOTES TO PAGES 114–122

24. Bonilla-Silva, "Feeling Race"; Matias, *Feeling White*.

25. Nicole Wetsman, "BSG to Introduce Articles of Impeachment Against Two Members," *Bowdoin Orient*, March 2, 2016, http://bowdoinorient.com/bonus/article/10992.

26. Meg Robbins and Harry Rube, "Students Debate Articles of Impeachment at BSG," *Bowdoin Orient*, March 4, 2016, http://bowdoinorient.com/bonus/article/11027.

27. Robbins and Rube, "Students Debate Articles of Impeachment."

28. Lauren Irwin, "White Normativity," in *Critical Whiteness Praxis in Higher Education*, ed. Zak Foste and Tenisha Tevis (Sterling, VA: Stylus, 2022), 57.

29. Nolan Cabrera, *White Guys on Campus: Racism, White Immunity, and the Myth of "Post-Racial" Higher Education* (New Brunswick, NJ: Rutgers University Press, 2019); Zeus Leonardo and Ronald Porter, "Pedagogy of Fear: Toward a Fanonian Theory of 'Safety' in Race Dialogue," *Race, Ethnicity, and Education* 13, no. 2 (2010): 139–57.

30. Jennifer Mueller, "Racial Ideology or Racial Ignorance? An Alternative Theory of Racial Cognition," Sociological Theory 38, no. 2 (2020).

31. Jessie Daniels, *Nice White Ladies: The Truth about White Supremacy, Our Role in It, and How We Can Help Dismantle It* (New York: Seal, 2021).

32. Matias, *Feeling White*.

33. Ingrid A. Nelson, Hannah J. Graham, and Natalie L. Rudin, "Saving Face While (Not) Talking about Race: How Undergraduates Inhabit Racialized Structures at an Elite and Predominantly White College," *Social Problems* 70, no. 2 (2023): 456–73, https://doi.org/10.1093/socpro/spab045.

34. Katherine Timpf, "School Reportedly Creates 'Safe Space' for Students Hurt by 'Tequila Party,' " *National Review*, March 2, 2016, https://www.nationalreview.com/2016/03/bowdoin-college-tequila-party-safe-space-students-offended/.

35. Koos Couve, "Students Offered Counselling Over Small Sombrero Hats at Tequila-Themed Birthday Party," *Independent*, March 6, 2016, accessed January 23, 2020, https://www.independent.co.uk/news/world/americas/students-offered-counselling-over-small-sombrero-hats-at-tequilathemed-birthday-party-a6915521.html.

36. Helena Horton, "Students Asked to Leave Halls, Put on 'Social Probation' and Offered Counselling over Fancy-Dress Sombreros," *Telegraph*, March 8, 2016, https://www.telegraph.co.uk/news/newstopics/howaboutthat/12187450/fancy-dress-sombreros-maine-cultural-appropriation-students-university.html.

37. Kim LaCapria, "Bowdoin Mini Sombrero Controversy," Snopes, March 8, 2016, https://www.snopes.com/fact-check/bowdoin-mini-sombrero-controversy/.

38. Catherine Rampell, "Political Correctness Devours Yet Another College, Fighting over Mini-Sombreros," *Washinton Post*, March 3, 2016, https://www.washingtonpost.com/opinions/party-culture/2016/03/03/fdb46cc4-e185-11e5-9c36-e1902f6b6571_story.html.

39. Catherine Rampell, "Why Write about Tiny Sombreros?" *Washington Post*, March 4, 2016, https://www.washingtonpost.com/news/rampage/wp/2016/03/04/why-write-about-tiny-sombreros/.

40. In her final follow-up, the author reported she had been tipped off by alumni about a photo booth at the college's reunion, less than a year prior to the Tequila party, that offered a sombrero among other "silly hats" for taking dress up photos. The "mixed messaging" she argued, was too much.

41. Gene Weingarten, "A Mea Culpa (No Offense to the Romans!)," *Washington Post*, March 31, 2016, https://www.washingtonpost.com/lifestyle/magazine/gene-weingarten-a-mea-culpa-no-offense-to-the-romans/2016/03/29/9ff3758c-e6e2-11e5-a6f3-21ccdbc5f74e_story.html.

42. Matias, *Feeling White*.

218   NOTES TO PAGES 124–135

43. Sarah Mayorga-Gallo, "The White-Centering Logic of Diversity Ideology," *American Behavioral Scientist* 63, no. 13 (2019): 1789–809.

44. James Callahan, "Effects of 'Tequila' Backlash Unknown, but Little Concern about Long Term Impact," *Bowdoin Orient*, April 1, 2016, http://bowdoinorient.com/bonus/article/11074.

Chapter Six

1. Annette Lareau, Unequal Childhoods: Class, Race, and Family Life (Berkeley: University of California Press, 2003).

2. James Callahan, "Effects of 'Tequila' Backlash Unknown, but Little Concern about Long Term Impact," *Bowdoin Orient*, April 1, 2016, http://bowdoinorient.com/bonus/article/11074.

3. Charlie Eaton, *Bankers in the Ivory Tower: The Troubling Rise of Financiers in U.S. Higher Education* (Chicago: University of Chicago Press, 2022).

4. Megan Neely, *Hedged Out: Inequality and Insecurity on Wall Street* (Berkeley: University of California Press, 2022).

5. Eaton, *Bankers in the Ivory Tower*, 69.

6. Victor Ray, "A Theory of Racialized Organizations," *American Sociological Review* 84, no. 1 (2019): 26–53.

7. Shamus Khan, *Privilege: The Making of an Adolescent Elite at St. Paul's School* (Princeton, NJ: Princeton University Press, 2011).

8. Mitchell Stevens, *Creating a Class: College Admissions and the Education of Elites* (Cambridge, MA: Harvard University Press, 2007).

9. Harry Rube, "BSG Approves New Impeachment Bylaws," *Bowdoin Orient*, April 1, 2016, http://bowdoinorient.com/bonus/article/11075.

10. Adira Polite, "Bias Incidents Revisited: By Taking Punitive Measures, the College Hinders Genuine Progress," *Bowdoin Orient*, May 6, 2016, http://bowdoinorient.com/bonus/article/11247.

11. Polite, "Bias Incidents Revisited."

12. Daniel Viellieu, "Culture Not Costume Photo Shoot to Show Solidarity," *Bowdoin Orient*, March 4, 2016, http://bowdoinorient.com/bonus/article/11024.

13. Viellieu, "Culture Not Costume Photo Shoot."

14. James Thomas, "Diversity Regimes and Racial Inequality: A Case Study of Diversity University," *Social Currents* 5, no. 2 (2018): 141.

15. Clayton Rose, "President Rose Responds to Reactions to 'Tequila' Party," *Bowdoin Orient*, March 4, 2016, http://bowdoinorient.com/bonus/article/11038.

16. Melvin Whitehead et al., "Disrupting the Big Lie: Higher Education and Whitelash in a Post/Colorblind Era," 2021, *Education Sciences* 11, no. 9 (2021): 486–500;

17. Rose, "President Rose Responds."

18. Rose, "President Rose Responds."

19. Wendy Moore and Joyce Bell, "The Right to Be Racist in College: Racist Speech, White Institutional Space, and the First Amendment," *Law & Policy* 39, no. 2 (2017): 99–120.

20. Sarah Mayorga-Gallo, "The White-Centering Logic of Diversity Ideology," *American Behavioral Scientist* 63, no. 13 (2019): 1789–809; Jennifer Mueller, "Racial Ideology or Racial Ignorance? An Alternative Theory of Racial Cognition," Sociological Theory 38, no. 2 (2020).

21. Meg Robbins and Harry Rube, "Students Debate Articles of Impeachment at BSG," *Bowdoin Orient*, March 4, 2016, http://bowdoinorient.com/bonus/article/11027.

NOTES TO PAGES 135–153

22. "Out of Focus," *Bowdoin Orient*, March 4, 2016, http://bowdoinorient.com/bonus/article/11035.

23. *Bowdoin Orient*, "Out of Focus."

24. Carlos Holguin, "Criticisms of Political Correctness Are No Excuse," *Bowdoin Orient*, March 4, 2016, http://bowdoinorient.com/bonus/article/11023.

25. Francisco Navarro, "The Ownership of Cultures Is Not a Simple Matter of Race and Ethnicity," *Bowdoin Orient*, March 4, 2016, http://bowdoinorient.com/bonus/article/11018.

26. Joe Lace, "Punitive Measures Not the Best Way Forward," *Bowdoin Orient*, March 4, 2016, http://bowdoinorient.com/bonus/article/11020.

27. Phoebe Kranefuss, "We Must Recognize Lingering Effects of Upbringings," *Bowdoin Orient*, March 4, 2016, http://bowdoinorient.com/bonus/article/11022.

28. Richard Arms, "Responding to My Critics and Expanding the Conversation," *Bowdoin Orient*, March 4, 2016, http://bowdoinorient.com/bonus/article/11019.

29. W. E. B. DuBois, "Does the Negro Need Separate Schools?," *Journal of Negro Education* 4, no. 3 (1935): 328–35; Mitchell Chang and Maria Ledesma, "The Diversity Rationale," in *Diversity in American Higher Education: Toward a More Comprehensive Approach*, ed. Lisa M. Stulberg and Sharon Lawner Weinberg (New York: Routledge, 2011), 74–85.

30. Leslie Picca and Joe Feagin, *Two-Faced Racism: Whites in the Backstage and Frontstage* (New York: Routledge, 2007).

31. Eduardo Bonilla-Silva, *Racism without Racists: Colorblind Racism and the Persistence of Racial Inequality in America* (Lanham, MD: Rowman & Littlefield, 2018).

32. Ray, "A Theory of Racialized Organizations."

33. Uncle Turtleboy, "Tequila Themed Party Deemed Racist by Bowdoin Students Who Had Their Feelings Hurt," *Turtleboy Sports*, February 29, 2016, https://turtleboysports.com/tequila-themed-party-deemed-racist-by-bowdoin-students-who-had-their-feelings-hurt/.

34. Mark Granovetter, "The Strength of Weak Ties," *American Journal of Sociology* 78, no. 6 (1973): 1360–80.

35. Robert Granfield and Thomas Koenig, "Learning Collective Eminence: Harvard Law School and the Social Production of Elite Lawyers," *Sociological Quarterly* 33, no. 4 (1992): 503–20.

36. Shamus Khan, "The Sociology of Elites," *Annual Review of Sociology* 38 (2012): 361–77.

37. Eaton, *Bankers in the Ivory Tower*.

38. Amy Binder and Kate Wood, *Becoming Right: How Campuses Shape Young Conservatives* (Princeton, NJ: Princeton University Press, 2013).

39. Julia Mead, "So Bye, Bowdoin: Reflecting on my Columns and Takes on Campus Events," *Bowdoin Orient*, May 6, 2016, http://bowdoinorient.com/bonus/article/11255.

Chapter Seven

1. Rachel Allen, "New Committee to Address Campus Inclusion," *Bowdoin Orient*, September 9, 2016, http://bowdoinorient.com/bonus/article/11299.

2. Clayton Rose, "Why We Need the Liberal Arts Now More Than Ever," *TIME*, August 30, 2017, https://time.com/4920389/bowdoin-college-liberal-arts-education/.

3. TIME Media Kit, "Audience Snapshot," *TIME*, January 25, 2023, https://time.com/mediakit/.

4. Faria Nasruddin, "Students Unite After Campus Bias Incident," *Bowdoin Orient*, Sept 8, 2017, https://bowdoinorient.com/2017/09/08/students-unite-after-campus-bias-incident/.

5. Osa Omoregie, "Comfort Versus Courage: Bowdoin's Culture Promotes Lazy Activism," *Bowdoin Orient*, Sept 22, 2017, https://bowdoinorient.com/2017/09/22/comfort-versus-courage-bowdoins-culture-promotes-lazy-activism/.

6. Zeus Leonardo and Michalinos Zembylas, "Whiteness as Technology of Affect: Implications for Educational Praxis," *Equity and Excellence in Education* 46, no. 1 (2013): 150–65.

7. Sarah Mayorga-Gallo, "The White-Centering Logic of Diversity Ideology," *American Behavioral Scientist* 63, no. 13 (2019): 1789–809.

8. Kevin Hernandez, "A Desire for Reconciliation with Minimal Reciprocity: Revisiting the 'Tequila' Party," *Bowdoin Orient*, February 23, 2018, https://bowdoinorient.com/2018/02/23/a-desire-for-reconciliation-with-minimal-reciprocity-revisiting-the-tequila-party/.

9. Justin Weathers, "Discussions from Brunch: On the Offer of the College and Its Unfulfilled Potential," *Bowdoin Orient*, March 2, 2018, https://bowdoinorient.com/2018/03/02/discussions-from-brunch-on-the-offer-of-the-college-and-its-unfulfilled-potential/.

10. Nora Cullen, "Discussions from Brunch: Thoughts on Passivity and Activity at Bowdoin," *Bowdoin Orient*, March 2, 2018, https://bowdoinorient.com/2018/03/02/discussions-from-brunch-on-passivity-and-activity/.

11. Rebkah Tesfamariam, "Discussions from Brunch: If You're Not Talking Then You're Not Learning," *Bowdoin Orient*, April 20, 2018, https://bowdoinorient.com/2018/04/20/discussions-from-brunch-if-youre-not-talking-then-youre-not-learning/.

12. Harrison Hawk, "Discussions from Brunch: Seeking Conversation to Be Proactive, Not Reactive," *Bowdoin Orient*, April 20, 2018, https://bowdoinorient.com/2018/04/20/discussions-from-brunch-seeking-conversation-to-be-proactive-not-reactive/.

13. Charles Mills, *The Racial Contract* (Ithaca, NY: Cornell University Press, 1997).

14. Sydney Avitia-Jacques, Hannah Berman, and Sophie Cowen, "Dorm(ant) divergence: unequal understandings of housing, self-segregation and inequity," *Bowdoin Orient*, March 30, 2018, https://bowdoinorient.com/2018/03/30/dormant-divergence-unequal-understandings-of-housing-self-segregation-and-inequity/.

15. Sydney Avitia-Jacques, Sophie Cowen, and Joyce Kim, "Untested Complicity, A+ Potential: Curricular Reform Can Relieve Students of Color from the Burden of Teaching Race," *Bowdoin Orient*, April 6, 2018, https://bowdoinorient.com/2018/04/06/diversity-in-higher-ed/.

16. Sophie Cowen et al., "Long Division: Polarizing Parties, Formulaic Discussions and Their Confusing Remainders," *Bowdoin Orient*, April 13, 2018, https://bowdoinorient.com/2018/04/13/long-division-polarizing-parties-formulaic-discussions-their-confusing-remainders/.

17. Sophie Cowen et al., "Discourses on Diversity: Between Buzzword and Reality," *Bowdoin Orient*, April 20, 2018, https://bowdoinorient.com/2018/04/20/discourses-on-diversity-between-buzzword-and-reality/.

18. Adira Polite, "Burglary, Prison, and Pedro O'Hara's: Revisiting the Infamous Bias Incidents," *Bowdoin Orient*, May 4, 2018, https://bowdoinorient.com/2018/05/04/burglary-prison-and-pedro-oharas-revisiting-the-infamous-bias-incidents/.

19. Clayton Rose, "Message to the Campus Community—June 11, 2020," Bowdoin College Office of the President, 2020, accessed January 30, 2023, https://www.bowdoin.edu/president/writings-and-addresses/messages-to-the-community/2020/june-11.html.

20. Victor Ray, "A Theory of Racialized Organizations," *American Sociological Review* 84, no. 1 (2019): 26–53.

21. Ray, "A Theory of Racialized Organizations."

NOTES TO PAGES 167–172

22. Charlie Eaton, *Bankers in the Ivory Tower: The Troubling Rise of Financiers in U.S. Higher Education* (Chicago: University of Chicago Press, 2022); Cheryl Harris, "Whiteness as Property," *Harvard Law Review* 106, no. 8 (1993): 1707–91; David Labaree, *A Perfect Mess: The Unlikely Ascendancy of American Higher Education* (Chicago: University of Chicago Press, 2017); Megan Neely, *Hedged Out: Inequality and Insecurity on Wall Street* (Berkeley: University of California Press, 2022).

Chapter Eight

1. Raul Perez, *The Souls of White Jokes: How Racist Humor Fuels White Supremacy* (Stanford, CA: Stanford University Press, 2022).

2. Adrienne Keene, "Representations Matter," *Journal Committed to Social Change on Race and Ethnicity* 1, no. 1 (2015): 102–11.

3. Rob Eschmann, *When the Hood Comes Off: Racism and Resistance in the Digital Age* (Berkeley: University of California Press, 2023), 214–15.

4. Amy Binder, "Afterword: New Institutional, Inhabited Institutional, and a Cultural-Organizational Approach to Studying Elites and Higher Education," in *Universities and the Production of Elites*, ed. Roland Bloch et al. (New York: Palgrave Macmillan, 2018).

5. Victor Ray, "A Theory of Racialized Organizations," *American Sociological Review* 84, no. 1 (2019): 36.

6. Mitchell Stevens and Josipa Roksa, "The Diversity Imperative in Elite Admissions," in *Diversity in American Higher Education: Toward a More Comprehensive Approach*, ed. Lisa M. Stulberg and Sharon Lawner Weinberg (New York: Routledge, 2011), 63–73; Lisa M. Stulberg and Anthony S. Chen, "The Origins of Race-Conscious Affirmative Action in Undergraduate Admissions: A Comparative Analysis of Institutional Change in Higher Education," *Sociology of Education* 87, no. 1 (2014): 36–52.

7. Paul DiMaggio and Walter Powell, "The Iron Cage Revisited: Collective Rationality and Institutional Isomorphism in Organizational Fields," *American Sociological Review* 48, no. 2 (1983): 147–60; Stevens and Roksa, "The Diversity Imperative."

8. Mitchell Chang and Maria Ledesma, "The Diversity Rationale," in *Diversity in American Higher Education*, 74–85; W. E. B. DuBois, "Does the Negro Need Separate Schools?," *Journal of Negro Education* 4, no. 3 (1935): 328–35.

9. David Brunsma, Eric Brown, and Peggy Placier, "Teaching Race at Historically White Colleges and Universities: Identifying and Dismantling the Walls of Whiteness," *Critical Sociology* 39, no. 5 (2013): 717–38; Joe R. Feagin, Hernan Vera, and Nikitah Imani, *The Agony of Education: Black Students at a White University* (New York: Routledge, 1996); Wendy Moore, *Reproducing Racism: White Space, Elite Law Schools, and Racial Inequality* (Lanham, MD: Rowman & Littlefield, 2008).

10. See Kirsten Hextrum, *Special Admission: How College Sports Recruitment Favors White Suburban Athletes* (New Brunswick, NJ: Rutgers University Press, 2021).

11. Natasha Warikoo, *The Diversity Bargain: And Other Dilemmas of Race, Admissions, and Meritocracy at Elite Universities* (Chicago: University of Chicago Press, 2016).

12. Eduardo Bonilla-Silva, *Racism without Racists: Colorblind Racism and the Persistence of Racial Inequality in America* (Lanham, MD: Rowman & Littlefield, 2018).

13. Bonilla-Silva, *Racism without Racists*.

14. Ruben Gaztambide-Fernandez and Leila Angod, "Approximating Whiteness: Race, Class, and Empire in the Making of Modern Elite/White Subjects," *Educational Theory* 69, no. 6

(2019): 719–43; Robert Granfield and Thomas Koenig, "Learning Collective Eminence: Harvard Law School and the Social Production of Elite Lawyers," *Sociological Quarterly* 33, no. 4 (1992): 503–20.

15. Shamus Khan, *Privilege: The Making of an Adolescent Elite at St. Paul's School* (Princeton, NJ: Princeton University Press, 2011).

16. Nancy Leong, "Racial Capitalism," *Harvard Law Review* 126, no. 8 (2013): 2151–226.

17. Candis Smith and Sarah Mayorga-Gallo, "The New Principle-Policy Gap: How Diversity Ideology Subverts Diversity Initiatives," *Sociological Perspectives* 60, no. 5 (2017): 889–911; Warikoo, *Diversity Bargain*.

18. DiMaggio and Powell, "The Iron Cage Revisited"; Ray, "A Theory of Racialized Organizations."

19. Lauren Rivera, *Pedigree: How Elite Students Get Elite Jobs* (Princeton, NJ: Princeton University Press, 2015).

20. Sara Ahmed, *On Being Included: Racism and Diversity in Institutional Life* (Durham, NC: Duke University Press, 2012), 44.

21. Jennifer Mueller, "Racial Ideology or Racial Ignorance? An Alternative Theory of Racial Cognition," *Sociological Theory* 38, no. 2 (2020).

22. George Lipsitz, *The Possessive Investment in Whiteness: How White People Profit from Identity Politics* (Philadelphia: Temple University Press, 1998).

23. Charles Mills, *The Racial Contract* (Ithaca, NY: Cornell University Press, 1997); Charles Mills, "White Ignorance," in *Race and Epistemologies of Ignorance*, ed. Shannon Sullivan and Nancy Tuana (Albany: State University of New York Press, 2007), 28.

24. Sarah Mayorga-Gallo, "The White-Centering Logic of Diversity Ideology," *American Behavioral Scientist* 63, no. 13 (2019): 1789–809.

25. Amy Binder and Kate Wood, *Becoming Right: How Campuses Shape Young Conservatives* (Princeton, NJ: Princeton University Press, 2013).

26. Ingrid A. Nelson, Hannah J. Graham, and Natalie L. Rudin, "Saving Face While (Not) Talking about Race: How Undergraduates Inhabit Racialized Structures at an Elite and Predominantly White College," *Social Problems* 70, no. 2 (2023): 456–73, https://doi.org/10.1093/socpro/spab045.

27. Veronica Lerma, Laura Hamilton, and Kelly Nielsen, "Racialized Equity Labor, University Appropriation and Student Resistance," *Social Problems* 67, no. 2 (2020): 286–303.

28. Zeus Leonardo, *Race, Whiteness, and Education* (New York: Routledge, 2009); Mayorga-Gallo, "White-Centering Logic"; Leslie Picca and Joe Feagin, *Two-Faced Racism: Whites in the Backstage and Frontstage* (New York: Routledge, 2007).

29. Warikoo, *Diversity Bargain*.

30. Shamus Khan, "The Sociology of Elites," *Annual Review of Sociology* 38 (2012): 361–77.

31. Picca and Feagin, Two-Faced Racism.

32. Ray, "A Theory of Racialized Organizations."

33. Charlie Eaton, *Bankers in the Ivory Tower: The Troubling Rise of Financiers in U.S. Higher Education* (Chicago: University of Chicago Press, 2022); Cheryl Harris, "Whiteness as Property," *Harvard Law Review* 106, no. 8 (1993): 1707–91; Leong, "Racial Capitalism."

34. E.g., Rivera, *Pedigree*.

35. Khan, *Privilege*.

36. Mitchell Stevens, *Creating a Class: College Admissions and the Education of Elites* (Cambridge, MA: Harvard University Press, 2007).

NOTES TO PAGES 179–186

37. Bianca Williams, Dian Squire, and Frank Tuitt, *Plantation Politics and Campus Rebellions: Power, Diversity, and the Emancipatory Struggle in Higher Education* (Albany: State University of New York Press, 2021).

38. Eaton, *Bankers in the Ivory Tower.*

39. Mark Granovetter, "The Strength of Weak Ties," *American Journal of Sociology* 78, no. 6 (1973): 1360–80.

40. Granfield and Koenig, "Learning Collective Eminence."

41. Khan, "The Sociology of Elites."

42. Eaton, *Bankers in the Ivory Tower.*

43. Randall Collins, *The Credential Society: An Historical Sociology of Education and Stratification* (New York: Academic, 1979).

44. Binder, "Afterword"; Ray, "A Theory of Racialized Organizations," 28.

45. James Thomas, "Diversity Regimes and Racial Inequality: A Case Study of Diversity University," *Social Currents* 5, no. 2 (2018): 140–56.

46. James Thomas, "The Economization of Diversity," *Sociology of Race and Ethnicity* 5, no. 4 (2019): 471–85.

47. Michael Hout, "Social and Economic Returns to College Education in the United States," *Annual Review of Sociology* 38 (2012): 379–400.

48. See also Gaztambide-Fernandez and Angod, "Approximating Whiteness."

49. Hout, "Social and Economic Returns."

50. Lawrence Bobo, "Group Conflict, Prejudice, and the Paradox of Contemporary Racial Attitudes," in *Eliminating Racism: Profiles in Controversy*, ed. Phyllis Katz and Dalmas Taylor (New York: Plenum, 1988), 85–144. Anna Boch, "The Limits of Tolerance: Extreme Speakers on Campus," *Social Problems* 69 (2022): 143–63.

51. Eaton, *Bankers in the Ivory Tower.*

52. Stulberg and Chen, "Origins of Race-Conscious Affirmative Action."

53. Ray, "A Theory of Racialized Organizations," 36.

54. For more on the intersection of housing and race, see Maya A. Beasley, *Opting Out: Losing the Potential of America's Young Black Elite* (Chicago: University of Chicago Press, 2012); and Warikoo, *Diversity Bargain.*

55. Eaton, *Bankers in the Ivory Tower.*

56. Arik Lifschitz, Michael Sauder, and Mitchell Stevens, "Football as a Status System in U.S. Higher Education," *Sociology of Education* 87, no. 3 (2014): 204–19.

57. Emilio Castilla and Ben Rissing, "Best in Class: The Returns on Application Endorsements in Higher Education," *Administrative Science Quarterly* 64, no. 1 (2019): 230–70.

58. Frank Dobbin and Alexandra Kalev, *Getting to Diversity: What Works and What Doesn't* (Cambridge, MA: Harvard University Press, 2022); Scott E. Page, *The Diversity Bonus: How Great Teams Pay Off in the Knowledge Economy* (Princeton, NJ: Princeton University Press, 2019).

Index

accountability, 60, 69–70, 107–8, 149, 164–66, 177. *See also* apologies; intent; punishments

administrators: delimiting definition of racism, 50, 67–68, 94, 109–10, 121–22, 134–35, 137–38, 149, 173–74; and diversity script, 27, 53, 62; lack of response from, 73–74; and naturalization script, 55; response to Cracksgiving party, 64–68, 72–74; response to Gangster party, 79–82, 87–91, 94–96; response to Tequila party, 108–11, 121–24, 134; student trust in, 89–90, 130–31. *See also* Bowdoin College; campus-wide emails; punishments

admissions: histories of selectiveness, 29–31; need-blind policies, 22, 32, 58, 170; and normative whiteness, 28–29, 31–35, 57, 168; privileging wealth, 129, 170–71; test-optional policies, 22. *See also* affirmative action; higher education

AfAm, 42–45, 89–90, 92–94, 96, 136, 151–52, 155

affirmative action, 30–31, 58, 67–68, 152. *See also* admissions

African American Society. *See* AfAm

Ahmed, Sara, 173

Alexander, Michelle, 5

Anderson, Elijah, 48

Angod, Leila, 18

Annamma, Subini, 49

anonymity: in campus communities, 17, 68–69, 182; and social media, 88–89; and targeted racism, 114–15, 176–77. *See also* social media; social networks

antiblackness, 5, 7, 18. *See also* white supremacy

anti-PC culture. *See* political correctness

apologies, 72, 76, 81, 86, 91–92, 116, 126, 142–43. *See also* accountability; intent

Arizona State University, 2

Armstrong, Elizabeth, 19

Arum, Richard, 19

Asian Student Association, 61, 96, 151

Bangor Daily News, 87

Barstool Sports, 113–14, 119, 136

Bell, Joyce, 15, 20, 134

Bias Incident Group, 28

Binder, Amy, 17, 68, 147

blackface, 7–8, 120–21, 168. *See also* racism

Black Girl Brunch (BGB), 79–80

Black Lives Matter (BLM) movement, 14, 59, 61, 64, 75, 99–100, 150, 168

Black Student Union. *See* AfAm

Black studies departments, 99–100

boarding schools, 32–33, 104, 128–29, 178

Bonilla-Silva, Eduardo, 49, 51, 109

Bowdoin College: alumni networks, 124, 127–28; balance of athletics and academics, 36, 100–101; early history of, 20–21, 77; lack of Greek life, 35, 101; perceptions of, 20, 32, 54–55, 153; structural changes at, 150–54, 166–67; student body demographics, 21–23, 26, 57–60, 62, 104–5. *See also* administrators; *Bowdoin Orient*; elite colleges; *and specific units and departments*

Bowdoin Orient: and "both sides" framings, 85–86, 134–35; columns about race and diversity, 83–84, 95, 100, 133–34, 147–48, 152, 160–63; coverage of BSG impeachment proceedings, 115–18; coverage of costume parties, 56, 59, 66, 110–11, 124, 132; limited discussions of race in, 62, 78; perceptions of, 25–26. *See also* Bowdoin College

Bowdoin Student Government (BSG): authority of, 25–26; impeachment proceedings, 115–18, 130–33, 160–61; members engaging in cultural appropriation, 59–60, 111–12, 115–18;

Bowdoin Student Government (BSG) (*cont.*)
representation of multicultural groups, 100, 151;
response to Cracksgiving party, 73; response to
Gangster party, 84; response to Tequila party, 111
Broderick, Alicia, 18
Brown, Michael, 61, 67, 149–50
BUCRO, 42
Bush, George H. W., 13

California State San Marcos, 2
campus housing: application processes, 101–2,
185–86; limiting off-campus housing, 46–47,
99, 151; and normative whiteness, 28–29, 45–49;
and social groups, 45–46. *See also* off-campus
housing; Tequila party
campus life: as bubble, 17, 27, 51, 58–59, 99–100,
166–67, 176–77; and feelings of belonging,
19–20, 32–33, 88, 114–15; and ideals of diversity,
3, 9, 16; and outside world, 104–6, 124–25,
128–29; and reputation, 118–21, 138, 144–45; and
sense of community, 68–69, 79–80; and social
networks, 18, 54, 71, 128–30, 137–38. *See also* de
facto social segregation; social capital
campus-wide emails, 66, 80–83, 94, 134. *See also*
administrators
Castile, Philando, 150
Chamberlain, Joshua, 21
Chen, Anthony, 58
civilized diversity discourse, 68–69, 73, 76–77,
81–82, 86, 96–98, 110–14, 126–27, 133–41, 143–44,
154–64, 174–76. *See also* diversity script; naturalization script; political correctness; race;
racialized equity labor; racism
civil rights movement, 5–6, 26–27, 30
Civil War, 5, 10
Claremont McKenna College, 2
class. *See* social class
Clery Act, 15
Colby College, 58
Cold War, 9–10
Cold War party, 120
Collins, Randall, 19
colorblindness. *See* color-evasiveness
color-evasiveness, 49–51, 55, 69, 134, 169. *See also*
race; racism; structural racism
"Compton Cookout," 2
Concerned Student 1950, 76
Confederate flag, 77
cornrows, 12, 79, 85–86. *See also* CROWN Act;
cultural appropriation; Gangster party
Cracksgiving party: acceptance of consequences,
69–71, 180; coverage in *Orient*, 67–68; individualistic response to, 64–66, 77; memory of, 74–
75, 104. *See also* off-campus housing; racially
charged college parties
"Crips and Bloods" party, 2

CROWN Act, 12. *See also* cornrows
Cullors, Patrisse, 59
cultural appropriation: alternative terms for, 110;
compared to assimilation, 12; education about,
133–34, 139; lack of familiarity with, 65, 70–71;
and political correctness, 13–14; and power
dynamics, 83–84, 92; recognition of harms of,
168–69. *See also* cornrows; Halloween costumes; racially charged college parties; racism
cultural capital, 27, 61, 100, 176. *See also* social capital

Dartmouth College, 2
Dean of Multicultural Affairs, 56
de facto social segregation, 53–55, 116–17, 163, 172.
See also campus life; race; social class; social
networks; students of color
Derek, Bo, 12
Diamond, John, 50
disabilities accommodations, 38
diversity ideology, 50–52, 55, 124, 169–71. *See also*
intent; "magical thinking"
"diversity regime," 181
diversity script: dominance of, 51, 170–71; and
homogenization of difference, 90–91; and
individualism, 72–73, 77, 130; performativity of,
151–52, 172, 180–81; promotion of, 51–53, 58, 62,
86, 137, 147–48; recognitions of limits of, 114–15;
and tokenization of people of color, 139–40;
and white ignorance, 29, 146. *See also* civilized
diversity discourse; "magical thinking"; naturalization script; race; racialized equity labor
Division I athletics, 35–36, 75–76
Division III athletics: and admissions, 36–37; and
normative whiteness, 28–29, 168; and white
spaces, 108, 177, 186. *See also* intercollegiate
athletics; New England Small College Athletic
Conference (NESCAC)
Dreer, Samuel Herman, 21
Dubose, Samuel, 77

Eaton, Charlie, 128
education about race: difficulty of accessing, 86–
87; effectiveness of, 70–72, 142–43, 147–48, 156,
164–66; as solution to racism, 56, 60, 69–70,
122, 133–34, 174; and structural changes, 82, 116–
17, 149–54, 174–75. *See also* punishments; race;
racialized equity labor
elite colleges: culture of, 26, 118–21; and first-
generation students, 153; increasing student
body sizes, 58; as market-driven organizations,
10, 16, 63, 128–29, 184–85; and meritocracy,
31–32; and reproducing racial hierarchies, 4,
49, 169–71, 182–83. *See also* Bowdoin College;
higher education; predominantly white institutions (PWI)
Ellis Island remembrance, 6

INDEX 227

English language, 9–10, 33
extracurricular activities, 11, 35, 42–45. *See also* inter-collegiate athletics; Outing Club; social networks

Fanon, Frantz, 69
Feagin, Joe, 137–38
Fisher v. University of Texas, 31
Floyd, George, 166, 185
free speech, 13–14, 73, 120, 134. *See also* political correctness

Gangster party: circulation on social media, 87–88; and civilized diversity discourse, 79–80, 96–98; lack of bystander objections, 103; memory of, 97, 157; sailing team's remorse for, 88–89, 91–92, 107–9, 117–18, 154–55, 180; student confusion about, 86–87; student-led education efforts in response to, 83–87, 136. *See also* cornrows; off-campus housing; racially charged college parties
Garland, Judy, 7
Garner, Eric, 61
Garza, Alicia, 59
Gaztambide-Fernandez, Ruben, 18
GI Bill, 30
Granovetter, Mark, 145, 180
Gratz v. Bollinger, 31
Great Depression, 29
Greek life, 11, 22, 101
Grutter v. Bollinger, 31

Halloween costumes, 2, 7, 11. *See also* cultural appropriation
Harris, Cheryl, 18
Harvard, 20–21, 30
Hatch, Louis, 21
Head, Payton, 75–76
Hextrum, Kirsten, 37
higher education: connections to other social institutions, 166–67, 172–73, 184–85; expanded access to, 10–11, 30; and private funding, 9–10, 27, 63, 68, 124–26, 153, 177–78; ranking systems, 17; and sustaining whiteness, 4, 9, 18, 203n68. *See also* admissions; elite colleges; intercollegiate athletics; predominantly white institutions (PWI)
Hotel and Restaurant Union, 12
hurt feelings, 81–82, 94, 134, 146, 175

ignorance. *See* white ignorance
indentured servants, 4–5
Independent, 1, 119
inhabited institutional theory, 16–18, 48, 181–83. *See also* racialized organizations theory
Instagram, 1, 106, 176. *See also* social media
institutional memory, 154–55, 157
intent, 65–66, 123–24, 141–42, 160. *See also* accountability; apologies; diversity ideology

intercollegiate athletics: and admissions, 10–11, 35–37, 57–58, 171, 186; and campus social life, 38–39, 43, 46, 100–101, 104–5, 171; and normative whiteness, 28–29, 168; and team hierarchies, 78–79, 108, 116, 146–47, 177–78. *See also* Division III athletics; extracurricular activities; higher education; Ivy League; New England Small College Athletic Conference (NESCAC)
Intergroup Dialogue (IGD) program, 62, 91–92, 101, 118, 151–52, 172
intersectionality, 90–91, 118. *See also* race
Ivy League, 36. *See also* intercollegiate athletics

Jackson, Darrell, 49
Jewish students, exclusion of, 29
Jim Crow segregation, 5–6
John Brown Russwurm House, 45

"Kanye Western" party, 2
Karabel, Jerome, 29–30
Kardashian, Kim, 12
Kelly, Megyn, 7
Khan, Shamus, 17–18, 129, 145–46, 178
King, Martin Luther, Jr., 2, 30, 151
KKK robes, 8
Korean Students Association (KASA), 44

Labaree, David, 9, 11
Lareau, Annette, 37
Latin American Student Organization (LASO), 111, 135–36, 141–42, 151–52, 155
Lee, Elizabeth, 63
Leonardo, Zeus, 18, 79
Lewis, Amanda, 50

"magical thinking," 26, 170–71. *See also* diversity ideology; diversity script
Martin, Trayvon, 59
Matias, Cheryl, 109
Mayorga, Sarah, 50–52, 160
"Meeting in the Union" event, 73–74, 100, 150
men's lacrosse team, 64–67, 69–70, 74, 155
meritocracy rhetoric, 18, 32, 34, 50, 178
microaggressions, 3, 44–45, 50, 152. *See also* racism
Mills, Charles, 6, 65, 174
money: power of, 128–33, 143–44, 149–50, 159, 178; significance of donors, 10, 147, 177–78, 184–85. *See also* social class
Moore, Wendy Leo, 15, 20, 134
Morrison, Deb, 49
Mueller, Jennifer, 6, 65, 174
Multicultural Coalition, 100

National Review Online, 119
Native American Students Association, 69–70, 74

naturalization script, 29, 51, 53–55, 130, 172. *See also* civilized diversity discourse; diversity script; race

Ndemanu, Michael, 76

need-blind admissions, 22, 32, 58, 170

Neely, Megan, 128

New England Small College Athletic Conference (NESCAC), 36, 38, 104. *See also* Division III athletics; intercollegiate athletics

New York Times, 13, 36

Obama, Barack, 14, 58–59, 149

Oberlin College, 14

off-campus housing: expansion of, 46–47; "passing down" houses, 47, 171–72; perceptions of, 48, 64–65; restrictions on, 46–47, 99, 151. *See also* campus housing; Cracksgiving party; Gangster party

Office of Development and Alumni Affairs, 124

Orient. See *Bowdoin Orient*

Outing Club, 35, 41–42, 62–63, 171. *See also* extracurricular activities

Pantaleo, Daniel, 61

Paris Fashion Week, 12

people of color. *See* students of color

Perez, Raul, 7

philanthropic homophily, 128–29, 179

Picca, Leslie, 137–38

"plantation politics," 19, 97–98

political correctness: backlash against, 4, 62–63, 73, 103, 113–14, 119; distinction from cultural appropriation, 85, 113–14; and free speech, 13–15. *See also* civilized diversity discourse; free speech

post-racial era, 58–59

Powell, Lewis F., 26, 31, 170

predominantly white institutions (PWI), 9, 18, 30, 44, 64, 163. *See also* elite colleges; higher education

punishments: and appealing decisions, 127–30, 141; demands for, 82–83, 116; limited nature of, 27, 56–57, 64–66; perceptions of, 134–35; privacy of, 56, 59, 66, 121, 173. *See also* accountability; administrators; education about race

race: and homogenization of difference, 23, 90–91, 151; and minstrelsy, 7, 11–12; opting in to or out of discussions about, 60–61, 78, 96–98, 116, 126–27, 137–41, 158–66, 172; perceived benefits of diversity, 26–27, 30–31; perceptions of post-race era, 59, 181–82; and resource allocation, 8–9, 17, 27–29, 44–45, 71, 93, 167, 182, 185–86; and self-identification, 5, 11, 23, 104, 212n4. *See also* civilized diversity discourse; color-evasiveness; de facto social segregation; diversity script;

education about race; intersectionality; naturalization script; racism; social class; whiteness

racialized equity labor, 27, 53, 55, 57, 60–61, 69, 75, 82–87, 92–93, 96–98, 111–13. *See also* civilized diversity discourse; diversity script; education about race; students of color

racialized organizations theory, 8–9, 17, 26, 28–29, 55, 59, 66–67, 167, 181–83. *See also* inhabited institutional theory

racially charged college parties: framing as hurt feelings, 81–82, 94, 134, 146, 175; media attention of, 1–2, 20–21, 66, 113–15, 118–21, 126–27, 176–78, 182; recurrence of, 3, 26–27, 169–79. *See also* Cracksgiving party; cultural appropriation; Gangster party; racism; Tequila party

racism: and anonymity, 88, 114–15, 176–77; claims of "reverse discrimination," 58; education as solution for, 56, 68–69; framing as individual act, 27, 49, 56–57, 59, 64–66, 74, 81–82, 121–25, 143–44, 150, 165, 173–74; hate crimes, 15–16; and hurt feelings, 81–82, 94, 134, 175; and intent, 65–66, 123–24, 141–42, 160; and passive complicity, 162; and violence, 30. *See also* blackface; civilized diversity discourse; color-evasiveness; cultural appropriation; microaggressions; race; racially charged college parties; slavery; structural racism

Ray, Victor, 8–9, 19, 167, 170, 177

Regents of the University of California v. Bakke, 31

research design, 20, 22–26, 195–97

Residential Life office, 45, 104, 151

resource allocation, 8–9, 17, 27–29, 44–45, 71, 93, 167, 182, 185–86

Resource Center for Gender and Sexual Diversity, 45, 151

Reyes, Daisy, 17

Rivera, Lauren, 18

Rockefeller Foundation, 68

Rooney, Mickey, 7

Russwurm, John Brown, 21

Russwurm African American Center, 89

"safe space" rhetoric, 2–3, 69, 84

sailing team, 78–82, 88–89, 91–92, 107–9, 117–18, 154–55, 162, 180

Sehgal, Parul, 13

September 11, 2001, 14

slavery, 4–5, 9, 62. *See also* racism

"smartness," 18, 29, 129–30

social capital, 27, 61, 100, 118–19, 127, 132, 160, 176–77. *See also* campus life; cultural capital; social networks

social class: distinctions of, 4, 18, 103–4, 128; perceptions of, 20, 104–5; and social networks, 32–33, 37–39, 115–16, 127–30, 145. *See also* de facto social segregation; money; race

INDEX

social media, 87, 106–8, 147. *See also* anonymity; Instagram; Yik Yak
social networks, 18, 32–33, 115–16, 127–30, 137–38, 145, 154–58, 164–65, 176, 180–81. *See also* anonymity; de facto social segregation; extracurricular activities; social capital; weak ties
South Asian Student Association, 152
Spanish language, 33
Squire, Dian, 19, 97–98
Sterling, Alton, 150
Stevens, Mitchell, 19, 31, 63
Stowe, Harriet Beecher, 21
structural racism: education about, 60, 92, 157–58; erasure of, 27, 129–30; general ignorance of, 6, 54–55, 62, 76, 83; recognition of, 3, 183–84. *See also* color-evasiveness; racism; whiteness; white supremacy
student activism, 2–3, 67–68, 73–74, 99–100, 111, 114, 117, 120–21, 132, 150–51
Student Center for Multicultural Life, 45, 53, 89–90, 133
Students for Fair Admissions v. Harvard, 31
students of color: and affinity groups for socialization, 44–45; disengaging from white-centered conversations, 93–94; and intercollegiate athletics, 40–41; labor of educating white peers, 27, 57, 60–61, 69, 75, 82–87, 92–93, 96–98, 111–13, 117–18, 139, 149, 173–74; pressure to do diversity work, 154, 179; self-identification as, 23–24; tokenization of, 19, 51–52, 101, 133–34, 139–40; validation of experiences, 157–58. *See also* de facto social segregation; racialized equity labor
Stulberg, Lisa, 58
Swarthmore College, 58

Telegraph, 119
Temple, Shirley, 7
Tequila party: administration response to, 108–11, 121–24; attendees acting as victims, 113–18, 126–30, 141–42, 180–81; and civilized diversity discourse, 99–100, 114–15; media coverage of, 1–2, 106–8, 113–15, 118–21, 126–27; memory of, 140, 154–68; opting in to conversations on race, 137–41, 144–45, 157–58; power of money to limit consequences, 128–33, 143–44. *See also* campus housing; racially charged college parties
Thomas, James, 93, 181
TIME, 153
Tometi, Opal, 59
transphobia, 152
Trudeau, Justin, 8
Trump, Donald, 14, 150, 152
Tuitt, Frank, 19, 97–98
Turtleboy Sports, 114

United States: founding of, 4–5, 13; funding for higher education, 9–10; immigration to, 5–6; national attention to racial justice, 3, 73, 114; 2016 presidential election, 14–15
"Unite the Right" rally, 152
University of California Davis, 31
University of California Los Angeles, 2
University of California San Diego, 2
University of Michigan, 2, 31
University of Missouri, 75–76, 96–97
USA Today, 7–8
U.S. News & World Report, 17

Warikoo, Natasha, 50
Washington Post, 119–20
Watts riots, 30
weak ties, 18, 145–46, 180. *See also* social networks
Weingarten, Gene, 120
white dominance, 4–9, 11, 15–16
white grievance, 3, 6
Whitehead, Melvin, 134
white ignorance, 4–9, 12, 19, 47–48, 52–54, 65, 71, 86–87, 91–97, 108–9, 116, 123, 126–27, 131, 136, 143, 162–63, 173–74, 183–84
white innocence, 109–10, 114
whiteness: and agency to "opt-out," 60–61, 96–98, 116, 126–27, 137–41, 158–66, 172; co-constitution with "smartness," 18, 29, 129–30; as credential, 28–29, 32, 65–66, 71, 158, 169, 182–83; and group identity, 5–6; markers of, 18, 33; self-identification of, 23–24. *See also* race; structural racism
white normativity, 18, 28–29, 31–35, 45–49, 57, 94, 162, 168
white spaces, 48, 55, 72–73, 101, 108
white supremacy: and organizational structures, 5–6, 8, 18, 97, 134; reproduction of, 3, 122, 149–50, 162, 184; and violence, 13. *See also* antiblackness; structural racism
"Why Do Issues of Race Matter If I'm White?" town hall, 95
Wilder, Craig, 9
Williams, Bianca, 19, 97–98
Wilson, Darren, 61, 67
Wolfe, Tim, 76
Women's Resource Center, 45, 151
Wood, Kate, 17, 68, 147

Yale University, 2
Yik Yak, 87–89, 106–8, 113, 117, 133, 135, 176. *See also* social media

Zabala, Pamela, 48
Zimmerman, George, 59